Living on the Other Side

"I came to *Living on the Other Side* as a former evangelical Christian who has spent decades immersed in earth-centered spiritual practices. I admire Lisa Hess for staying with her root faith tradition, for wrestling with it, and renewing it in a deeply personal, transformative way. The author's teaching voice in this book is engaging, but it really comes alive when she recounts her personal stories of grief, rage, struggle, body wisdom, connection, and renewal."

—**Joanna Powell Colbert**, author of *The Gaian Tarot: Healing the Earth, Healing Ourselves*

"Welcome to a spirited, pleasurable, and difficult journey with Lisa Hess as your wise, autobiographical guide. Her riveting story resonates in those wrestling with a faith that has failed, with a religion revealed as demonic, with a spirituality that denigrates who and what you are. This poetically vibrant pilgrimage opens a way to living joy-filled on the other side, to claiming one's truth and dwelling more fully in the divine."

—**Robert K Martin**, editor, *Journal of Religious Leadership*

"Simultaneously fierce and tender, this book stands at the intersection of bravely personal spiritual autobiography and deeply learned theology, both made accessible through Hess's unique combination of honesty, intimacy, wisdom and scholarship."

—**Brad Hirschfield**, president, Center for Learning and Leadership

"The root meaning of respect means to look again, and *Living on the Other Side* invites you into this query with every chapter. In a rupture that she names her own 'faith trauma,' Hess stirs the cauldron as she holds accountable her own faith traditions for the abandonment and betrayal of her as a woman. Rising rage in women can be a bellwether, capable of shifting directions and coursing new internal maps in our psyches for not only our wellbeing but our homecoming. This book is a deep mirror for women of faith to look bravely and no longer suffocate in the silence that perpetuates the wounds. As Hess concludes, yes, 'we are this woman, each of us, all of us.'"

—**ALisa Starkweather**, founder of the Red Tent Temple Movement

"Through scholarship and lived experience, Lisa Hess undertakes an act of 're-storying' herself within Christian theology, speaking what has been ignored and unspoken. *Living on the Other Side* takes courage. These pages are full of heart and meaning for feminist thinkers and allies who seek a broader and deeper understanding of what Hess calls 'root tradition.' Story is the guide through this rite of passage."

—**Christina Baldwin**, author of *Storycatcher*

Living on the Other Side

Sacred Bewilderment, Holy Rage, and a Freedom Beyond Forgiveness

Lisa M. Hess

CASCADE Books • Eugene, Oregon

LIVING ON THE OTHER SIDE
Sacred Bewilderment, Holy Rage, and a Freedom Beyond Forgiveness

Copyright © 2025 Lisa M. Hess. All rights reserved. Except for brief quotations in critical publications or reviews, no part of this book may be reproduced in any manner without prior written permission from the publisher. Write: Permissions, Wipf and Stock Publishers, 199 W. 8th Ave., Suite 3, Eugene, OR 97401.

Cascade Books
An Imprint of Wipf and Stock Publishers
199 W. 8th Ave., Suite 3
Eugene, OR 97401

www.wipfandstock.com

PAPERBACK ISBN: 979-8-3852-2914-7
HARDCOVER ISBN: 979-8-3852-2915-4
EBOOK ISBN: 979-8-3852-2916-1

Cataloguing-in-Publication data:

Names: Hess, Lisa M., author.

Title: Living on the other side : sacred bewilderment, holy rage, and a freedom beyond forgiveness / by Lisa M. Hess.

Description: Eugene, OR : Cascade Books, 2025 | Includes bibliographical references and index.

Identifiers: ISBN 979-8-3852-2914-7 (paperback) | ISBN 979-8-3852-2915-4 (hardcover) | ISBN 979-8-3852-2916-1 (ebook)

Subjects: LCSH: Christian education. | Theology—Study and teaching. | Theology, Practical. | Spiritual formation. | Psychic trauma—Religious aspects—Christianity. | Spiritual healing.

Classification: BV1464 .H48 2025 (paperback) | BV1464 .H48 (ebook)

VERSION NUMBER 05/14/25

New Revised Standard Version Bible, copyright © 1989 National Council of the Churches of Christ in the United States of America. Used by permission. All rights reserved worldwide.

Dedicated to

Ruth and Ben
of blessed memory

May you be pleased,
or even better,
proud

*For the glory of God is a living human being, and
the life of a human being is the vision of God.*
—Ireneaus of Lyons, *Against Heresies*

The prohibitive cost of denying Otherness could not be more crucial to the survival of the human race. Our mass refusal to face the "Other within" has engendered a regimen of sociopolitical atrocities, genocidal horrors and environmental devastations—a virulent storm of global proportions. Contrary to the tenets of foreign policy and social activism, a remedy for this aggressive pandemic cannot be mediated, legislated, or enforced at a global, regional or municipal level; it can only begin at the root, within each individual (intra-personally) and within our nearest and most intimate relations (inter-personally). It is therefore in this small and most private of territories that the potential for a truly humane society begins.
—Daniel Deardorff, *The Other Within*

You can't hate someone whose story you know.
—Margaret Wheatley

Contents

Preface | xi

Introduction | 1

Chapter One: A Woman's Economic Trinity and Crucible | 15
Chapter Two: Anger Become Conscious, Become Holy | 43
Chapter Three: Awakening to an Unknown Inside—Return to the Body | 73
Chapter Four: Problem of Prayer Well Met in a Trinitarian Möbius | 94
Chapter Five: Forgiving the Divine: It Has Something to Do With Grief | 124
Chapter Six: The Teaching No One Wants: Surrender | 148
Chapter Seven: The Body of Humanity, Scripture, & Faith ... Oh My | 167
Epilogue: Ancestral Wounds Healing—Absence Becomes Presence | 196

Appendix: Resources for Open-Space Communities of Practice | 205
Bibliography | 211
Index | 219

Decades of rage holy and righteous well-earned
in a world dangerous for so many
laughter in my belly
clean, reconfigured, revealing
disconnection
into deep connection,
ruptures
redeemed in faith and family
suffering
surrendered
embodied
eyes shining,
being shown:
irreconcilables
can dance
together in love
in a freedom song
found somehow beyond
forgiveness without will,
holy rage set apart
bewilderment become sacred,
grief hidden within as praise.
Abandonment can become sacred
held in the Body of Humanity.

Prayer becomes devotion,
waiting learns to be active,
yearning becomes desire
becomes pleasure circling
patiently for years, forever
within me, us, them
healing wounded ones
into many now gathering.
Regrounded trust unearned
in this world's cracked
cement pavement, broken open
just one fragile thready life
forgiving the divine as an amaryllis,
such expressive delight blossoms
in mercy, hope, lovingkindness,
faith refreshed to companion
sometimes even transfigured
suffering into belonging
only the body knows
in belly laughter
bewildered
I AM AS I AM

Preface

POETRY GIVES A SHAPE and felt-sense of things that would otherwise take thousands of words. The poem on the preceding pages, for instance, whether read top to bottom or bottom to top. *Living on the Other Side* is the thousands-words interpretation of the poem, with which my ninth-grade English teacher might smile (*z"l*). This book attests to the paradoxical sufferings as a woman within my root wisdom tradition, Christianity, within which I continue to live, breathe, and serve as both clergywoman and practical theologian. It is an oft-painful recounting of the unseen, persistently unconscious abandonment of women as women by the church configured as congregation today, by other women and men in faith, by families imagined only with a domineering presence at the helm, in traditional institutions and historic root traditions whose co-creation by both women- and men-identified human beings has disadvantaged women and the unseen for millennia. All of this is historically and theologically demonstrable, even as there is also an *other side*, no less true.

The storied-life here in Christian roots and streams also embodies an intensely delight-filled, theologically-themed arc of utter grace in diverse continuities, relentless belonging, and ancient communal wisdoms digested over decades so to sing anew in a woman's form, finally in the cadence and shape-singing of *women*. It is a work of self-implicated integration: an exile from congregational Christianity healed and healing in what I call the Body of Humanity—a non-sectarian *ecclesia*[1] of ancient but new open-space wisdoms, multiple lineages of circle-way in which human beings are (re)learning to gather, (re)learning to deepen consciousness, to

---

1. In its original Greek sense, *ecclesia* simply means "assembly" or "gathering," those "called out" to gather. Those refused by or unable to breathe within today's congregational forms are yet "called out to gather," I argue. For clarity's sake, *ecclesial* is reserved mainly for *congregational* Christian settings.

listen more deeply to the wounding stories of others, to honor the utter dignity of every sentient being within and beyond our tribal factions so polarized today. The deeply cathartic belly laughter to which the poem testifies signals the resulting life abundant, freeing, in Love.

It is odd to be writing a book on the interconnectedness of things—of deepening our capacities to perceive such a luminous thread—amidst separations we know today. It takes a return to the body, a willingness to see patterns in intergenerational lineages, a courage—*coeur-rage*[2]—to disrupt forces of unforgiveness in hope of healing. Not certainty, by any means, but a just hope. Organized into a chiasmic narrative for theological resonance with that hope, the stories recounted here have all been felt viscerally, then emotionally, spiritually-theologically in my own body, so to metabolize the pain and joy, to learn and even demonstrate how to grieve and praise anew, to enter into abundance, ultimately to offer gratitude and praise for *all of it*.

The excruciating stories are the ones able to uncover the use of faith language and practice that imprisons and disempowers, binding and dissociating human beings from their bodies in wisdom traditions meant to heal and liberate. Here we catch glimpses of ancestral lineages long-wounded, even as they are long-loving. Intergenerational healing, trauma-informed spiritual practice, and persistent congregational engagement weave together in lament, and some weary laughter. It's laugh or cry, or in my case, *both*. The paired stories of assurance, surprise and redemption counter these confining-binding tendencies in congregational communities today, so to point to a different way of perceiving informed by what might be called an *imaginal realm*. Though nonlinear and seemingly serendipitous, this *seeing with the eye of the heart* points to a deepening spiritual maturity within and beyond congregational walls, in bewilderment, rage, grief, ultimately surrender in a return to the body, in the Body of Humanity. Both painful and assuring stories shared here have been integrated, explored, and mined for a purpose of healing, wholeness and invitation: to imagine renewed and renewing faith language and practice that might better liberate, heal and beckon us all into shared risk, exploratory collaborations, ultimately emergent wisdoms more nourishing of life abundant, merciful, hopeful, and loving.

Barbara Brown Taylor observes that *solar* Christianity *loves* the triumphalistic stories of faith grounded in certainty and the familiar,

---

2. Quanita Roberson, personal conversation.

expertly argued interpretations of Scripture. Always trusting in Light alone, this sense of tradition is not to be challenged or stretched into something more subtle, flexible, grounded in a divinely-sparked human body. *Lunar* Christianity, in contrast, models a way to *walk in the dark* in a deeply embodied faith ever seeking understanding, ever surrendering into a love unseen but palpable in desire well met, well refined, faithfully shaped *in the flesh*.[3] *Living on the Other Side* is more lunar Christianity than anything else. It is a lengthy, viscerally grounded proclamation of both the divine abandonment of women by the church and the unexpected, even unwilled freedom that breathes into a body beyond *forgiving the divine*, an admittedly incomprehensible phrase with the proverbial digital-Easter-egg hidden within.

Tending to Interconnection: Ungainly Words, Punctuation, Parentheses

Tending to this interconnectedness begins in unexpected places, like common word choices and even the very grammar or language that can analytically fragment what is viscerally experienced in the body as whole. The woundedness so apparent in our world today can be understood in as many ways as there are human beings with stories, though we attempt to describe it most urgently from our own injuries alone. For my part, I honor this complexity with a persistent effort to refuse the word *patriarchy* and *patriarchal* throughout the text, as well as many of our identity-politics language that arises out of that wound. For one, *patriarchy* becomes a bit of a straw-man and lightning rod in conversations we need to be open-ended, curious, whether with family members or in faith community life. Patriarchy is only one way many have historically pointed to the persistent injustices remaining relevant in all areas of shared human endeavor—home, work, civic spaces, government, business, religion, etc. It has served us well, as far as it could. Jungian Marion Woodman provided a helpful reminder, however: *patriarchy* is an abuse of the *power principle* in collective human life, the collective unconscious. It's not masculine, nor about "men."[4] Our power-over habits of mind and practice have deeply wounded men and women, nonbinary and queer.

---

3. Taylor, *Learning to Walk in the Dark*, 7–8.
4. Woodman, *Sitting by the Well*, lecture six.

Not surprisingly, then, a *lot* of our ideological language arises out of this wound. Including the word, *feminist*, by the way, which I continue to use for the unhealed part of myself still needing to be seen and heard into wholeness, reconnection. These words have sacred purpose for healing in the Body of Humanity *and* there comes a time to relinquish them. To rejoin a larger community of being human. A woman of African descent would use "womanist," for instance, and *should*, as long as it serves her purposes for being seen and heard in her storying. As our communal fabric continues to tear, there will always be more words necessary from those who are not being heard or seen with the current words we have. While it becomes somewhat ungainly in prose, I therefore try to use combination phrases like power-over or abuse of the power-principle to focus attentions on the *communal-fabric-tearing dynamic* in our forces of unforgiveness around gender, dualisms, even orientation discourses so prevalent in our world. I honor the use of those words for the advocacy functions they serve *and* all of those categories arise out of the wound, the torn communal fabric of being-human-together. None of those words—in my experience—creates deeper capacity for connectedness, which in the end is what this work hopes to contribute. I do not expect this to be easy to digest in a culture drenched in unresolved rages, of course.

We need to use language that we need, if we are to stand with integrity in our embodied diversities. My use of the word "God" is complemented by a neo-logism that found me along the way in F/feminine awakening: *Godde*. It is pronounced just like the traditional word, yet in written form, honors a middle way between God and Goddess. I can no longer be complicit in the silencing of the F/feminine by suggesting language doesn't matter. It does. Yet *Goddess* is not a term that has ever landed easily in me, given it is demonized in Hebrew and Christian Scriptures and therefore internalized as dangerous in most people of faith I encounter. *Godde* honors the collective-traditionalist ecclesia's apparent unwillingness and unreadiness to welcome the F/feminine while honoring my need for integrity if/when I am to be present there. It even has a whiff of Germanic-heritage (*Gott*), which suits my own ancestral lineages. So every time I speak in public, I use feminine pronouns in liturgy and say *Godde* as what honors my own body's experience, even when all those around me refuse it, or me. Then as this manuscript drew to completion, a new combination emerged with some resistance in me, but also a sense of integrity. God and Godde retained a division not congruent with the Oneness I experience in my faith today.

So *God/de* emerged in prose, honoring this Oneness I profess. The usage of it is growing on me, but I cannot use it when I feel the F/feminine is silenced or refused, abused. Of course, in tending others' words, I retain their word choices within traditional expectation.

Even ungainly grammatical choices of our language can highlight an intention for connectedness amidst analytical language that tends to fragment and divide. Consider my frequent use of parentheses and forward slashes with capital/small letters. Let's start with (un)conscious. I regularly experience colleagues and family members as hostile to the F/feminine, to the most fundamental way I am in the world. The majority of instances when I feel pained are not malicious, nor even ostensibly conscious. Yet judging another's "woke-ness" is dehumanizing and offensive, ultimately distrusting of the sacred purpose in our differences because of un-metabolized pain in the perceiver. (Un)conscious is my way to honor human dignity and my pain-body at the same time. I experience behaviors as conscious, with intention, when they hurt; long-loving relationships attest to love, lack of awareness more than malice, unwillingness for reasons I cannot resolve within *me*. We all act according to the (religious-social-civic-intimate) scripts we know most, right? Consciousness is signaled by curiosity for me; those closest to us can struggle most to see anew in curiosity, to honor our newest intimate changes. Congregations, even families, are rarely that curious, particularly if it requires growth unchosen and undesired. (Un)conscious honors my experience and their love at the same time. I therefore practice this nonjudgmental stance—emphasis on *practice*—by saying I continue to serve in academic and ecclesial environments *(un)consciously* hostile to the F/feminine.

The use of a forward-slash with capital letters serves a unifying intention as well. The use of capital letters to signify the divine or a popularly perceived collective is a convention I still find useful. It's been absolutely crucial for me to distinguish the Feminine from a clearly masculinized God in ancient text and wisdom tradition. Feminine can be understood archetypally—small letter warranted—or more viscerally, as Spirited life in bodies—capital letter warranted. I speak therefore of awakening to the F/feminine which points to both archetypal nuance—small letter—and to the divine spark within each of us, stunningly Spirit-instigated or prayed into my very flesh—capital letter. The gift of the F/feminine is this very unity, *in the flesh*, dissociated and shamed by most traditionalist (Christian) theologies. Spirit-spirit intimacy is how my own mentor, James Loder, urged. S/spirit would mean the same thing.

Living on the Other Side is therefore a harvest book for the interconnectedness of things, pointed to in the grammars shaped largely by men, reshaped to match and name what I've been given to know within a woman-identified body. It's my own sense-making in the luminous perception of it all, in a bewildering life both in exile from congregational Christianity and in my return to a renewed trinitarian faith as the wholehearted, wholly embodied woman my tradition may never recognize nor honor as sacred.

"I once wrote a book . . . in order to make sense of my own journey and my own emotional confusion," confessed Elizabeth Gilbert, author of *Eat, Pray, Love*. "All I was trying to do with that book was figure myself out. In the process, though, I wrote a story that apparently helped a lot of other people figure themselves out—but that was never my intention."[5] This spoke to me deeply, even as Gilbert presses her point in a way that discomforts too. "Please don't try to help me. . . . Whenever anybody tells me they want to write a book in order to help other people, I always think, *Oh please don't.*"[6] I struggled with her sentiment for *years*, given most everything in my own psychological-spiritual makeup is *honed to help*. Seminary professor. Educator. Scholar. Clergywoman. Wife. Daughter. But here, considering the whole story arc, I understand. I even agree. For the first time, I have written aiming to be utterly honest *with myself* in my experience(s) as a woman, finally conscious of being in a woman's body, in a world quite dangerous for women, often made moreso by historic wisdom traditions.

Decades of feminist, womanist, mujerista, and conscious feminine scholars have wrestled with how to live with integrity and conscience as a woman in traditions and institutions (un)consciously hostile to the F/feminine. I bow deeply to all who have come before me, so many voices and beloveds who have co-created ancient and new healing paths for women-identified bodies to come more fully into their own sacred worth. Even so, I found the majority of today's much more contemporary-specialized disciplinary offerings in response to this challenge insufficient for what I have faced, what I needed. We have decades of fragmented and increasingly (if professionally-formal) enraged expertise that simply could not help me *with my rage*. As Toni Morrison purportedly said, "If there is a book you want to read, but it hasn't been written yet, then you must write it."[7]

5. Gilbert, *Big Magic*, 98–99.
6. Gilbert, *Big Magic*, 99.
7. Morrison, "Ohio Arts Council Speech."

This is the book I wish I could have found when it was time for me to become more fully the human being, fully alive, I was always meant to be. It is one thesis of this book that no one is fully alive without the F/feminine awakened and welcomed within, regardless of gender, which requires in every human being a willingness to delve deeply within their own bodies, becoming responsible for their own part of healing personal and intergenerational wounds ripping us apart today. Unbidden by me, grounded in an everpresent sacred bewilderment known in my body as desire, palpable as pleasure, it is a renewed and renewing Trinitarianism enlivened in the Body of Humanity Who brought me safely here, a side with no sides, immersed in Belonging.

My hope is to sketch a vision—only one—as given to me over three decades of theological formation, for living on the other side of what some call this Great Turning.[8] A time of great chaos amidst our climate crisis, political unrest, ecclesial discord, familial refusals, refusals of our human embodiment and our interconnection to every living being, widely understood. I've been given just a glimpse of what a faith-filled, deeply rooted practitioner's life *could* be, welcoming sacred bewilderment, holy rage, and the freedom that is inexplicably connected to forgiveness most of us are not yet seeking, from anyone. It begins with a *return to the body*, a willingness to reconsider *faith* and *community* shaped deeply but not solely by historic wisdom traditions, and participation-presence in what I've called the Body of Humanity, a (re)gathering ecclesia able to hold space, witness pain that cannot be fixed, and trust each of us to grow up, show up, offer and receive generously for the good of Earth and all.

I am thankful to Charlie Collier at Cascade Books whose persistent stewardship of innovative scholarship and creative writing over the years helped me catch the courage I needed for this volume, feasibly a final offering from one who never expected to land in higher theological education in the first place. I never planned to write another book but knowing there might be a place for it to land helped me stay the course. He is probably the best one to see and know I've been writing the same book, with *all* my books, for over twenty years. Deep gratitude to United Theological Seminary and its Board of Trustees for the timely sabbatical, without which I would not have labored so deeply, for so long. Woven in as faculty consultant to the doctoral cohort of Dr. C. Anthony

---

8. Macy and Serrante, "We Are the Great Turning."

Hunt—Enacting MLK, Jr's Beloved Community—I have been blessed with fellow pilgrims in the fertile-crescent of human rights in Alabama. My hope is that our journeying is palpable here, with deep gratitude. Without the faithfulness (and fragility) of my students, I would not have seriously considered delving into Trinitarian theological discourses as the conscious feminine theologian I am. Honoring them requires me always to attempt building bridges between their congregational worlds and my own Spirit-led integration of the sacred mysteries within and *beyond* such systems. Particularly for stewarding the gifts and challenges of awakening to and healing within the Feminine in all of us, desired or not. Finally, a smile for Holy Wisdom Monastery in Madison, Wisconsin, with abbess Lynne Smith: before my final sabbatical week in your contemplative midst, praying the hours, being on the land you steward, I had lost hope that a woman could *viscerally* feel such belonging in historic Christian community. Your faithful labor in liturgical tradition and ecumenical welcome honors the F/feminine so deeply, I knew I had found a Home, even if I don't get to visit as often as I would like. Just knowing you are (all) there gives a woman her heart back in fearful times.

To spirit-friends, near and far, you have given me hope when despair came knocking—you sent the random text or email; you made the phone call or nudge of inquiry seemingly out of the blue but so well timed in Spirit. Deep gratitude to you all, especially Susan Hagemann, Irwin Kula, Brad and Becky Hirschfield, LaTanya Wilson, Jean Jensen, Karol Dyer, Beth Lodge-Rigal, Libby Smith, Wendy Farmer, Saida Harle, Éva Porpáczy, Cynthia Thompson, Robbie Brandon, Tenneson Woolf, and Nicole Frederickson. Girlfriend Theology sisters—Ellen Nygaard, Mary Coffey, and Ginger Meeks held the retreat space for the three stories to emerge. Fire & Water peeps hold a larger container of deepening listening, shared lament and laughter—our monthly Zoom coffee circles mean more than I could say. David Watson, I am thankful for your sacred vocation as scholar and dean, but moreso, for the ways in which you live into intellectual virtue and your own version of bewilderment as you have witnessed Spirit's workings in my own life, so divergent from your own. Let us continue The Conversation for as long as Spirit decides, eh? Two elder stateswomen of faith—Cheryl Bridges Johns and poet Alicia Ostriker gave me hope and words precisely when I needed them. To the upcoming conscious feminine scholars—Amy Chavez, Heather Husted, and Jill Harman—you are calling forth a side of me I didn't know I even wanted to retrieve. A pastor of deep Heart companioned me through the surrender into a preacher's wife voice this past year—Kelley Shin—with blessed pots of tea. My CrossFit community of practice held space in ways mostly unknown to them but deeply, viscerally significant. You matter so very much in my return to the body, my capacity to be a balanced, non-reactive presence amidst people of faith: Wendy Thompson, Nicki and Jim Hagler, Andy Kerschbaum, and Matt, especially Melissa Mitchell. The Body of Humanity arguably formed most fully in the last decades (and some) of song-artists who accompanied my deep-feelings most accessible in music. A playlist called *Living on the Other Side* can be found on Spotify.

While my family and I have made this book what it is, there are three spirit-friends—elder, anam cara, and soul-hitched spouse—whose fidelity to their own sacred work and tenacity in loving me held space for all that follows. Quanita Roberson, whom I'm blessed now to call an elder, came into my life in an Essence of Circle training before the pandemic. Her eyes, laughter, and Wind-Warrior way drew me into the final leg of this very long journey I didn't even know I needed. She really *is* the promise of forgiveness and reconciliation in the world, as her Facebook page reads. This book is evidentiary exhibit A. *Anam cara* and local co-conspirator (in all things circle, spiritual direction, SoulCollage, and now returning to the Land), Lisa Michael Heckaman blew into my life over a decade ago, walking with me through the deep valleys and luminous mountaintops of this journey. We all need folks who can hold the rope when we are lowered into holy darkness; she held that rope more times than either of us can count. With her husband, Chris, they are an intimate weft-and-warp for surviving and thriving in such a crucible. May campfires and the Caribbean always beckon us into the mysteries that faith invites. Finally, Brian D. Maguire is the soul-hitched man who regularly takes my breath away in his capacity to love beyond injury and persist beyond hurt into grace undeserved. His love of swords makes me smile because he was the proverbial *midwife* of everything here. He is the most healed and healing man I know, embodying a deep feminine wisdom within an attractive, intensely romantic masculine. All of our marriages to one another have blessed me, even saved me, in the covenantal Love that continues to save us for sacred work more important than how we may feel about it on any given day. When is our next cruise again?

Lisa Magdalena Hess

July 22, 2024
Feast Day of Mary Magdalene

Introduction

LIVING ON THE OTHER *Side* was written first and foremost to invite soul-nourishing life on the other side of rage. I see unredressed, unresolved rage as one of the most pressing challenges in our communal worlds today, whether we understand "communal" as ecclesial, civic, political, ethnic, or religious. Part of the difficulty is that we've dressed rage up in a variety of clothes more acceptable for the power-dynamics in which we live, depending upon the *body* in which we live. Sometimes rage is cloaked in words of faith, when it wields other words as weapons like *belief, Orthodoxy, Scripture, heresy,* and *tradition*. Words of faith traditions are quite apparent in their use to fragment and divide, accuse and justify whatever is desired: purity, connection, justice, truth, certainty, etc. Sometimes it's expertise itself that parades our rage, decked out in professional roles assuring some offense "is not personal," or the now socially accepted, conceptually violent speech we call discourse today. Rage itself, particularly in bodies without power or perceived agency, comes to us dressed in clothing we've been taught to find ugly, even dirty: inherited and ingested shame, scapegoating projections onto others, refusals of our own body's *humus* or earth, let alone its wisdom, signaled in nonverbal but ultimately effective languages of chronic disease and ill-health. The fruit of rage is division, discord, polarization, neglect, refusal, accusation—none of which mirrors the fruit of Spirit we say we seek.

As the writing deepened over two years, perhaps even over a decade, a variety of other referents emerged with the question, *on the other side of what?* Just like prayer, a word of infinite Referent. Today, I find myself on the other side of *sides*, polarizations, though it's so easy to get pulled back into fideistic dualisms in faith and politics. I'm more often on the other side of *outside*, which becomes *inside*, regularly. Somatic work, it's sometimes called. An unsought awakening to the conscious feminine drew me deeply within my own bodysoul, which blessedly did lead me to the other side of imposed shames, then to sacred work resonant within but outside of more traditionally institutional roles, personas. I wondered for a time whether I might someday find myself on the other side of *grief*, though we never get fully on the other side of that unless we also numb ourselves out of *praise*.[1] I have been *bewildered* more often than confident in these last years, so I can say that bewilderment is certainly on the other side of certainty. Ultimately, I know I yearn for us all as people of rooted traditions or none to live on the other side of *fear*, for all our sakes. Fear is the most visceral yet cloaked engine for rage out of all of them.

So I offer my most grounded, gentling redress and response to the unresolved angers—rage—in my own life, with my own expertise and professionalism held loosely in the wings. I bring the deepest storying I have as a seminary professor and clergywoman through the most grace-filled, healing spiritual, theological, communal resources that have found me for largely two primary aims. One, I hope to imagine with you in a public way that there could be other ways to be deeply heard in this world and know a freedom that cannot be taken away. There *are* other ways than experts cloaking their unresolved angers in formalized discourses that never invite us *inward* to know if their wisdom resonates. There are better ways than the rest of us having to scream or storm the institutions of government and religion to be heard. Each of us is a nonexpert in many more areas of our lives than any in which we may claim even minor expertise. "It is therefore in this small and most private of territories that the potential for a truly humane society begins,"[2] observes Daniel Deardorff. "Although attempting to bring about world peace through the internal transformation of individuals is difficult, it is the only way,"[3] cautions the Dalai Lama. From my own root tradition, I turn to Irenaeus of Lyons, *Gloria Dei vivens homo*, usually translated "The glory of God is man fully alive."[4] Or *woman*, in my case.

Two, and more theologically themed, I point to a renewal of faith through a return to the body and a forming and re-forming Body of Humanity able to hold, witness, and invite healing of intergenerational woundedness quite diverse yet also honoring commonalities in all of us.

---

1. Prechtel, *Smell of Rain on Dust*, xii.
2. Deardorff, *Other Within*, xviii.
3. The Dalai Lama, foreword to Thich Nhat Hanh, *Peace is Every Step*, cited in May, "From Cruelty to Compassion," 165.
4. Irenaeus of Lyons, *Against Heresies*, 309.

Given my root tradition, the language for the driveshaft of all of that is a *renewed and renewing Trinitarianism*, the ever outward-inward reaching of divine love. There *are* ways to invite even fearful congregations into deepening spiritual maturity in which intergenerational healing can happen. We simply haven't traditioned this wisdom of serpents and innocence of doves very well . . . yet. The narrative aims to invite a more vibrant, healing life—personal and shared—toward more abundance and Mystery than rage or argued righteousness in faith could ever provide. God's glory is a human being *fully alive*. In my own words, living an expressive delight able to companion the suffering of self and other.

Mostly, this is a journey to the other side of certainty as we crave it, with something more grounding in an everpresent sacred. Contrary to much philosophical speculation, this renewing Sacred is *not* Secular,[5] though it is heresy in my home to say so. We simply do not speak wisely of this One . . . yet. Made possible because of a stunning web of spirit-friends—practitioners of deep observance in multiple wisdom traditions and none—I am returned as whole to my root tradition, though I now know it as a rootedness without walls or lid. Or even much congregation. I know it more in my body and this larger Body of Humanity than I know it in any Christian congregation or denominational sense today. Non-sectarian definitions and languaging. Accountability but not confinement, nor imprisonment to the past alone. Community held by those capable of witnessing humans' pain, this centuries-long divine abandonment, without attempting to fix it in known categories or silence it as unfaithful. A Body of Humanity, across traditions and none, trusting me to do the healing work of transfiguration within a Force and Flow intimately within me yet irrepressibly beyond me,[6] Who never lets us go, Who breathes so deeply in each of us that we cannot escape if we tried.

Living on the Other Side will attest to the re-storying and practices that found me, that are necessary on this other side of certainty. Returning to the body, risking practices that disrupt the cycles of unforgiveness

---

5. Taylor, *Secular Age*. See also Smith, *How (Not) to Be Secular*. I honor how this pervasive stream of literature is speaking so deeply to so many I love. I also recognize it speaks primarily to populations grieving the loss of a felt-sense of centrality and voice amidst a proliferation of human voices and experiences.

6. The use of "transfigured" is intentional. *Transfiguration* doesn't remove the wounds even as they may be healed. See Ross, *Silence: a User's Guide*. *Transformation* was more familiar, with my mentor's *transforming moment*, so I had used solely that term, for decades. *Transfigured* attests that this woundedness of the F/feminine is a crucial part of the sacred in all of us.

in our day, we can live and breathe in a gracious-unnerving space of *bewilderment* that does become *sacred*. It requires unending contextual discernments, relational deepening of authentic connection across difference(s), and theologically, an unexpected freedom and peace that does not depend upon the conditions of peace.[7] It does not relinquish my own felt sense of absolute truth within which I've been conditioned to think, but it does require a deeply engaged humility and intellectual virtue in commitment to listen to everyone, maintaining integrity *and* living open-heartedly, with compassion, able to companion the suffering of self and others.[8] It requires strengthening skills to set boundaries, "the distance at which I can love you and me simultaneously."[9] Most of all, it requires living humbly in the sense of finally in my own *humus*, my own flesh, revealed to me now as holy, sanctified and sanctifying. If the earth, if all people, are to be able to breathe and live in their unalienable dignity, we will need to hold our bodies and our lived-traditions differently than we were taught. The wisdom of the F/feminine arrives precisely in H/her own time, for just that purpose, for those willing to receive H/her.

Ancestral Lineages—Wounded and Healing

I can still remember the pancake breakfast nearly fifteen years ago at which I literally *felt in my bones* that I was going to write about my (mostly paternal) family. I was enjoying the extended Hess family reunion in Estes Park Colorado. We are an intense people with a deep love for one another and an impassioned intellectual–faith history. At one point, I even thought I would do a scholarly study of the hymn tune, *Grosser Gott*, or sometimes *Grosser Gott wir loben dich*, which is a beloved family table blessing we've sung for generations. It's known in Protestant hymnals today as "Holy God, We Praise Your Name." Goosebumps arise on my arms just remembering how we sound when we sing it together over a meal, the uncles singing parts. My beloved Brian knew I needed some reprive, so out for pancakes we went.

Tears began as I became viscerally aware that someday, I would write into the mythically-tinged *ethos* of who we are, undergirded by a cherished history in faith, family, belonging, and service. *I am because*

---

7. Levandoski and Finley, *Sanctuary*.
8. See also Kula and Loewenthal, *Yearnings*: "humble absolutes."
9. Hemphill, *What It Takes to Heal*.

we are who we have been, a salty paraphrase of the African ubuntu wisdom. My paternal great-grandfather's diaries are cited in a Brethren in Christ history of the denomination.[10] Our faith-roots run deep in Pennsylvania-Dutch (Deutsch) streams of these United States. We laugh knowingly today, as my paternal grandmother was involved in the revision of the Brethren in Christ hymnal. Family lore has it that she didn't know how to play—or perhaps would not play *well*—the hymns she didn't like. Holy rascal, I think she'd smile to be named. She was arguably the first real writer in our family, as she wrote the family letter to each of her four boys every week, *for forty years*. If you persistently received the faintest copy from the carbon-copied typewriter, we'd joke about having done something to offend her. She laughed, smiling slyly without comment. So I come from a long line of deeply loving, faithful people both pleased and proud of our penchant for stories, for honoring others by asking for and remembering their stories.[11]

What I had in mind over those pancakes well over ten years ago had nothing to do with intergenerational healing of long-inherited wounds and wounding behaviors in my own ancestral lineage(s). Unadulterated hagiography was more what I was feeling and thinking. How marvelous to write about a family with no growing edges at all, right? Unrealistic and untruthful, in the end. These pages do give homage to the freedom, abundance, forgiveness and grace I know today because of my family. No less true: this healing work has been excruciating for me, *and for them*. To that, I bow, even as I proceed. These pages offer what I hope is a healthy lament for how families sometimes cannot hold spaces for one another, for our own best selves, particularly when it is time to differentiate or grow up. We try to maintain connection and love across difference, even as sometimes, we fail for precisely the reasons necessary for our personal and communal healing.

Midway through my forties, then, a mentor-elder asked a question that made me guffaw out loud, bowing in deep gratitude to my family as I also began to see a new name for myself in our midst. The context was a circle gathering exploring the disruption of generational trauma,

---

10. Wittlinger, *Quest for Piety and Obedience*.

11. My grandmother Ruth Berger Hess was known for preferring "I am pleased" to "I am proud" when assessing one's own accomplishments. "Pleased" prioritized God's gift and agency in all things, "proud" prioritized the self. Some of her friends were offended when her son eulogized her at her memorial service, *how proud she was* of her sons. Our language is *so precise* together that all the rest of us *howled*. He was right: she was *proud*, blessed and deservedly so.

what it meant to be a *cycle-breaker* for patterns of unconscious pain in one's own current and ancestral lineages. "How do you think *they* feel about having *you* in the family?" she asked us.[12] I was so painfully immersed in the family "Troubles" that had come upon me-with-them that I'd never thought to ask what it must be like *for them*. I laughed aloud, for quite a while. It felt good. Cathartic somehow. I could finally imagine what *a pain* I must be for them, for most of my extended family in that moment. I even felt sorry for them. Did that lead to a softening of the Troubles? Actually, it did. I felt seen and heard in that workshop, enough to grieve this woundedness I experience in my woman's body in my ancestral lineages. I felt the sadness fully if just for a moment *and* the laughter released some of it. As I softened, changed, so my family could draw closer, get more curious.

I take delight then, in being precisely who and from where I've come. My own ancestral lineages are deeply wounded, though you'll never hear a Pennsylvania-Dutch complaint or emotional outburst from most of us. It's simply *not done*. Which is part of the wounding, of course. We are highly educated, white, publicly cisgendered human beings with a high value of family—as the family has been known, guided, governed by the four boys (now three, upon the death of my uncle on Easter Sunday 2022, around whose bed we sang our family's blessing). Most of us track in impassioned discussions of intellectual fervor, a small majority focused upon matters of faith and theology, the other portion of us speaking through philosophy, spirituality, and the life and human sciences. We love getting together, laboring hard to have one-on-one conversations with everyone we can in the short time a reunion offers. We love good food, good wine or beer (though Grandma Ruth was a teetotaller), lots of laughter and connecting deeply with one another as we may. Mostly, we see ourselves in an intense relationality without much expressiveness of it with one another, standing in the blessed Ruth and Benjamin Hess line. For a variety of reasons, most of us choose to simply not talk about things that will bring deep feelings, which no one will know how to process themselves, let alone in the company of others.

And...I am as I am. My father has often shared an image that amuses him in being a father. Maybe even *my* father. I have an older sister, always one he said would stand (metaphorically) on the highest hill within a field, using binoculars to see the fence-lines, the potential openings, anything

---

12. Nsoroma, workshop teaching, 2022. See also *The Wisdom Walk to Self-Mastery*.

she might see "beyond." I, on the other hand, preferred walking right up to the fences, pushing against them for any weak points or gates I could find. When I found one that would let me, I'd explore whatever was beyond, come hell or highwater. Hence, Dad would say, looking heavenward, "If Kathy turns out okay, thank you, blessed Jesus. But if *Lisa* turns out okay? Jesus, You are *welcome*." He usually gets a laugh, able to name his own frustration, if pride too. I was difficult to rear well, I have no doubt. I like to think my parents are *proud*, as well as pleased. These pages do represent my own rattling of the fence lines cherished by my largely paternal family, however, for sake of the freedom offered on the other side. Few of them will probably understand their own lives this way. This is also not their book. Throughout all of it, I am so very blessed to have landed in the ancestral lineages that I am privileged to call "my own."

Structure of the Book

A couple observations about the structure of things to come. Like my previous work in text and classroom, this restorative narrative and sense-making here arise in a chiasmic pattern, rippling out from a center visible only when *seeing with the eye of the heart* first, before the eyes and the mind. In my earliest scholarly work, I called this commitment to an unseen center a *contemplative empiricism,* because I needed to have a scholarly method with an articulate name. This way of being/doing—when one is willing to risk into it—invites a way of encountering, participating in, and interpreting a life of faith from a *felt*-center instead of the more familiar linear-causal rationality(ies) within which our past and present understandings of God/de must conform (mind-eye approach). "Chiasm is a traditional literary form," explains Cynthia Bourgeault. "It consists of paired events arranged symmetrically around a center core."[13] It's essentially like a stone thrown into a pond with concentric circles fanning out around it. "The simplest form is B, A, B', with A representing the center and B the symmetrical wings. The next more complicated level is C,B,A,B',C', and the sequence continues on from there."[14] You begin to see a pattern, organized spatially or three-four dimensionally instead of linear, two-dimensional thinking. She even offers her monastic mentor's

---

13. Bourgeault, *Eye of the Heart*, 69.
14. Bourgeault, *Eye of the Heart*, 69.

imaginal reconstruction of the *Gospel of John* on the basis of chiasm to demonstrate its scriptural nuance.[15]

We are so accustomed to perceiving our world with only linear causation: *this* causes *that*, *that* caused *this* in a linear pattern *ad infinitum*. We define problems from within the habits of mind within which the problems have arisen, which never resolves them. Most of our rationalities function that way. From time to time, however, we experience serendipities or coincidences that seem so very extraordinary. Bourgeault's point with chiasmic patterning is these serendipities point to a deeper way of ordering, of perceiving and understanding our lives with deep integrity from a felt-center, more than a "before and after" conceptuality. These serendipities alert us to a larger patterning at play, one with trustworthiness. Bourgeault observes that beginning to perceive this way begins with *finding the center*, which can only really be learned by studying patterns. "The center is that which will allow all the pieces to fall into place in a balanced and harmonious order, revealing hitherto undetected correspondences. You eventually get a feeling for it,"[16] she concludes.

In this way of perceiving, meaning is caught by the heart, or in my case, *the body*, which leads us human beings today closer to the ancient-scriptural wholeness intended by *heart*. The heart experiences resonances or coherence, "correspondences" that "announce their logic by the strength of the connectivity" established between them.[17] Much like finally receiving the larger frame of reference within which dissonant opposites can find harmony together in a transformational logic,[18] "the revelation of the larger pattern restores an overall sense of spaciousness and calm. Something, someone, is in charge here; it is not all just random and tragic."[19] Unexpectedly, and certainly not from within my own wounded causation, a *renewed and renewing Trinitarianism* was the center around which all stories found their place, within which an overall sense of spaciousness and calm landed in my body. A *contemplative empiricism* within an *artisanal way* had bought me legitimacy long ago in practical theological contribution to the discipline of Christian spirituality.[20] Only in the last

---

15. Barnhart, *Good Wine*, cited in Bourgeault, *Eye of the Heart*, 71.
16. Bourgeault, *Eye of the Heart*, 69.
17. Bourgeault, *Eye of the Heart*, 68
18. Loder, *Transforming Moment*, 35–44.
19. Bourgeault, *Eye of the Heart*, 75.
20. *Artisanal* describes a theological perspective that embodies ten characteristics of *artisanal* bread-baking: it is of human scale, relatively raw and untransformed,

year did I encounter Sarah Coakley's *theologie totale*, which is much more systematic and traditionally oriented, but deeply resonant with the language I had needed long ago, needed in this work. Her words, which we will delve into in due course: a primacy of God's desire, an *ontology of desire*, gifted viscerally in the power of the Spirit—awakening, intensifying, refining-being-refined, shaping into kenotic self-offering. Her *theologie totale* prioritizes contemplation in all things, as do I, making explicit this *return to the body* held in healing work in what I call the Body of Humanity, of which Christian wisdom traditions are one tribe. The structure of the book that follows is therefore a glimpse of my own pond, I guess you could say, with a renewed and renewing Trinitarianism, awakened in desire, dropped into my life as center, rippling outward.

Chapter 1 offers the comprehensive grounding for all to come in devotion, discipline, and prayer amidst a trifecta of stories holding the plot tensions of the journey: divine abandonment of me as a woman, an incredibly early awakening to sensual desire when I was but six years old, and an unbidden anointing of my body in a DC coffee shop. Those closest to me know that my relationship with God broke in the spring of 2014, when what I call my "Days in the Weeds" overwhelmed all cognitive capacities I had with an excruciating, seemingly unending visceral awareness of abandonment. Utter abandonment by God. Void. Nothingness. Terror. Unstoppable tears. Nearly twenty-four hours the first day; about six hours, the second day two months later. Given I was awakened to desire when I was six years old, I (un)consciously knew the power of desire, even as it was submerged to survive in my ancestral lineage's woundedness around the body, deep feeling, and imposed-inherited shames. The anointing—unbidden and inexplicable to my scholarly-Presbyterian self—somehow held in place, even when my Days in the Weeds stripped all else away. This first chapter names the prayerful-grounding and three-storied crucible out of which everything else follows: abandonment back to awakening, all rage deeply viscerally held in place by means of an irrefutable, inexplicable anointing.

Chapter 2 begins a more linear approach to naming, claiming, and understanding the conscious feminine as well as the rage of someone in a woman-identified body claiming to have been abandoned by the God of the church. Those well acquainted with rage of their own are invited to

---

unbranded, personalized, transparent, authentic, local, "tasty but without pretence," and simplified. See Hess, *Artisanal Theology* and *Learning in a Musical Key*, 172–73. Original source Reinhart, "What Is an Artisanal Loaf?" 157–65.

skip this chapter entirely. It *is* for those who (un)consciously resist seeing or hearing any shadow side of the church, unwilling to even hear, let alone listen to the stories of us who are trying to be heard. A theological overview sketches three approaches to understand the rage: *prosecutorial*, *historical* with a *herstory* addendum, and a *scriptural–archaeological* approach centered within my root tradition.

Chapter 3 enfleshes the *bewilderment* of *becoming conscious* of living in a woman's body. This chapter contributes to conscious feminine reflection that honors both the awakening of feminist–womanist–womyn consciousness and the utter dignity of a woman's choice in her own life, even when she chooses *not* to align with what I call the F/feminine. I admit I am also hopeful to offer at least a *less-gendered* glimpse into journeying into the *inside of the human body* in sensation, receiving of the sacred in experiences legitimate and valid even when—or most especially when—inarticulate. Human bewilderment is non-gendered, all-inclusive, when we're honest. We need to learn skills of staying with bewilderment that can become sacred when welcomed, healed, and gifted within and beyond the self in a witnessing community.

Chapter 4 then lands us into the center of the project—deeply embodied prayer within which a renewed and renewing Trinitarianism gifts us with awakening to desire, palpable in pleasure, back into prayer, forever in an infinitely flowing Möbius pattern.[21] *Prayer* is what brings us to the chicken-egg or theory-practice problem about which theologians have been arguing forever, *which comes first*. Linear causation does not matter here, particularly as the answer is "yes." The Möbius pattern demonstrates the relationship—always both-in-one, while remaining inseparable, indivisible, unchangeable, and unconfused.[22] But prayer does become a *problem* here. How is a woman deeply steeped in Christian devotion and prayer, yet abandoned as a woman for centuries by God and the church, to make sense of *prayer*? What *is* prayer that is not complicit with one's own silencing in such a wisdom tradition? The gentle dance between embodied prayer and theological systematics offered by both Cynthia Bourgeault and Sarah Coakley offers reprieve, surprisingly. We land in an inductive approach to an embodied-spirited understanding of the Trinity, the *praying the Trinity* or Trinity as *participation* argued by two women-contemplatives deeply invested in historic Christian

---

21. Loder, *Knight's Move*, 35ff.
22. Christian theological readers, please note the Chalcedonian formulation.

traditions. For me, this process-practice-prayer counters what has always felt disembodied and solely masculine, even toxic, for my body. My hope is that even those outside of my own root tradition can feel their way into Bourgeault's *seeing with the eye of the heart*,[23] willing to enter into the dimensions of encounter in a Spirit-led ontology of desire made palpable in pleasure, translatable into their own worldview or wisdom.

Chapter 5 harvests the fruit of all that comes before, beginning to explore the bewildering and unsought forgiveness that can find us if/when we're willing to receive, to surrender, to participate in our own liberation within a community able to witness our pain, hold us to heal, trust us to return. It has something to do with learning to grieve, learning the limitations of rage. It also has something to do with a community able to do new and differently collective, collaborative work together: holding open spaces, trusting what emerges, learning to slow down and listen more deeply, on multiple levels. Because here on this "other side of rage" beckons an abundance and graciousness I could never have imagined on my own. I never consciously sought *forgiveness*, but this Force or Flow insisted, poking my theological acumen with a completely incomprehensible phrase, gift, problem: *forgiving the divine*. Through it, freedom was borne.

Chapter 6 demonstrates the pathway to the *forgiveness that finds us* even as it necessarily comes through a voice neglected and disenfranchised by the church: the preacher's wife/spouse. Offering gentle invitations for congregational awakening to *seeing with the eye of the heart*, this chapter also illustrates the significance of surrender for deeply intimate, covenantally undergirded love and belonging. Visible in my twenty-year-long street fight against it, *surrender* is yet the unspoken, undesired, unchosen invitation in a faith-filled life that none of our current practices of theological formation can teach, name or describe well, if at all. In a role and function *unchosen* and *undesired* by me, I've learned the most about covenant, empathy, surrender and desire unto raw intimacy with God, Godde, begrudgingly God/de as One.

Chapter 7 brings an economic trinity of voices into one voice to respond to constructive practical theological matters yet to be reconciled in such a journey as this one amidst congregational forms of wisdom-traditional faith life: *community* evolving into the Body of Humanity, *Scripture* reconsidered, and *faith*. Can today's declining and socialized

---

23. Bourgeault, *Wisdom Way of Knowing*, 88.

faith language and practice become transfigured into new forms better able to steward bewilderment, rage, and a forgiveness that can find us, especially when we are not seeking it?

Epilogue: the journey of a renewed and renewing Trinitarianism, awakened in desire made palpable in pleasure, emerges as one woman's plumbline for an expressive theological delight able to companion the suffering of self and others. The familiar quest for certainty is transfigured into a quest for assurance,[24] blessedly met. Ancestral wounds can indeed be healed when held in the Body of Humanity. Divine abandonment, absence, can become Presence in the most unexpected ways.

---

24. Marion, *Erotic Phenomenon*, 75.

Feminist: [femənəst] *n.* an advocate of women's rights on the basis of the equality of the sexes; a person who supports feminism, i.e., "all genders having equal rights and opportunities"; "respecting diverse women's experiences, identities, knowledge and strengths, and striving to empower all women to realise their full rights." (*International Women's Development Agency*) *n.* A term originating from the wound of patriarchy. (~Quanita Roberson)

Conscious Feminine Theologian: a formally trained Christian-theological scholar who *consciously embodies* the archetype of the feminine, in a rhythmic dance with the archetypal masculine, remaining present, actively serving in historical and contemporary settings (un)consciously hostile to the F/feminine

Preacher's Wife: the covenantal partner of a congregational minister; i.e., the recipient of multiple unconscious projections of well-meaning but unaware congregational members

["I love it when people offer up their list of expectations regarding my role, said no pastors' wife . . . ever." Or "If a pastor's wife wrote a book about life in the ministry, would it be classified under humor, horror, or fiction?" *Som(ee)cards*]

Chapter One
A Woman's Economic Trinity and Crucible

I AM A FEMINIST with a forgiveness problem, though probably not the one you expect. My problem is not in forgiving the obvious sins or sinners in power-over abusive histories exacted on all our bodies over centuries within religious traditions. I am regularly angry, even enraged, of course, to be in our world so demonstrably dangerous. No, my problem is that *I have been found by a forgiveness I was not seeking to offer. Anyone.* The spaciousness, abundance, and sacred freedom—the belonging I know deeply in my flesh and bones—is worth more to me than anything I have ever known. This is the belonging I would like us to consider, even as it retains a sacred bewilderment, inarticulate surrender, and delight with mystery to which all of our wisdom traditions point. All this does make being a feminist in today's environs a problem, however, particularly as historic traditions are conceived as *the problem* for so many of us. Forbearance of injury looks like, *could be*, complicity. Forgiveness looks weak to impossible in the habits of today's over-culture.[1]

I am also a conscious feminine theologian, trained at an establishment, East Coast seminary as a student of the Spirit-found and Spirit-healed James E. Loder.[2] After his unexpected death in 2001, I landed

---

1. A poetic term used by Clarissa Pinkola Estes to denote the psychological-societal-and-cultural forces that shape even our perception of self and other. See *Untie the Strong Woman*, 81ff.

2. James E. Loder was a Kierkegaardian, science-and-theology practical theologian who was brought into Princeton Theological Seminary's Christian Education department in the early 1960s, remaining there to teach and write into the forming discipline of practical theology for nearly forty years. He was a bit of an iconoclast, serving well underneath the academic norms of the time to invite students into the life of the Spirit he had experienced, crystallizing in his *Transforming Moment* of healing and encounter

in the vocation of seminary teaching at a freestanding seminary in the Midwest. Shortly into my tenure there, I also landed in two disparate but *consciously feminine* communities: a Red Tent/Temple circle of wilding women meeting often at the New Moon,[3] and a circle of women writers, living in celebration of the individual voice in practices of community, so to bring the feminine more fully to expression in the world.[4] This means I am an established, ecclesially located theological scholar who now embodies *consciously* this complementary *F/feminine* in traditional ecclesial settings quite unfamiliar with her or her characteristics—receptivity, hospitality, circle-way gathering, capacity to hold paradox, celebration of the individual voice in practices of egalitarian community, etc. Mostly, fearful congregations today simply can't be bothered. Beloved human beings with whom I love, serve, and live persistently refuse to see, hear, or get curious about the experience of human beings who are *acutely conscious of being women* in our world, even more so in our root wisdom traditions. So I remain present but silent in honor of the silenced, neglected F/feminine in declining, increasingly insular communities of well-meaning congregational members and theological-school personnel (un)consciously hostile to the F/feminine.

Lastly, I am a preacher's wife, a pathway clearly chosen of God/de for my soul-hitched, beloved Brian, yet a role of imposed presumption and inflicted visceral-spiritual pain for me as a woman and theologian. My own years of seminary formation taught me to avoid becoming a preacher's wife, almost at all costs. Theological students in my day regularly mimicked and made fun of the subordinate role, the secondary chair, the unending impositions of ludicrous tasks by well-socialized congregational members who (unconsciously) viewed the spouse as addendum. After dating a pastor myself—who was actually a PhD student, in my world—I swore I'd never date a pastor again. I have not. I got engaged to my first love from college days, reconnecting with him when he was a litigating-attorney with a deep passion for theology. Perfect. Or so I thought. Because here I write, a preacher's wife companioning a pastor's ministry of well over two decades. God's *bait-and-switch*, I've called it. Which is illegal in international law, by the way, if not the Kin-dom.

---

of the Spirit of Christ on the roadside of the New York State Thruway. See Wright, "Biography of James E. Loder."

3. ALisa Starkweather and Isadora Leidenfrost, *Red Tent Movement*.

4. Women Writing for (a) Change, founded by Mary Pierce Brosmer in 1991. See Brosmer, *Women Writing for (a) Change*.

So, welcome into my very own *economic trinity*, by which I mean who I am with the differentiated roles, modes, and activities in which I relate to the world(s) around me. I say this with an impish smile, half tongue-in-cheek to irritate theological types who will protest my woman-handling of doctrinal things, half in grieving-impishness to alter our reified habits of mind in Christian traditions. I do demur from the capital "T" so to honor traditional habits of the Christian community denoting the Divine. The *economic Trinity* is a longstanding Christian idea developed in the early patristic era, largely associated with church fathers Irenaeus of Lyon and Tertullian. It refers to the Triune God's relationship to and work in the world in salvation history with respect to creation, atonement, and perfection. It is complemented by, persistently interwoven with, the *immanent Trinity*, which refers to the inner Life of the Triune God, how the Three relate and yet exist as One. Lots of ink (and blood) have been spilled over the centuries in the variety of ecclesial disagreements in theological interpretation and contradictions. Resonant with that tradition, my *economic trinity* found her voice in these immanent things. S/she must therefore be holy and mundane, earthy and sacred. Each will speak in her own voice, yet we speak as one too. A deep feeling woman with an incredibly complicated, faith-ruptured, raw-intimate relationship to the One who called her into being (Ps 139), resourcing her with devotion, active waiting—prayer—from beginning to this present tense. Any renewed and renewing Trinitarianism emerges from the dance or invited relationship between, within, amidst our voices, our bodies, attuned as one in praise.

Creating the Theological Crucible

In the trifecta of stories to come, I as a conscious feminine theologian smile to see the seeds of my own theological method gifted to me for the scholarly vocation that would form. These seeds in earliest expression were simply *writing as prayer*, intensification of deep feeling into *devotion*, then *waiting actively* to allow Truth to breathe into its unexpected forms as gifts I could attempt to name in prose. I would eventually create my own neologism to describe how I learned best in Spirit's tether—a *contemplative empiricism*[5]—but make no mistake: I was making it up as I went in the early days. Today, I call it a method of *sacred bewilderment*,

---

5. Hess, "Contemplative Empiricism."

but it's the same practices, given more contemporary language. I didn't know to think of it as a *crucible*.

Those closest to me know that relationship with God broke in the spring of 2014, when what I call my *Days in the Weeds* overwhelmed all cognitive capacities I had with an excruciating, seemingly unending visceral awareness of abandonment. Utter abandonment by God. Void. Nothingness. Terror. Unstoppable tears. Nearly twenty-four hours the first day; about six hours, the second day two months later. There was no distinction in me at that time between God of the church and the Spirit of God. I suppose there still isn't, from the healed side. But this was utter abandonment by all I knew as Sacred. No One was present to help, heal, comfort, or assuage the terror. Few colleagues in ministry know this, of course, as I continued to labor in the proverbial vineyard as a professor of practical theology in a freestanding seminary in the Midwest, also as an ordained Presbyterian clergywoman of good standing in the specialized ministry of theological education. For the sake of my own integrity, I assumed I was on my way out of the theological-ecclesial business entirely. How could a woman made painfully aware of her own abandonment *as a woman* by centuries of tradition in God's name, *remain in a seminary*, teaching fledgling theological students? Clearly, I had to leave.

The *idea* of departure from my job terrified my security-minded husband, however. So began years of negotiations. Delays in my departure if not my desire to leave. For years. Eventually, in a covenantal compromise, we prepared our finances so I could resign on a moment's notice, if and when I needed. If and when the rage or dissonance simply became too much. His need for security was met. My ability to depart was available to me. Then the preparations freeing me to leave unexpectedly freed something inside of me to stay. No longer did I *have* to stay. I could stay or I could go. Staying for what purpose, I could not imagine. For how long?!? I regularly beseeched No One in Particular. Still a little surprised if now grateful, I remain to this day in ecclesial and academic systems that I find triumphalist, often patronizing, rarely feeling like the Sacred I attest to in these pages. Even in the bewildered-received language I can use. Hubris, foolishness, humility, cowardice? I do not know for sure. But well over twenty years ago I learned my job was not my work, per se. It was my work that was being drawn forth by Something or Someone beyond me, beyond all of us, decades ago and still ongoing today.[6]

---

6. Rev. Laurie Ferguson.

Which means, in the end, that my relationship with God, whom I know in prose as *Godde*, never broke. Rarely did I lose a sense of embodied-enspirited *prayer* as practice to sustain my way. The times I did, faithful practitioners—in my root tradition or in other wisdom traditions—held faith, trust, confidence in the larger purposes of God/de *for me*. For decades, non-traditional, non-sectarian communities *able to witness my pain without denying it* helped me to trust more deeply. Throughout, I have had to learn to prioritize trust in my body and in intimate spirit-friends who again and again demonstrated their love of me, their expressed commitment to my best interests. Historic religious traditions have never had the best interests of women as women as a priority, after all. The Body of Humanity could hold it all, without denial or refusal. Providentially brought into my life, these spirit-friends and circle-way communities could hold sacred-healing-listening spaces more than my traditionalist family members or colleagues. More than any ecclesial community, attempting to keep me in line with socialized, stale expectation.

Today, I can finally see this decade after the Days in the Weeds as a prolonged testing of my vocational method in a theological crucible, which also can finally *bemuse me* as a theologian. I was gifted with a *theo*-logical container that *could* hold all that would come, even when my own tradition's congregations *would not be able*. Years of prayer, intensified into devotion, active waiting. An undesired and unchosen *surrender*, long ago conditioned as trusting a felt-sense of deep-belly fire, sustained in active waiting within texts, practices, writings. Most of my graduate training was in theo-*logical* method, however: linear rationalities, cognitive discourse, and the like. Years later, I would learn from Jean-Luc Marion, "Theology can reach its authentically *theo*logi*cal* status only if it does not cease to break with all theo*logy*."[7] They were connected, yet ruptured for my own woman's body. *Dancing* across this chasm, my entire theological journey has been a slow-and-steady *return to the body*, which was then well-met by the *Body of Humanity* I had not had access to in my graduate school years. In the larger, more deeply *incarnational* container of this Body, honoring of its various tribalistic expressions as well as none, my embodied-enspirited method became more whole for what I hope to share here, how I yearn for congregational communities to mature in deeper spiritual resilience, wholeheartedness, and *koinonia*. And yet...

---

7. Marion, *God Without Being*, 139.

I felt the abandonment of God viscerally, completely, in my Days in the Weeds. Terrified.

I never walked alone. Not one day.

Both are utterly true, which I can only say today by the grace of Godde.

Writing as Devotion and Active Waiting

Hindsight is a gift, waiting for insight, craving foresight.[8] Sometimes a yearning comes upon you, an ache for what used to be, always remembered as easier than it actually was. Shortly before beginning to write anything here, I ached for my graduate student self who had been exiled for many years amidst awakening to the F/feminine. In hindsight, she was a charming survivor, a loyal-soldier who had insured my protection and successful progress in my choices, at least as much as possible. She was the one with foresight, I'd say today. Arriving into midlife, however, those wars were *over*. A deep Invitation was beginning to be tendered, to explore my own tendernesses that had been unwise back then. Impossible, even. Waiting for insight, I returned to my old journals from graduate school days, startled to find similar questions I'd been asking and newly answering about deep feeling, about my body, about *prayer*. In my bones, when I drop my mind into my heart, I am easily returned to the echoes of when I first learned *devotion* as *prayer*. That was the center of all I knew as sacred. I had been shown and taught that theological center for decades. It was in graduate school that writing became the pathway Spirit chose to shape my own body, mind, spirit in what I have written about elsewhere as *devotion*.[9]

All of me, when centered in heart even now, can *feel* me writing a final paper during Christmas break for a directed study with the man who would become my dissertation advisor three years down the road. I had felt unspeakably drawn to him—his faith, his *gravitas*, his erudite yet gentle humor. His unbidden tears in class lectures moved me. His areas of inquiry touched seeds that had been planted in me in college—science, Kierkegaard, theology. "I want to learn *how* you've woven together *what* you've woven with science, theology, Kierkegaard, Spirit . . . " I remember

8. Ginwright, *Four Pivots*, 42, though I organized my first scholarly paper for doctoral comprehensive exams this way back in 1998, a convergence of patterning decades apart.

9. Hess, *Companionable Way*, 70–77.

saying to him nervously, in a meeting I had requested. The directed study was born. I was to study with James Loder for the next seven years, eventually to sit by his bedside, singing hymns, when the aneurysm took his conscious mind. I was his final PhD graduate before he died in 2001. Writing my first thesis for him in the masters program was an *act of devotion*. To him or to God, it was hard to differentiate.

I worked for hours at a time the week after semester's end, drafting paragraphs, refining my argument on "Metaphor as Method," relying on Paul Ricouer's work, opening with Emily Dickinson's poetry. *Tell all the Truth but tell it slant — / Success in Circuit lies* . . . I found myself falling in love with this Truth, to be honest. Something ancient, something new. Beckoning me forward, intellectually, but viscerally too. All it took was *discipline*—which I had stumbled into years before in my Kierkegaard class. And *curiosity*, inherited from my father and his brothers over years of family reunions, well-seasoned and bubbling out of me. And a strange new fire I had begun to feel, in my belly. About which I knew nothing, of course. It was a *something more* that landed me in that study carrel day after day, a week after the semester ended. It had a feeling of sacred attention, with visceral intensity, urgency. There was a palpable presence in the work somehow, an abundance egging me on to look around the next corner, to explore the next page. Ultimately, to write to this Truth with whom I had fallen in love, offering up my curiosity, my fledgling disciplined habits.

There was also a sense that the Truth was writing *me*, regardless of the inherited and ingested shames deep within my body. However frail or hidden, this Truth felt *within* me somehow. Stunning to me today, given my wholeness then did not include either conscious sensation or any visceral feminine. Writing, reading, thinking, praying had become a sacred hide-and-seek game between God and me. An intense attention with sacred intent, hue, purpose. Not will, per se, nor intellect. *Devotion*. Not the proscribed "moments with God's word" I had learned about growing up, but an irresistible, utterly sacred force, somehow felt and leading me within my very own body to the next paragraph, the next texts.

Today, I see how I was being shaped in a radical *trust*. I was learning in the sensations of a sacred hide and seek that I could trust, lean in. I was being called deeper and deeper within, though I only knew how to shape my mind outwardly to the tasks ahead. Gently, I was being shown that curiosity and discipline, offered in faith, would lead to where Truth could be found. Or could find me; speak in me. Which I still believe to this day, though it has been sorely tried. This God did not protect me from abandonment, even betrayal, as a woman by my root tradition professing unconditional, gospel love while condemning and demonizing the F/feminine particularly in Scripture professed as sacred. As the Dickinson poem continues, *Too bright for our infirm Delight / The Truth's superb surprise.* That Christmastide so long ago, I was not yet prepared to become the woman I was intended to become all along.

Writing as an act of devotion seeded in me what I might call now an *active waiting on God*, an intensification of devotion in conflict or pain, resulting in stronger muscles of trust. "We do not obtain the most precious gifts by going in search of them but by waiting for them," wrote Simone Weil.[10] Capacity to withstand and sustain dissonances deepened as I knew then to focus, explore, discover this Truth that was writing me. It required active intention to show up at the page, then to wait for what might inspire. Enspirited listening, receiving, writing. *Active waiting*, which still resonates in all my sacred work today.

The *sensate* experience of it all, however, was compelling, energizing, even intimate underneath and beyond all I knew or yearned for. My work *did* catch the attention of my scholar-mentor, such that our work expanded into the next seven years. I experienced a connection and belonging in scholarly research and writing that scratched an itch within me. I came to understand this way of showing up at the page, of setting time and effort toward some "thought-project" as my sacred path. Today, I see how the *sensate experience* of it all—while never spoken aloud, nor even really honored as significant to me then—created a sign and seal, a protection of some kind. One might even call it *a veil*, with some conservative impishness.

Devotion and Active Waiting Embodies Prayer

Writing as devotion, in active waiting, *is* what Simone Weil describes as *prayer*. "The key to a Christian conception of studies is the realization that prayer consists of attention. It is the orientation of all the attention of which the soul is capable toward God. The quality of attention counts for much in the quality of prayer. Warmth of heart cannot make up for it."[11] I felt closest to the sacred when I was curious, disciplined, and writing, studying

---

10. Weil, "Right Use of School Studies," 57.
11. Weil, "Right Use of School Studies," 57.

theological and scriptural works. So I appreciate Weil's words, smiling at the wisdom of them for my own seminary students to come.

Yet I balk too. "Warmth of heart" *was constitutive*, even *protective* for me. It was the palpable, sensate presence that led me during that Christmastide so long ago. It's the memory of that sensate-leading in my own body that has guided me ever since. It was this sensate-leading that shaped my entire life's work as a *return to the body*, first through music,[12] then through covenantal companionship,[13] then through encounter with human beings of other traditions or none.[14] I now call this "warmth of heart" my *visceral awareness*, eventually *womanheart*, which can contradict more egoic-cognitive habits. If I pay attention to my own body, that is. Most of us leading in seminary contexts have been shaped to suspect the body, even utterly disregard it.

At the time, I had no reason to imagine that my physical body was distinctive in any respect. Ultimately, it is not; my body is like everyone else's body in potential and sacred intention. But I am now able to receive and perceive intuitively, sensually, dependably in ways underneath and beyond the formal theological training I was receiving. I have lived for decades into a deeply embodied, practical theological method for which I first made up words, then was found by the words of other theologically rooted women contemplatives whose language resonated with mine. The conscious feminine language I use today? From the very beginning, I was gifted with a *theological enfleshed container* that would be able to withstand all that would come: prayer, intensified into devotion by curiosity and discipline, active waiting in deepening attention. All of which led me into the Body of Humanity without which I could never have sustained what was coming. *Truth's superb surprise* bearable only in a *life of prayer*, held in a gathering-regathering ecclesia about to witness without judgment, holding me in trust I could sense was *holy*. On the one hand, I had been prepared for this journey my entire life; on the other, I was *not* prepared.

---

12. Hess, *Learning in a Musical Key*.
13. Hess, *Artisanal Theology*.
14. Hess, *Companionable Way*.

Abandonment

Those well shaped in the memorized promises of Scripture and in the socializing practices of congregational life today struggle to understand how someone like me could say she has been abandoned by God. I get it. I didn't experience any of this in my body until I was well into my forties. Classic mid-life "falling upwards" that Richard Rohr names in his book of the same title.[15] Wisdom traditions of all kinds point to void-spaces prevalent in a deepening intimacy with God. My own tradition speaks of a "dark night of the soul." Others point to midlife suffering that refines a human being's consciousness unto enlightenment or nirvana. Rafe, the abler-soul companion of Cynthia Bourgeault, foreshadowed this for me, unknowingly at the time I read his words. "That's the beginning of it. That's when you're getting somewhere. If you can only just stay present in that bare self, you'll begin to discover how the absence of God is the presence of God."[16] Ultimately, I landed in words like *mystery*, then *sacred bewilderment*.[17] Nothing about these Days offered certainty, except a certainty immersed in terror, then rage.

Write about your *Days in the Weeds*, urged a spirit-friend, early on in my journey into the conscious feminine. I had learned the phrase decades before, waiting tables at our local pizza joint when I was an adolescent. When you got slammed with too many tables at once, you let others know you were "in the weeds," so to receive help, or at least space as you whizzed around corners with drinks and often-late food deliveries. These two days in March and May of 2014, when I was in my mid-forties, landed an existential weight of Nothingness or Void onto my established spiritual frame, just barely strong enough to withstand it. Or perhaps *not* strong enough to withstand it. Terror. Loss. Rage. Today, I see this unfolding as Godde's revelation to me of my own lineage's ancestral wound regarding the body. In 2014, I had no context for that yet. It was simply something "too much" landing on "too little" in me.

As for any truly transformative journey, its instigation was innocuous, an innocent replaying of patterns so familiar as to be unconscious. On the way to Quaker meeting for worship, I listened to a song that

---

15. Rohr, *Falling Upward*.
16. Rafe, cited in Bourgeault, *Love Is Stronger Than Death*, 61.
17. I used to say simply *bewilderment*, because discernment is required for whether it is for sacred purpose. Sacred bewilderment is always *uncertainly* sacred, otherwise we'd call it certainty and move on.

unexpectedly, completely undid me. "This is to Mother You," sung by Jennifer Berezan. Her rendition of Sinead O'Connor's song[18] left my calm, collected clergywoman and theologian sobbing by the side of the road. *I had no idea why I was crying.* As I often did with anything I was struggling to understand, I wrote out my listenings in an email to a couple elder family members. It forefronted more emotional weather than was our usual, but I was so moved by the graciousness of the maternal energy, the dulcet tones of this lullaby that is also a gentle lament—a sadness for how one is often not seen or held, loved, as needed in our earliest years. Which happens to *all of us,* because infants cannot name their own needs and the disconnect ultimately serves as developmental fodder toward our own maturity.[19] Except our world has little felt-sense of this F/feminine, which the song forefronts with gentle force. I had sobbed and sobbed, being touched so deeply in ways I could not understand nor articulate. I suspect today this was final straw in an increasingly foreign-feeling and sounding path my elder-family simply could not understand, nor feel, given our ancestral refusals of feeling. The (un)conscious fears were about to erupt our ancestral wound open, raw, projected onto my own body. We were about to enter a period I deemed "The Troubles" in which my own journey was to seriously differentiate from theirs.

The awful—now awe-full—was so predictable, even innocent. I sensed their discomfort with my email so I stopped by their home en route to meeting with a new friend to allay their concerns. My earliest safety had taught me how to buffer and tend to my family whenever they were uncomfortable, even angry (which we also didn't *do* in our home). Unaware, I was afraid of their displeasure, even in my forties. And much to my distress and utter dismay, I was no longer able to assure them as I had hoped. We began to talk about things they heard that made them uncomfortable. There was a new energy in my life, which I knew as the conscious feminine, which I knew to trust in the circles of women which had begun to hold space for me. They had no frame of reference for this energy except their own unconscious fears of the body, with sexual-overtones and disgust in an erotic they could not process. Whatever all that was, it was unacceptable to them, to who they were at that time.

As I tried to rationalize with one of them about the F/feminine, what I was learning, what was so very nourishing for me, I witnessed his

---

18. Berezan, "This Is to Mother You."
19. Berman, *Coming to Our Senses*, 25–32.

face contort with disgust. Seemingly for the first time, though I'm sure it was not. Even the mention of the F/feminine triggered something in him that was deep and shaming, which he projected rather assertively *outward*. He refused any wisdom S/she might have to offer in my own experience, for anyone's experience. He lashed out at me in disgust. Then I could not unsee my other family member's silence and withdrawal, the emotional abandonment of me as a daughter, being overtly shamed by another family member, lashing out. Ashamed, I acquiesced to their need and refusal. I "made nice" and the coffee chat ended without any more conflict. I probably changed the subject and they were relieved. Here was the unexposed raw wound of my origin-family's relationship with the body, with the F/feminine, completely segregated, even demonized, in our lineage of Christian faith. I wore the searing brand on my flesh as I drove up to be in prayer-listening with my new friend.

Of course, finally at a safe distance, I began to fume. I had seen so very clearly, for the very first time, my own family's utter abandonment of a daughter's emotional experience, their complete incapacity to honor or even allow the deep pain that was clearly within me, the healing that was being offered, the nourishment I was receiving in communities of women. Processing it three years later in 2017, my journal records my own re-parenting voice I'd learn in the years that would follow, in grounded conscious feminine disbelief: *What family would not break open with the tender fear and overwhelming pain I had named? What guardian could not but hold with delicate care the beautiful and vulnerable way I named my own tender body fears? The grace in how wounds and pains could finally be held, healed, in circles of women, in a new spirit-friendship Gifted to me by God? All the language was intimate but chaste, bounded, attentive to covenant and ecclesial expectation. And still they lashed out. Shaming their own younger one, silencing her, unconsciously pushing her worst fears deep into her own flesh. The sadness rises even now, because I (seemingly) had to cower inside, retreat, contorting myself to stay within their good graces. The familiar feelings trying to grab hold of me, that I was dirty, ugly, even bad for my own body's deep feeling and inherited wounds.*

Today, I know how to answer my originating question, of course. They were being human beings wounded as they are, just as I was. I'm sure my story-telling to my family-elders was not as vulnerable and gently-tendered as I play it out in my journal. In my own fears, my voice probably had anger and rage just under the surface. But we were family, caught in our own ancestral wounds, without malice or conscious intention, transmitted to generation upon generation, all the same. "That which is not transformed will be transmitted," says Richard Rohr.[20] Or Jojopahmaria Nsoroma, "I want you and every human being on this planet to believe and learn that emotional pain can be transformed rather than transferred."[21] That day, I didn't know any of this. I arrived at the chapel to visit with my new spirit-friend, who was understandably afraid of damaging me in my own family line. I felt her begin to withdraw, wondering if our friendship was creating this family-rupture. I did my best to keep a stiff upper lip, as my inherited responses had shaped me, as any respectable academic professional would do. By the time I returned to my car, I could not stop the tears. The first Day in the Weeds had begun.

Unending tears. A rather dangerous highway drive home, difficulty seeing. Coming home to a husband uncertain how to hold space for such tears. Collapsing into bed, sleeping for a time, awakening to more tears. That day, complex thought was inaccessible. My speech was that of a three-year-old. I tried to pray. Nothing. I eventually fell to my knees, crying out to anything or all I had known as Sacred. Nothing. I remember wondering what someone was supposed to do for a *psychological-spiritual* emergency. Where was someone even supposed to go? I made a phone call to my coach, who lived in NYC area. She kindly set up a time for us to check-in by phone at 4 p.m. Around 3:45 p.m., "it," whatever "it" was, seemed to be waning. I could feel an ending of sorts, blessed by someone who was expecting me to call at 4 p.m. I made the call, walking outside to the front yard when my husband arrived home. I named my sensations, the unstoppable tears, the excruciating awareness of abandonment, utter terror. My language was coming back. The tears were stopping. Wisely, my coach listened, receiving, assuring, holding. Nothing more, but it was enough. My body was exhausted, but my mind seemed to becoming more itself again. The first Day in the Weeds was ending.

The second Day in the Weeds happened about two months later, though this time I felt it coming on. A spirit-friend had promised to attend a day-long conference with me in Columbus. A family obligation she could not refuse meant this time together was *not* going to happen after all. Another abandonment I could not withstand was beginning, no matter how my mind tried to change its perception. I did everything in my power to meet my needs that day—visiting with two other women

---

20. Rohr, *Daily Meditations*, October 17, 2018.
21. Nsoroma, *Wisdom Walk to Self-Mastery*, loc. 112–18.

friends, honoring my spirit-friend's choices, tending to myself—but to no avail. On the side of the road about twenty miles south of home, walking myself behind a mound of earth, I let "it" have me, seemingly without choice. Unstoppable tears. Utter terror. Isolated and alone. No speech at all this time. After about six hours, "it" seemed to begin to wane, enough for me to drive home. I went upstairs and slept for hours.

I have a variety of stories and language about these Days in the Weeds, their purposes ultimately in returning me to *visceral awareness in my own body* as the woman I am. Recalling it here, I can still feel the echoes of it in my cells, the whispers of terror. I know to honor my body's experience, how it completely shaped the years immediately following—the utter terror of being abandoned again at any whiff of "not being met" as I had expected, of becoming completely incapacitated for hours on end, with no confidence that Anyone or anything Sacred would come close to protect, soothe, assure me *at all*. Because Nothing Sacred *did*. Everything I knew as Holy was silent as the grave. Void. Nothingness. Utter isolation. Alone. Abandoned, utterly viscerally undeniable.

The first resourcing that found me, to make sense of the *sensate visceral consciousness* of abandonment, emerged from transcendental psychology, which I found at the local university library after the first Day. "Regression in the service of transcendence" was the formal phrase, acknowledging the mysterious return of a body to physical sensations or awarenesses of trauma in previous years of life.[22] It made sense to me, immediately after the event. It spoke my own body's plausible return to particular moments of terror, when my mind and body dissociated in self-preservation. For instance, I remember one instance when I experienced my mother's rage. The details are unimportant, but I was about three years old. In my mind's—and now body's—eye, I can still see the stairs I was sitting on as I wailed terrified tears. Perhaps I was being returned to this visceral memory, this time in an echo of my little girl's body in my adult woman's body.

An uncanny discovery confirmed a plausible storyline for the second Day in the Weeds. I was organizing my family's "archival files" I keep in various tubs in my house. Pictures, keepsakes, letters, even some books. From the most recent tub came a gallon ziplock baggie with various memorabilia from my first year of life. Pictures of me as an infant I don't remember ever seeing. The list of gifts from the baby

---

22. Washburn, *The Ego and the Dynamic Ground*, 171–202. See also his *Embodied Spirituality in a Sacred World*.

shower, with who gave what. And then, a single sheet of paper with my mother's handwriting on both sides. Tears arose, in wonder, gratitude: a *first-hand, intimate recollection of my birth*. My mother's recollection of her labor, her time in the hospital in Tegucigalpa, Honduras, the precise time of my birth, the first weeks of life. And her need to wean me from visceral connection to her body at one month old, as we prepared to fly back to the States. A glimpse of an event of separation that was not considered anything but mundane at the time. Lots of infants never nursed with visceral connection to their mothers' bodies at all, being moved straight to formula. Perhaps my own little infant body was overwhelmed by the loss of contact, because my midlife self cried from deep belly spaces when I saw my own mother's handwriting. It resonated so deeply as confirmation of what my body had already said when I was forty-five. The visceral realities my newborn-into-28-year-old self learned to contain in silence: an ancestral inheritance of bodily-disconnection, feelings unspoken and silenced, silencing.

This is not an historical accounting, remember. This is an approach via *resonance*, through intuition, deep-feeling-sensation and interconnection known in alignment or correspondences, connectivity.[23] The first story makes sense of my experience, attuned to the "This is to Mother You" song awakening me to all that I had yearned for in a F/feminine juicy and nourishing of my deepest being. The lack I have known was not malicious nor conscious, but an inherited ancestral wound of disconnection, dissociation, a chosen or unchosen *inability to feel*. The second story makes sense of six hours of tears with literally no words, an infant unable to speak to the loss of physical connection. There is nothing quite as terrifying as being unable to speak, at least when you're a seminary professor whose words *have built your life*. It was the ancestral wound—the familial refusal of my embodied experience—that instigated the entire unfolding. My covenantal partner, long steeped in precisely the same familial dynamics refusing embodied experience and deep-feeling, was completely at a loss to help me hold the experience. I attempted to abandon my own experience in hopes of staying connected with him, but it would not be denied. It was a visceral thing in my own body. These Days in the Weeds had planted an undeniable, irrefutable visceral sensate awareness of *abandonment* with little external interest from those who loved me. That the refusal would

---

23. Bourgeault, *Eye of the Heart*, 85.

be familial, faith-communal, and even divine on pilgrimage in the holy land made the sense of abandonment utterly complete.

Ecclesial-Communal Abandonment

When I reflected upon these Days in the Weeds during my first Shalem Intensive in 2017, I could no longer *unsee* my faith community's abandonment of my experience. On the first day, participants were asked to reflect upon significant encounters with God, guided by four to five questions. I *knew* I was to reflect on my Days in the Weeds, though the questions to reflect on God's Presence in important moments of our lives didn't really make sense for me. How can one speak to God's Presence experienced in two Days of utter Absence? Yet it felt this was the Nudge. This was part of why I was there in the first place. I sat for the thirty minutes of contemplative space/time, trying to understand, to hear, to pray. Was this some significant encounter(s) with God . . . or if not God, then Void, Nothingness? Was this the God who had abandoned me trying to show me something?

When we returned to the large hall, fellow participants began to share their experiences. I grew more and more quiet. No one was sharing anything about abandonment as a significant event. Finally, I raised my hand and gave a brief contour of my experience. No one said anything. Abandonment was apparently not an allowable or conceivable "event" for folks of faith there. The seeds of anger began to root deeply within me. I began to suspect it was true that God *had* abandoned me, *confirmed as true in the similar abandonment by the ecclesia*. Of course I know *now* that our collective gatherings simply do not know how to receive or hold well any experiences that discomfort public truth, experiences that won't confirm faith as certainty. Shalem leaders and participants were present with me, but few knew what to say. All I could feel was the community had abandoned me, disallowing my felt-experience in their own fears and refusals.

Divine Abandonment

About seven months after my Days in the Weeds, a trip to the holy land/Israel/Palestinian Territories confirmed this story of the abandonment of me as a woman, the abandonment of women by God for centuries as *divine abandonment*. In my role as seminary professor, I was co-leading a pilgrimage to "walk where Jesus walked," though companioned by a Modern Orthodox rabbi and spirit-friend for a curriculum we have continued to develop in these ten years.[24] The visceral-awareness in my body was born, and was being borne by steady contact with spirit-friends and women's circles. Church and academy were more and more toxic for me in these months, but into the Temple Mount we went, a group of 27 pilgrims and a raw, wounded conscious feminine theologian unseen, becoming shaped by the F/feminine.

The only place I could breathe in the entire site was a little grove of trees, sheltering the paved sidewalk path toward the door. Olive trees, perhaps some rosemary bushes nearby, were allowing me to breathe in the impressive and oppressive energy coursing through my body. This religious, historic, and mythic hotspot on our planet Earth is one of the most important religious sites in the world. Jews venerate it as the location of the First and Second Temples, the first destroyed by Babylonians, a second one rebuilt then destroyed by the Roman Empire in 70 CE. The Temple Mount is known to Muslims as the Haram al-Sharif, "the Noble Sanctuary" and third holiest site in Islam (in Sunni strands of Islam). The Jewish prophets venerated by Islam are honored here. The sacred al-Aqsa Mosque and Dome of the Rock (completed in 692 CE) were commissioned by early caliphs, a sanctuary and a shrine commemorating Muhammad's night journey, ascending to heaven. Jews consider this location to be where Abraham nearly sacrificed Isaac (but didn't). In other words, this is one of the most conflicted religious sites in the Middle East, a center of the Arab-Israeli conflict, and a prime location for the utter disregard of the F/feminine by these historic religious traditions "of the Book." I felt it all in my body, suffocating. Once we left the plaza, I breathed a sigh of relief to be out of there, on our way on the Via Dolorosa toward the Church of the Holy Sepulchre, one of the holiest Christian sites in Jerusalem.

Our group was shepherded out of the Temple Mount onto a narrow street, walking toward a right turn up the street. A small garbage truck was in the middle of the road, forcing us to squeeze into single file, each turning right at the corner. About three-fourths of the group was in front of me, talking animatedly, curious what our pilgrimage would show them next. I think all of us were a little relieved to be out of the Temple Mount.

---

24. See Hess and Hirschfield, "It's More Complicated Than We Know," 116–34.

I squeezed past the truck and turned the corner. This lady stopped me in my tracks.

She was black, bruised, smashed into pieces, laying bereft on the stone-cobbled street of the Holy City. A deep sob erupted from my belly. I couldn't move. The person behind me bumped into me, then stopped behind me. I pulled out my phone and took this picture. *Rage*. Rage was all I could feel. Searing deep belly screaming and tears I was not allowed or supposed to cry. S/she took my breath away . . . and yet the group pushed me forward, animated in its eagerness to get to the next site on our list. I was dazed, hiding, cramming everything erupting within me into my gut and my belly. I was there to companion Christian pilgrims, even be one myself. There was no time or place for me to even begin to name what had happened in my body on a narrow street in the Old City of the holy land. We entered into the Church of the Sisters of Zion, to descend into the stone-prison-chambers, where tradition has it that Jesus was held for trial. It is configured to allow groups to enter in, find a seat on a stone bench somewhere, and pray, reflect, sing, share. The timbre of the group quieted, and the emotional energy became heavy, pregnant even.

I don't even remember what chant-like song I began to sing, because it was my role or function to lead us in song in various sites. I was out of my body, for the most part. All I could hear was the raging-screaming inside *this woman's body*, now even left by me too. I didn't know how to stay with her. Our group was focused upon the *suffering of one man*. We had passed *an icon of the suffering of nearly all the women in the world*, and most of the group stepped over her, with utter disregard. No one seemed to see it, except my spirit-friend with me. I don't know how I choked a quiet song out of my vocal cords, but this Force, this Source of . . . unsure . . . was showing me *something*, to make the flow move. The rage began to be released about an hour later, in a private but companioned way, with a spirit-friend who saw me, who could help me stay with my feeling, stay with my body's experience. It happened at the Church of the Holy Sepulchre, in a concerted, clearly Purposeful way, at the side-shrine at which I had sat by myself the year before. The shrine tradition holds "the women waited, at the bottom of the cross . . . "

Crucible Wound

My Story of Abandonment became complete. I felt abandoned by my family of origin, who refused to welcome this terrifying journey I seemed to be on or any of the learning that might come because of it. My body was returned to a visceral sense of abandonment—terror, isolation, aloneness—that still companions me today, when I feel into these years. The Christian community as configured today abandons women who awaken and begin to advocate for women's rights, women's experience, women's voices to be heard. Not out of malice nor completely conscious intention. (Un)conscious abandonment all the same. Then the *piéce de resistance*, the pilgrimage to the Holy Land confirmed all this as *divine abandonment*. As a little girl, as an adolescent, as a young woman dissociated from her own body, the abandonment of me as a woman by us all was undeniable. Especially in the academy. Especially in the local congregations of the Christian church.

Denial of *who I was becoming* for the sake of protecting historic traditions crafted largely by men. Denial of the experiences of women, even when offered in their own voices. Denial of the systemic realities of institutions that keep the injury, abuse, neglect, and abandonment of women persistently in practice today. Denial of women's cadence in the Scriptures written largely by men. I was finally *conscious* of it all, *feeling* the sensations of this abandonment in my cells, flesh, bones. Rage at an irrevocable, impossible-to-reconcile loss of my own body's sensation, my own feminine, *for decades*. Most of my life, a deeper life of intimacy and participation in pleasure was taken from me, without even a thought that it could matter.

The Days in the Weeds were terrifying, exhausting, excruciating. Yet the *denial* by everyone around me in my familial-congregational-marital life was almost worse than the terror. What I can say today is the only One large enough to withstand the Accusation—righteous as it is—is the One I now call Godde, eventually God/de, if I am pressed by community to One-ness. God of the church had abandoned me, clearly, yet the utter refusal of my experience was made bearable only by those spirit-friends and women's circles who knew how to witness, without judgment. Communities of sacred, non-sectarian commitments to what I now call the Body of Humanity held me, honoring the human dignity of *each of us*, no matter what. There was still some Flow or Force in this Body of Humanity who kept showing me *just enough of a sign* for me to stay, to learn prayer in my body, relinquish my own words and actively wait. Christians might say "at the foot of the cross," but know that language would have exacerbated the woundedness in me. I literally could have punched you in the face.

With a little foreshadowing for material to come in later chapters, a bi-furcated journey into a deeper integration was beginning. It erupted as a deep-belly grief, a sadness unknown as sadness while it is experienced as rage. Michael Lerner highlights this experience as the "second gate of grief" in Francis Weller's work, which we will explore in detail later. While we all know the first gate of grief, Lerner says, "the second gate surprises us: *the places that have not known love*."[25] He cites Weller's words directly, "These are the places within us that have been wrapped

---

25. Lerner in Weller, *Wild Edge of Sorrow*, xiii.

in shame and banished to the farthest shores of our lives . . . These neglected pieces of soul live in utter despair . . . The proper response to any loss is grief, but *we cannot grieve for something that we feel is outside the circle of worth.*"[26] My entire life, being a woman in a woman's body was *outside of the circle of worth* in my lineages. Without malice. (Un)conscious. The F/feminine was simply suppressed, disempowered, disdained. As was human desire, for that matter. Bodies were to be functional and cleaned regularly. They were never to be explored nor loved from the inside. No one in my lineages had ever known what that could be like. Which of course, *paradoxologically,*[27] gave me my life's work: *a return to the body.* Unless the Abandonment were complete, including by the God of the church, I would never have been required to move beyond into all that was beckoning me, that beckons all of us. Inarticulate. Bewildered. Rebirthing and reshaping wisdom. I'm not writing an uncritical "thank you note" for this Story of Abandonment, but it was what absolutely required me to return to where Godde always meets us: desire, palpable in the body as pleasure.

Awakening

Most of my work as a theologian could be roughly understood as a *return to the body* in theological perspective and faith practice(s). Today, I see the seed of this work planted so very early in my life. At the age of six years, I experienced a sensual awakening I knew to be wondrous, enlivening, *beautiful,* even as it also had to go psychologically underground for decades in order for me to survive it in my Protestant ecclesially dominated environs. From my earliest years into my late twenties, this event was the source of deepest shame and greatest fear. Isolated within it, both by my own wisdom and my family's ancestral wounds, I told no one until I was 28 years old, when the requirements for my professional formation in the ministry met the demands of the rigorous, healing work possible in well-supervised clinical pastoral education. If I wanted to continue in deepening ministry practice, healthily, my supervisor insisted I "talk to someone" about a splinter in my spirit-body she had intuited but did not know. Sister Shirley Nugent (of blessed memory) was irritatingly perceptive that way. I'm forever grateful to her today.

26. Lerner in Weller, *Wild Edge of Sorrow,* xiii.
27. Winter, *Paradoxology,* 13.

It's actually quite innocent. Even simple. I injured my toe when I was just over six years old, losing my big toenail. So painful, achy for weeks. Then itchy as it healed. We had gotten a dog earlier that year "so Lisa would learn to show emotion." Sitting around the family room one night, the dog kept licking my toes. I liked it. It relieved the itch. Family was laughing and paying little attention. Without any context for the mysteries and power of a human body's sensuality, I experienced an overwhelming pleasure in my entire body, fanning out from between my legs. For that instant, I froze. My six-year-old self had no idea feet could connect to other parts of my body, nor that pleasure was what pleasure could be. Bodies were disciplined and cleaned in my Puritan-esque family. They were dirty and to be untouched, especially *there*. I just *knew* that what happened to me, in the presence of everyone, was bad, something of greatest shame. I hid all sign of it, covering it up with laughter with my family. Laughing from being tickled was okay. What *this* was, surely was *not*. So for over twenty years, I never told a soul . . .

Yet the proverbial door to the body had opened, a completely premature Awakening about which I have raged at God, Godde, for decades. Why land such pleasure, sacred overwhelm, in a little girl's body so unprepared for it? In a deeply Christian family so unprepared to assist her in it? In such danger of imposed shames? Had I been born into an Indigenous family, for example, with an unbroken relationship to the Land, to the entire web of creation, my sensual awakening would have been considered innocent, not unusual, natural. There would have been no imposed shame or dissociation necessary. Assisted by elders comfortable in their own bodies as sacred vehicles of nature, I would have grown into an already wilded and wondrous mystery of belonging as part of our Earth, our Mother. As it was, only shame took root. A good four decades later, after the Days in the Weeds, my disbelief and rage used this story as just another example of being abandoned by God. God of the church *cannot* withstand the erotic awakening of human beings, so I thought for years. Knowing then the irrepressible force of desire, the exquisite sensations so pleasurable—sexual or not—explorations of it all began in my isolated, curious, shamed self, irrepressible and growing stronger and stronger. I found more ways to find release into pleasure—by myself—than you could possibly imagine. I was clever, after all.

Blessed or cursed—could be either or both—it *was* early enough that by the time adolescence arrived in full, I was practiced at self-isolation such that I did not experiment with anyone. I could imagine this intensive drive pushing me into anything with anyone, but I was practiced at isolating by the time others my age were entering into their body-awakenings. I had learned to keep my own secrets, presumably to the grave. At age seventeen, an unaware but proto-feminist, I finally crafted my own body-dissociation ritual, tearing all sensation from my mind. Anything to do with pleasure went into a local river with appropriate vow to quiet this sensation, split from it, leave it all behind. It mostly worked until I got into Clinical Pastoral Education at age twenty-eight. Ages seventeen to twenty-eight, I had numbed, feeling sacredly virtuous while chastising myself for lapses with the occasional proactive partner. One year of dating in college began some reknitting of my body and spirit, with the gentlest, softest-eyed, patient and romantic soul I'd ever met (which is probably why I married him ten years later). When he got too close, however, I made sure my irritation moved us both to call "us" off. For eleven years, I insured that any pleasure my body felt was kept as discrete and as unconscious in my awareness as possible. Desire was shameful, even sinful. God was never to be known in the human body, but only in the Spirit.

From another angle, this story is a repeat demonstration of my own ancestral lineage, deeply severed from body and feeling, theologically severed from any felt-sense connection to the Land, to nature or creation, as we'd call it. The body secrecies and dissociation in my family of origin traumatized all of us . . . beginning well before my parents' generation, let alone my sister's and mine. All this could also be understood within *whiteness*, in a Pennsylvania-Dutch/German-American disregard of body, emotions, feeling.[28] We have traditioned disconnecting hearts from bodies, necessary rationalization of emotion *or* feeling before honoring body responses, even though I cherish how we are also a deeply faithful and loving family. What I know today includes more and more *what my body carries*, generationally, intuitively, within my own capacity for self-reflection, discernment, and an increasingly practiced willingness to feel.

This is part of the *gift* of the awakening, even if it was so bloody early in my body. Even with all the self- and divine-abandonment, I knew how to feel deeply because it had been awoken in me so very early. I could sense something or Someone, an embodied F/feminine wisdom that has always been a part of me somehow. Today, with my re-mothered consciousness[29]

---

28. Jennings, *After Whiteness*, 8–9.
29. Webster, *Discovering the Inner Mother*, 244–53.

and a much more healed sensate self, I marvel at the intuitive wisdom of my six year old self. Some part of me was wise enough to *not speak* what my family of origin could not negotiate peacefully, without more shame. It meant I participated in my own body's silencing, which is complicated and complicating, part of the wound. Yet I knew enough even then to protect myself, to trust my own body's wisdom. In an oblique conversation with my folks, shortly before their eighty-year-old selves departed for a new home across country, my father confirmed this little girl's wisdom. I spoke of my sensual awakening to the body, though without much detail. Dad said, "Yeah, knowing who that man was, as a father of that age? I'd not have known how to handle such news well." He smiled sadly, but it felt like we finally connected on this side of all that. We had both survived so many disconnections, somehow, together, for which I am so very grateful to him, for him, to me, for us.

Today, I see this sensual awakening as both ancestral-lineage wound and overwhelming gift for healing. What had been co-created in my own lineages as shame and harm has become a cornerstone of reconnection, a pathway to abundance and grace. At a most innocent, visceral level, my F/feminine body was awakened and then grounded to grow into her mature expressions today, continuing to deepen, be transformed and transfigured, both. My sacred work was seeded here, in an awakened, deeply feeling sensual self in a protectively-injuriously dissociated human body. In my flesh. I do smile today, because Godde knew it would arguably be the safest place for Her Wisdom to reside. A Pennsylvania-Dutch (Deutsch), disciplinarily-trained theologian *would never look for Godde in her own body*. A body that was to be anointed for its sacred purposes unfolding beyond expectation.

Anointing

About the same time as my scholarly work began in the mid-1990s, the re-integration of bodily sensation also began in supervised clinical education (CPE). Inexplicable to me then, variously significant to me over the years, I received an unexpected Spirit's in-breaking which created a crucible able to hold and point toward the untameable and wilding Flow or Force in my life. My body received an indelible and unavoidable sign and seal which held me together when I no longer could on my own, i.e., after the Days in the Weeds. The timing of it strikes me today as deeply significant: Spirit's transformative work can rarely happen with fragile human beings outside of containers strong enough to hold the dissonances and usually-inhibitive fears. CPE is one of the best containers I know for this kind of healing-integrative work. I was well into my own clinical training, being returned to my body so to receive what I would need.

The event itself has meant different things over the decades I've held it in my cells, my mind, my spirit. Sometimes it's been legitimating, supportive, encouraging for trusting God in the face of suffering. Other times it's been frustrating, binding, and irrefutable that God/de is always more than our ways, especially in the face of rage, anger, and grief. In brief, one August morning in 1998, I was prayerfully anointed with oil by two Assembly of God Christians in a coffee shop in DC. This description offers none of the bodily experience of it but does give a bare bones testimony to my own re-enchanted world, reclaimed as part of the imaginal realm dancing within and around me ever since.

I was facing the tasks and sublimating the fears of my doctoral comprehensive exams. I had driven to visit my best friend from high school. While she worked, I took my work to a local coffee shop. A pile of books rested on my table, with the smallest on top: a small-print Bible. The next table over was a group of women, clearly in Bible study together. Irritation flashed through me. I was much more an old-school Presbyterian in those days, with a strong sense of places where such intimate conversations should happen: at home or in church. Flaunting one's faith language in a public sphere felt like an imposition in the larger society that may or may not be interested. Two of them approached me when the Bible study was done, seeing my own Bible. They were just being friendly. I was irritated but I didn't want to be rude. "Yes, I'm a doctoral student in practical theology, studying for my comprehensives," I explained to them, needing a reason for my own Bible to be on display. "May we pray for you?" one asked. Anticipating a Presbyterian prayer—closing our eyes and listening to some words spoken aloud for a while—I said, "Sure." Again, I didn't want to be rude. I did say *yes*, which is significant in these holy things.

They moved to either side of me, and one began to speak in completely unintelligible (to me) sounds. Because my body had been awakened long ago, I could feel the energies around me heighten, deepen. The air seemed to grow charged and so I opened my eyes. Their eyes were closed. Then the one who seemed to be in the lead paused, opened her eyes, to look at her friend, "Would you find the last chapter of Habakkuk in your

Bible?" I remember suppressing a giggle, with the idea that an Evangelical or Charismatic (in this case) couldn't find the minor prophets at the end of the Old Testament either. The Bible was opened, and the opening verses of Habakkuk 3 entered into the room in her friend's voice, reading aloud. *Though the fig tree does not blossom, and no fruit is on the vines; though the produce of the olive fails and the fields yield no food; though the flock is cut off from the fold and there is no herd in the stalls; I will exult in the God of my salvation. God, the Lord, is my strength; he makes my feet like the feet of a deer, and makes me tread upon the heights* (Hab 3:17–19).

Then the leader opened her eyes again, pausing her unintelligible speech for the second time. "May we lay our hands on you," she asked respectfully. Wordless by now, I nodded my *yes*. She reached into her purse, searching for something. She brought out a small vial of oil. Dabbing her finger in the oil a bit, she made the sign of the cross on my forehead, then put the vial back on the table. She laid one hand on my shoulder, one on the crown of my head. Her friend placed both hands on my shoulders. Words I could understand were then spoken, though I only remember one phrase to this day. *Lion of Judah*. I have no idea what else was prayed aloud, nor whether what I know today was *speaking in tongues* continued.

Tears streamed down my cheeks, as even I as a Presbyterian could recognize all of the scriptural fingerprints of this unfolding. There were two of them. They had been in Bible study in a larger community. They were hospitable, friendly, concerned for me in my fears. At each point, my permission was asked. At each point, I granted permission. The oil is when I lost all composure. I'd never seen or experienced an anointing, but I'd read about them *in Scripture*. I remember a deep body awareness confirming something deep inside of me that the sacred threads in Scripture were *real. Real.* Not a figment of mystical imagination alone, but alive and loose in this world around and within me. *Lion of Judah . . . Lion of Judah . . .* I will never forget this, even though I had no idea what it could mean. Experience of anointing or this scriptural phrase. After what felt an eternity, they stopped speaking, praying.

The pager worn by the leader beeped, startling all of us out of wherever we had been into the moment we were in next. She looked at the message, then in a most ordinary voice, turned to her friend. "Lacey is having a pool party at 2 p.m." Then she looked at me. "Would you like to come?" I nearly laughed aloud. Wordlessly, I shook my head, no. "Thanks anyway," I managed to whisper. "I think I need to sit for a while . . ." She smiled, writing down her phone number on a scrap of paper pulled from her purse. "Well, call us if you change your mind!" And with that, they trundled off to their car and the 2 p.m. pool party. I remember packing up my things, slowly. I put them into the car, then noticed a chain bookstore next door. I wandered in there to browse, which I often do when I am restless, cannot resolve something inside of me. I stumbled across Alasdair MacIntyre's work, purchasing the volume which eventually undergirded almost my entire dissertation work to come.[30]

Knowing what I know *now*, the leader of the twosome was *speaking in tongues*. I had never experienced nor heard anything like it before in the Presbyterian church. I know also that such an anointing is a common practice of prayer in such Charismatic communities of faith. They were not doing anything out of the ordinary for them, though it was completely *extraordinary* to me. I have (of course) returned to the Habakkuk text from time to time, seeking the energetics of what I experienced in that moment. It has never read or felt the same since. It sometimes feels like I'm sitting with C. S. Lewis, waiting before the proverbial Wardrobe, knowing viscerally now the mysteries contained yet also hidden within it. In sum, this turning point of anointing planted something so visceral and unmovable in my cells that even when everything I knew was stripped away, this visceral something *was not*. It's like there was an energetic seal upon me, from that point on, about which I could do little to nothing to argue.

Said in hindsight, of course. At that time, I had no idea that The Greatest Argument with God, my own complete rupture in abandonment, was yet to come in about fifteen years. Awakened, anointed, in a Force or Flow beyond my ecclesially-shaped expectation, I would become viscerally conscious of the primary wounding of my life—an early body-sense of pain, fear, isolation, terror—even as it would be the very seed for my own life's purpose to grow, blossom, flower. The coffee shop anointing was a colorful thread that held the fragile and irreconcilable pieces together when nothing else could. Godde's seal of faith on my very flesh.

There is unimaginable freedom here on the other side of nothingness, injury, fear, and rage. The other side of being abandoned by those slated to care for us but unable to tend to their own ancestral wounds, so to tend us in a Love beyond judgment. The other side of anger, spilling over into rage, running rampant in a culture and families unskilled in how *not* to project it ever-outward. The other side in which we get to live

---

30. MacIntyre, *After Virtue*.

more fully into this mysterious life we've been given, alone and together, drenched in fear as we all are. Undesired by me as the deeply wounded and abandoned woman of faith I have been, I know this today only because of this Force or Flow Who would never let me go, Who breathes so deeply within me I scarce can imagine. Godde, who showed me *anger can become conscious*, that even *rage* can be *holy* as an embodied wisdom left untapped, a cauldron for all the sacred work to come.

_____ Chapter Two

Anger Become Conscious, Become Holy

MOST PEOPLE OF FAITH have an uneasy relationship to anger, let alone rage, which makes this one of the most pressing challenges needing redress today if communities and human beings within them are to evolve, mature, heal. Perhaps I should qualify that statement as *conscious* relationship. Most people of faith have an uneasy, (un)conscious relationship with anger. I know this intimately in my own Pennsylvania-Dutch, Scottish-British lineages of family and faith. Cognitive strategies control embodied sensation and expression. Communal pressure and condemnation of anger means suppression, refusal of awareness of the anger, even when justified, healthy or righteous. Safety from explosive tempers—the presumption of the only expression of anger—requires dissociation and suppression. I have inherited these defense-mechanisms, yet I have also sustained a long-term, seemingly unending conscious relationship with anger while understanding its clear limitations. Our need to relinquish it, when it's time, is a gift to be received.

It's telling that in the writing process, I wondered whether this chapter would distract, perhaps even obstruct the abundant grace I know on the peaceable side of rage. I omitted and reinstated the chapter more times than I could count. It remains because rage needs to be honored, seen, heard, received by a witnessing community, when it's time to finally release the angers. "The dimension of authenticity is 'depth': looking through the mirror to interiority, ancestry, primality. . . . First is the 'cauldron' . . . which endows the gift of poetic wisdom—the knowledge of past, present and future."[1] Perhaps you are well familiar with the depths

1. Deardorff, *Other Within*, 90.

of your own rage. If so, skip this entire chapter. It won't illuminate or educate you on anything you aren't already feeling. If you are always wondering why so many people today refuse any engagement with faith or anything transcendent, then this chapter is for you. My hope is that it will illuminate, in the gentlest way I know how, the necessary fires of anger that have defended my body, my integrity, and my own spirit as led by Spirit. It is also my way of honoring all those who simply could no longer stay within a human collective utterly disregarding human dignity of so many. So many of "you" constitute the Body of Humanity that has blessed me so. I aim to demonstrate it *is* possible to hold this fire of rage and to know the holy waters of baptism that poured through my suffering woman's body—both at the same time.

Anger Becomes Conscious, for Sacred Purpose(s)

I can name the time in my life when anger at God became conscious, breaking open this most sacred relationship I could still name God. I was serving as an intern at a battered-woman's shelter in Trenton, New Jersey. It was part of the degree plan. While I didn't know why I was there, I was a good student. I was not remotely *prepared* for the work invitations that came. The social worker on-call was doing "an Intake," getting the information and details from a woman arriving to the shelter from a threatening situation. "Do you want to sit in?" I was asked. "Sure," I said, not doing anything else obviously useful.

I remember sitting in the terrified, wounded, and bewildered energies of an older Christian woman. She reminded me a little of my mother. After this woman's husband died, she had entered into a romantic relationship with a man who over a period of months swindled her of all her resources, all her money, eventually battering her black and blue, kicking her out of her own home. She landed in this social worker's office, with a completely unmoored seminary student "sitting in." This woman told her story and we sat together, speechless but holding her hands, in her bewilderment, her terror. We bore witness to her and held space for her—language I know now for what we were doing. Something in me unhinged. I did not know it unhinged, but it did.

It wasn't until I was almost home, having driven from blue-collar Trenton into white-intellectual Princeton, that I realized I was crying. Had been crying for some time, by the look and feel of my clothes. Dazed, I parked my car in the student lot by the library, and walked toward my dorm. I felt nauseous with the idea of going into the hallway, making chit-chat with dorm sisters on the floor. I didn't know where to go, what building would even be open this late. I landed in the chapel, the only public building with lights on inside. Someone was playing the organ, practicing. She was a woman I didn't know but recognized from choir practice on Thursday nights. I sat quietly in a pew, about midway back.

She approached me on her way out of the sanctuary, having completed her practicing. "Would you be interested in singing in a small a capella group we are forming? We need a strong alto voice, and you would be a good fit, we think." I was so stunned by the inquiry that I nodded, "Sure . . . " I didn't realize she even knew who I was. I felt shy that a forming singing group had even noticed my voice. "I would like that." I said, more confidently and steadily. "Great! We'll sort it out before choir practice tomorrow, okay?" I nodded. I made sure it was late and lights were off before I went "home" to my room.

An *explicit* journey of anger had begun, ultimately a fierceness for women fired by rage. Theological studies seemed pointless and flat. Had I not been in the touring choir, had I not been woven into that small group of a capella singers, I probably would have withdrawn from seminary entirely. Church made no sense. Proclamation of any good news tasted like sawdust. About six months later, sitting at an outside table at the Met Opera in New York City with an elder choral member I'll call Rosemary, I finally named my rage. I let myself be seen in the inability to integrate the bewildering violence against women with anything or anyone Sacred just standing by. "Don't you think God is large enough to handle your anger?" she asked, sipping her chardonnay with an impish smile.

It was probably the first time anyone had ever framed a way anger was not to be repressed, not to be hidden. That it was not a sin but an invitation to consider being seen in *relationship*. Up to that point, I could not imagine that anger could be sacredly held in relationship, even for a holy purpose. This was the first of many teachings where I learned: anger did not erase God, it honored me in my body. Anger that was *conscious* could become a container for deepening intimacy. It eventually became a cauldron for all that was, is, to come. Something More was larger than any of it, could hold all of it, which then allowed me to see the other gift-elements of my own story.

That serendipitous-providential invitation in the chapel sanctuary opened and formed a small community—a container built around music and laughter—that would hold me for the remaining years of Masters work at the seminary. In hindsight, it struck me as significant that this Invitation arrived nearly immediately after a dissociating, shattering encounter with the world as I had ever known. Something or Someone in the Universe knew what I would need to stay, *and provided it*, if I would choose to join. Time and time again in my journey, this serendipitous Flow can be felt, known in my body, if I allow it within my cells, my flesh and bones.

As something unhinged in me that night at the shelter, as I was unaware of it driving home, so it was in these last years, raised exponentially to the point of utter rupture, what I now call my own "faith trauma." As a woman, I too am that elder Christian woman, battered, swindled, betrayed. As a woman theological student, I had already been abandoned, betrayed *as a woman* by a church and seminary's baptizing its betrayals as sacred in the world. I just didn't see it yet. For both good and ill, then, that night in the shelter was the one in which anger, as its collective expression, rage, really took hold of me. Anger moved into my bones, my cells, my blood. She looks like that older woman, a widow with battered face and body. She identifies in me as a Christian, self-sacrificing and loving others with disregard of herself *as she was taught to do*. Which means utter abandonment, of course. As we do, so does the world. She is me and I am her in some fashion. It was the work of Marion Woodman, held in a circle of wilding and writing women, that introduced me to the *conscious feminine*.

The Conscious Feminine

My understanding and experience of the F/feminine today arose within communities of practice deeply drawn to Holy Wisdom yet intentionally shaped in non-traditional, non-sectarian ways. Most of us *know* that human beings are created for relationship. Being held in love and accountability matters for evolution and maturity in love. Most I have been blessed to know in non-sectarian communities had or have also been deeply wounded by historic wisdom traditions, institutionally organized. So *those* communities became unavailable for those of us deeply wounded. But for *intentional community*, in other words, I would never have awakened to the grace and abundance I know today. This F/feminine is deeply sacred, if silenced and made persistently peripheral in historic tradition(s). S/he is Divine and human, both. Not ideologically defined or confined to gender, but instructive, illuminating for all who are willing to receive her. Clearly, few of us in traditional communities *are* willing, but that does not alter Her audacious love. As Jan Richardson observes H/her, "She will wait outside the city gates as long as it takes, as long as the arguments over her rage, as long as brave souls hazard conversations with her through chinks in the city walls, as long as there are those who risk breathing her name. And when she returns, she will bring with her the others who were outcast, who were lost, who were expelled because of the way they looked or how they acted or what they believed or whom they loved."[2] *This* is the F/feminine I know today, most often articulate in the phrase *conscious feminine*.

Entering into the *conscious feminine* within the Women Writing for (a) Change communities, alongside the less formal *womanheart* of Red Tent circles, gave me grounded language for embodied experiences refused by ecclesial-academic communities yet deeply spiritually rooted in practices of community. Books addressing this general area of inquiry—whether framed as gender, or biology, or sexuality, or identity-ideologies—do bandy about a wide variety of words popularly assumed to be referring to women, both biologically determined and gender-specific in my midwestern contexts. Move to the coasts or university campuses, and you will get an earful about the ignorant slurs on my own mental habits here, which in progressive estimation should "wake up" to use terms like womyn, womxn, wimmin, birth-able humans, and/or the like. A lot of energy is expended here. These distinctions are highly valued by many human beings, often younger generations of us, so I *do* bow to their usage. And . . . I am the mid-fifties white, cisgendered woman that I am, with my own navigation of these dynamics in the terms that assisted my own integration: sexual fluidity, archetypal energies of feminine and masculine, and a deeply appreciated queering move into non-binary alongside us more binary folks, men and women. Given my eventually-trinitarian reframing, you could understand why I love the queering move, even as I make the most sense to myself within the binary in which I matured, even awoke (dare I say?). I will use the language that resonates most deeply in my own storying, therefore, asking your forbearance if you experience such habits as offensive. Think of it as opportunity to forbear, even to forgive, whereby you become more

---

2. "Prologue: Wisdom in Exile," In Richardson, *In Wisdom's Path*.

and more free, regardless of *which* language some human being uses, sitting across from you in person or on social media.

It was the 2013 Conscious Feminine Leadership Academy that began to shape my bodysoul, mind, and spirit into these strands of practice and thought, rooted in Jungian streams of archetypal psychology. The founder of this non-traditional writing school, Mary Pierce Brosmer, landed on the phrase *conscious feminine* as used by Jungian Marion Woodman, foundational thinker for her/our continuing leadership formation work. The early years of this entrance into the conscious feminine were bumpy, but not rupturing. I had learned quiet-accommodation quite well. As my own F/feminine became stronger, more and more conscious, S/she became more important to honor than anyone else around me who could not see H/her, would not welcome her. The "Troubles" were not far behind.

Woodman often said she was still asking and answering the question as to what the conscious feminine *is*, so it is understandable that so many in my life struggled to see or honor this F/feminine within me. Woodman writes,

> Like all the questions in my life, I cannot know the meaning of the question until I have found the answer. I cannot know Sophia, the feminine nature of God, until I have experienced her love radiating in my cells. I cannot experience that radiation until I love the reality of my cells, a reality that is constantly renewing itself in their death and rebirth. Nor can I love the reality of my cells until I have known them, felt their anguish, heard their purring, seen them with my fingers, ears and eyes. And perceived their dying and reviving dance in the fire of my imagination.. . . . The question still remains. Each time I try to answer it, I answer from where I am. One thing I do know. The answer asks the question.[3]

What I hear today is Woodman's wise refusal to fragment her own experience for someone else's habits of mind. She refuses the question even as she also answers it in an exquisitely conscious feminine way— fierce for unity, integrity, wholeness *first*. She honors the "is-ness" of the conscious feminine that is impossible to define in words for analytical, fragmenting minds.

Mary Pierce Brosmer gave the phrase some of her own language as she described the founding of her school, Women Writing for (a) Change

---

3. Woodman, *Conscious Femininity*, 7.

in Cincinnati, Ohio, in 1991. She writes, "I am describing the "Feminine" as an "energy of life and leadership available to both women and men, expressing values of transparency, hospitality, capacity to hold paradox, nurture-with-rigor, and a model of community [that] supports individual gifts but not at the expense of societal or planetary well-being."[4] As I received her wisdom, I drew out several focal points converging with my own artisanal theological work. The Conscious Feminine is an *energy*, first and foremost. *Embodied*. Arising as an energy of *life* and *leadership*. It's a *receptive passion*, able to companion the suffering of self and others. An expressive delight, rooted in the deepest core of who you are, whether male/female or you refuse the binary altogether . . . rooted in who you have been shaped to be . . . from which you cannot help but overflow into blessing, to serve, offer, receive, learn *ad infinitum*. Making this sense of *feminine* perceivable or even desirable in my own ecclesial and academic contexts was mostly impossible, however, or at least implausible. Systems like stability and stasis. Most prefer stasis to actually listening to an awakening woman's experience(s).

Alice Walker's conscious feminine wisdom seasoned this even further for me, though I recognize I will always be a "befriended outsider" to womanist work. Walker is more fierce than most I've encountered for the *communal*, the *Folk*, regardless. She defines *womanist*

> From *womanish*. (Opp of 'girlish', i.e., frivolous, irresponsible, not serious.) A black feminist or feminist of color. From the black folk expression of mothers to female children, "you acting womanish," i.e., like a woman. Usually referring to outrageous, audacious, courageous or willful behavior. Wanting to know more and in greater depth than is considered "good" for one. . . . Responsible. In charge. Serious. 2. *Also*: A woman who loves other women, sexually and/or nonsexually. Appreciates and prefers women's culture, women's emotional flexibility (values tears as natural counterbalance of laughter), and women's strength. Committed to survival and wholeness of entire people, male *and* female. Not a separatist, except periodically, for health. . . . 3. Loves music. Loves dance. Loves the moon. Loves the Spirit. Loves love and food and roundness. Loves struggle. Loves the Folk. Loves herself. *Regardless*. 4. Womanist is to feminist as purple to lavender.[5]

---

4. Brosmer, *Women Writing for (a) Change*, 7.
5. Walker, *In Search of Our Mothers' Gardens*, xi–xii.

Here, we can sense how the Conscious Feminine is fierce, outrageous, audacious, courageous, serious, and loves across all divides. S/she is committed to survival and wholeness of entire people, not just her own. The Conscious Feminine in women and men begins in love of self in partnership with others, no matter what. In my own language, offered in a doctoral plenary years back, I argued this phrase within my own root-tradition's terms, weaving both Brosmer's energetics-focus and Walker's fierceness for all. "The Conscious Feminine is an energy of the Trinity, balanced with the Masculine, both relating and interconnecting all things toward wholeness and belonging. In our day, the Conscious Feminine is also an *awakening consciousness*, an expansive way of being in the world, seeing and sensing the world(s) around you in wholeness and available mystery."[6]

Another Jungian, Jean Shinoda Bolen, observes similarly: "This growing feminine edge of consciousness is known through intuition, archetypal or mythic consciousness, body perceptions, images and imagination, or ritual expression. It calls upon the soul/psyche to participate and be emotionally and spiritually affected by the experience through which it knows more, which is different from the impersonal detachment in which the mind works best—as different as reading about a baby is from giving birth to one."[7] Before her, Helen Luke describes this F/feminine as "energies . . . in the ability to connect theories encountered, emotions aroused, and the symbolic life within."[8] In this active, integrative work, *who she is in her body* coheres with what she is encountering in the worlds around her. A felt sense of resonance, of connection, of belonging emerges.

The *unconscious* provides for healing here in Luke's estimation, "for no amount of rational analysis can bring healing."[9] Her sense of the word feminine does have an essentialism about it that would trouble gender theorists today, but she draws connections with spirit and creativity that I find most helpful, accurate to my own experience. She describes her "basic feminine nature" as that which "receives, nourishes, and gives birth on all levels of being through her awareness of the earth and her ability to bring up the water of life from under the earth. All her true

---

6. Hess, "Conscious Feminine Leadership," 3.

7. Bolen, "Athena, Artemis, Aphrodite, and Initiation into the Conscious Feminine," 221.

8. Luke, *Woman Earth and Spirit*, 2.

9. Luke, *Woman Earth and Spirit*, 2.

creativeness springs from this."[10] The intent here is *archetypal*, available to *all* human beings, regardless of gender (or gender-refusal). It is this contrasexual wisdom that I find most resonant today, still, these many years further into the journey. I use the word *feminine* to refer to this balancing wisdom so badly needed in our world so *out of balance*. Receptive. Transparent. Integrative. Capacity to hold paradox. Commitment to nurture with rigor. The feminine is an archetypal energy—a human collective energy of the body for life—always amidst cycles of birth, life, death, and new life. It is available to all human beings, however their biology is configured, however their sexuality, gender, and orientations shape them from within and without.

The Spirit-ed sense of this energy then becomes the Feminine, both in the human body at once, F/feminine. Woodman and Luke both argue for a F/feminine intimately attuned to the word become flesh, an incarnational moment upon moment available in every human life awakening. The Divine Feminine usually describes this, except our power-over habits of mind make Her a female counterpart to the God we have today. Unacceptable. As argued here, it is the Feminine in a top-down thinking, the feminine in a down-up thinking that is *O/one*. F/feminine. We receive an integration of embodied experience(s) into cognitive terms and deepening awarenesses (often nonattached-cognitive in form) in Spirit, en-spirited, always unfolding in time. Whatever breaks us open so to sense the whole more fully . . . that is what the F/feminine is and has been for me. This is the pain and—if held well, witnessed and entrusted in community to heal—the blessing that the feminine is as archetypal force, when dancing with a conscious masculine newly finding his way. This F/feminine is embodied by enraged women—righteously enraged, legitimate, valid—who face into the abandonment, abuse, and silencing by screaming to be heard or, with great cost, aligning with toxic patterns so to lead. One of the gifts for me has been honoring that this rage is righteous and when set apart for healing purpose, *holy*.

The Righteousness of Rage Legitimated and Validated in Embodied History(ies)

A conscious feminine theologian can offer the minds of those faithful (any who are curious or willing to listen) some linear, logical and

---

10. Luke, *Woman Earth and Spirit*, 2–3.

utterly reasonable origins for the rage that abounds today. The desire to be heard, seen, and understood never goes away, even if one habituates to irrevocable loss. So my conscious feminine theologian continues to steward the gifts she's been given, pointing to the various approaches she's taken to redress the wound, to make meaning even out of abandonment. In this role, I am indebted to and have digested so many contributions of those who have come before me.

The archaeological, historical, integrative journey arises in largely three "approaches" expressive of rage yet also hoping to educate, illuminate, so to *know who we have been*. Such is my intention here. A *prosecutorial approach* offers clear data, almost speaking for itself about the abuse, abandonment and silencing of women's voices in international-global view. The feminist-historical work so ably researched, imagined, and written offers a plausible *historical approach* for understanding how intelligent, fierce women co-created a world in which women are yet subordinated, increasingly vulnerable to the power-over of men. The cadence of women's voices—the focal point of women's souls, bodies, spirits . . . what I call *womanheart*—is strikingly absent from historic Scriptures, practices, traditions of our histories. Therefore, a dip into pure *her-story* can fascinate, illuminate. Lastly, and closer to home in my own root tradition is the *scriptural-archaeological* approach, laboring to honor the presence and voices of women in sacred Scripture when few to none are actually recorded in ancient texts. Women are always faced with "proving a negative," which basically proves the point. The sacred purpose of rage, at its best, is to hold us all accountable by mirroring experiences not being considered. The approaches named here provide the groundwork to see what soil we must work with today: prosecutorial, historical (her-story, for the feeling of it), and scriptural-archeaological approaches.

A Prosecutorial Approach

Violence against women in our world today is indisputable, yet remains disputed or at least ignored, perhaps with a sense of overwhelm and hopelessness, perhaps with a persistent unconsciousness that refuses what we've co-created for generations. It is exacted upon women and women-identified human beings voraciously *every day*. One day, in frustration, I heard the voice of Captain Jack Ross, US Marine JAG Corps prosecutor played by Kevin Bacon in the 1992 movie, *A Few Good Men*: "The facts of the case are these . . . These are the facts of the case, and they are undisputed."[11] We continue to live and serve in a world hostile to women, serving in traditional institutions resistant to change, resistant to their own complicity and active aggression in the abandonment, abuse, and neglect of the F/feminine. Even in the face of "indisputable facts," we project responsibility onto others, onto "them," whomever "they" may be.

The United Nations defines violence against women as "any act of gender-based violence that results in, or is likely to result in, physical, sexual, or mental harm or suffering to women, including threats of such acts, coercion or arbitrary deprivation of liberty, whether occurring in public or in private life."[12] The prevalence estimates of lifetime intimate partner violence range from country to country, but it is estimated 1 in 3 women worldwide have been subjected to either physical and/or sexual intimate partner violence or non-partner sexual violence in their lifetime. It's a global phenomenon, showing heightened presence with clear risk factors from lower levels of education to community norms that privilege or ascribe higher status to men and lower status to women, from low levels of women's access to paid employment to history of exposure to child and partner maltreatment. Historic religious traditions are regularly employed to exacerbate violence against women, though most traditionalists point only to how religious faith comforts and liberates.

My own holy rage is directed at my root tradition of Protestant Christianity, even as I am blessed to live in a country in which I have unbounded freedom to speak, mirror my experience, confront for the future (at least so far). The specific religious tradition matters little, in the end. "The reality is that regardless of the particular religious affiliation, alongside the trauma of violence, a majority of women will be dealing with some aspect of religious beliefs and teachings which will serve either as a resource or a roadblock."[13] Rev. Dr. Marie Fortune and Rabbi Cindy Enger argue that the task for religious and secular leadership requires recognizing this ambivalent role religious traditions can play in the safety of women as well as advocating for deeper critical awakening to the conflictual and often dangerous interpretations of sacred texts for women. Toward that end, Fortune and Enger give a brief listing of the story after story of violence against women in the Hebrew Bible and Christian

---

11. Dir. Rob Reiner, Columbia Pictures, 1992.
12. World Health Organization, "Violence Against Women."
13. Fortune and Enger, "Violence Against Women and the Role of Religion."

New Testament.[14] Later Christian texts and earlier and later Jewish and Muslim texts also condone male violence against women and the domination of women. "Proof-texting (the selective use of a text, usually out of context, to support one's position) is a common ploy by those who seek to simply justify their actions. It is not difficult to prooftext a man's prerogative to dominate and control a woman within patriarchal western religious traditions."[15] *The facts of the case are these . . . these are the facts of the case, and they are undisputed.*

What is a woman to do to hold her own root tradition accountable for the betrayal of her as a woman, the *sanctification* of that betrayal as sacred? The question drives even more deeply when women become complicit in their own silencing, their own abandonment. Like I have been, for over forty-five years. No wonder I hear Kevin Bacon's voice as Captain Jack Ross in my ear. He was ultimately called to prosecute a case that the Armed Forces had given to an attorney renown for plea bargains and no courtroom legitimation. The case was never supposed to see the light of day in a courtroom. Captain Jack Ross was predestined in the movie to *lose the case*. Likewise, scholars shaped for decades in the practices and habits of mind of higher education—seminaries, in particular—will rarely confront the injustices so fully ingrained into a life of sacred service. *The facts of the case are these . . . These are the facts of the case, and they are undisputed.*

An Historical Approach—Reassessing History within the Gaze of Women

While I suspect the energy of the prosecutorial lies underneath many of the other approaches we might pursue, a most familiar approach has been an historical one: researching and writing *women's* history so to rebalance, even confront or complement, accepted historical narratives, rooted in the gaze of the imbalanced power-over masculine. Several scholars have been fundamental for me here in feeling my way to a woman-centric way of living, listening, seeing, loving.

Gerda Lerner is a now classical voice in employing historical methods to unearth women's history, which she sees as fundamental to

---

14. E.g., Dinah (Gen 34), Tamar (2 Sam 13), the Levite's concubine (Judg 19), Jephthah's daughter (Judg 11), Vashti (Esth 1), Susanna (Dan 13), and probably the persistent widow in Luke's Gospel (Luke 18).

15. Fortune and Enger, "Violence Against Women and the Role of Religion."

women's emancipation from power-over behaviors and habits of mind (in women as well as men, non-binary, queer). Demonstrable in multiple disciplines of scholarship—anthropology, literary studies, even liberation theology—knowing one's *own history, herstory* in my case, empowers perception, agency, and courage. Uncovering a plausible narrative for any woman-centric history faces seemingly insurmountable challenges, however. Near complete omission from written records. Written records solely within the voices and assumptions of men, usually elitist men. It's also difficult to sustain critical historical methods that acknowledge such limitations while resisting the temptations to make causal claims where none exist or interpretive leaps that fit one's hopes more than the other multiple interpretations possible. Lerner navigates this Scylla and Charybdis fairly well, all things considered, providing a plausible historical narrative for how women have had agency in their own lives and yet co-created a social system that subordinates women.

Lerner insists upon the active agency of women over popular accusations of victimization. While one could clearly provide evidence for victimization (see prosecutorial case above), Lerner insists "it is a fundamental error to try to conceptualize women primarily as victims. To do so at once obscures what must be assumed as a given of women's historical situation: Women are essential and central to creating society; they are and always have been actors and agents in history, either their own or that of men."[16] Seeing one plausible storyline for this strand of the co-creative journey has often provided women courage to confront their own disempowerment, coming to voice about their own actual historical experience, yearning to redress the rage inherited from one broken motherline to the next. Lerner therefore provides a brief summary-overview of relevant theoretical formulations for the subordination of women before providing her own "working hypothesis" for the *creation of patriarchy* as ideology and presumption. Human beings have co-created this power-over bastardization of the masculine, in other words, historically, which means it can be *uncreated* in conscious collaboration.

The strands of Lerner's argument and method are these: 1). Men and women built civilization jointly. 2). Our search is for the history of the patriarchal system, resisting "single-factor explanations," given how global the system is. It would have evolved distinctively in different cultural contexts, in other words, though clearly some common characteristics

---

16. Lerner, *Creation of Patriarchy*, 5.

remain. She cautions against improper analytical-causal interpretations, persuasive with both material evidence and written sourcework. Scholars are never objective, after all, so causal-interpretative moves often say more about the hopes of the scholar than the plausibility of the history. You can see this play out in the question of *matriarchy* as an historical phenomenon, for example. Was *matriarchy* the historical precursor to *patriarchy*? Lerner disagrees with this proposed historical narrative, arguing the historical and archaeological evidence is simply *not there*. She begins, instead, with the first and most basic dyad of human being—mother and child—for a working hypothesis of society's persistent abuse of the power-principle.

A most distinctive characteristic of human being is the "prolonged and helpless infancy of the human child," requiring proximity of elders for care unto survival, elders who were gifted to forage and gather more than hunt and kill. This infant-helplessness had evolutionary biological origins, of course—bipedalism, walking upright, narrowed female pelvis and birth canal, smaller-headed children to get *through* the birth canal, infants born at greater immaturity, requiring prolonged, completely dependent care. Lerner highlights the necessity of this bond for survival, the necessity of ready nutrition and social interaction in "foraging for food," that then created the initial division of labor by which women do the mothering. Her argument is that this is an historical unfolding more than a biological one. "For millennia group survival depended upon it, and no alternative was available." In contrast to any whiff of biological determinism, Lerner clarifies, "I will show that male dominance is a *historic* phenomenon in that it arose out of a biologically determined given situation and became a culturally created and enforced structure over time."[17] Not essentialist, in other words, but historically plausible for the sake of group survival in the Neanderthal period (100,000 BCE). The pervasive veneration of the Mother-Goddess accompanied this development, given the psychological power and necessity of the mother-child bond. (The ready archaeological evidence can be found in the innumerable hand-size figurines pervasive in Eastern Europe, which some point to as the human need to hold the hand of Our Lady, by whatever name ye may call Her.[18])

---

17. Lerner, *Creation of Patriarchy*, 40.
18. Strand and Finn, *Way of the Rose*, 8.

Lerner provides an overview of the variety of interpretations for women's roles in the Neolithic era, the variety of ways women have co-created our societies today, but she hones her argument upon Claude Levi-Strauss's "exchange of women" for the historic origins of the abuse of the power-principle today. This "exchange" took a variety of forms—aversion of the incest taboo, the forceful removal of women from their home tribe (bride stealing), ritual defloration or rape, negotiated marriages—but the practice reified women into dehumanized objects, antecedents to a sense of "property." C. D. Darlington sees *exogamy*—the practice of marrying outside a community or clan—as a cultural innovation that ultimately offered evolutionary advantage. More women, more offspring. Women easier to coerce than male warriors, whose bond to offspring was less than the mother's bond (with rape, especially, which would produce offspring). More offspring, closer ties of keeping a mother in the new clan. The "exchange of women" for intertribal peace, for conquest, for evolutionary advantage can be seen at different times in different parts of the world. It yet provides a plausible argument of pattern and outcome toward patriarchy, right on the cusp of the rise of the agricultural era when private property develops and kinship arrangements tend to shift from matriliny to patriliny. The intensity of the mother-child bond becomes the avenue through which women (un)consciously co-create a system within which women systemically, culturally, become property.

The development of agricultural conditions required more group cohesiveness and continuity over time. One production cycle depended upon the seed and harvest of the previous one. This strengthened the influence of older males and it increased the incentive for acquiring more women. Elder males begin to control knowledge pertaining to production, controlling food, knowledge and women. Women's sexuality becomes controlled within the needs and requirements of one home, or a group of homes. And "in a situation in which ecological conditions and irregularities in biological reproduction threatened the survival of the group, people would search for more reproducers—that is, women.... Thus the first appropriation of private property consists of the appropriation of the labor of women as *reproducers*."[19] Therefore, at least in this argument, the exploitation of human labor and the sexual exploitation of women become interwoven. In all this, Lerner posits a narrative where women would agree to a sexual division of labor, grounded in the

---

19. Lerner, *Creation of Patriarchy*, 52. Lerner does not say it, but one could also see the seeds of chattel slavery here, in the drive for *reproducers*.

power of the mother-child bond and a division of labor necessary for group survival. All without anticipation of that which would ultimately disadvantage women.

Toward the end of her argument, Lerner yet takes on the role of historic wisdom traditions in this subordination and omission of women from history. It was the emergence of Hebraic monotheism that attacked the widespread cults of various fertility goddesses. Not only that, but the establishment of the covenant with this God relies on a basic symbolism and actual contract that assumes the subordination of women and their exclusion: circumcision. Women's only access to God and to the holy community is in their function as mothers. She posits the originating question to be "Who creates life?" which lies at the core of religious belief systems. "Generativity encompasses both creativity—the ability to create something out of nothing—and procreativity—the capacity to produce offspring."[20] Yet Genesis begins the explicit omission of women in stories of generativity *which would be impossible without women.*

For example: "And it came to pass, when men began to multiply on the face of the earth, and daughters were born unto them . . . " (Gen 6:1–4). Lerner points out the ironies here. "To my mind, what is significant in the text is the reference to human women as the daughters born to men. . . . It is not explained how men came to multiply, but the omission of women from the process seems to me highly significant."[21] She concludes that this formation of the text shows the abusive power-principle assumptions about procreation were already well established. "Procreation itself has been turned into a male act. There are no mothers involved in it."[22] Naturally, then, the decisive change in the relationship of man to God that happens via *covenant* is defined in such a way as to exclude woman. To the question "Who creates life?," Genesis answers, "Yahweh and the God-like male he created."[23]

Speaking as the conscious feminine theologian I am: No wonder I chose a childless path. A choice, but a choiceless choice for a woman so dissociated from her own body that welcoming another life into it felt like murdering herself. I had ingested the male-centric, patriarchal system fully, placing myself as one who lived in these worlds of men, successfully. It wasn't until I found myself in woman-centric spaces that I could even

20. Lerner, *Creation of Patriarchy*, 180.
21. Lerner, *Creation of Patriarchy*, 186–87.
22. Lerner, *Creation of Patriarchy*, 187.
23. Lerner, *Creation of Patriarchy*, 193.

imagine anything else. To offer you a felt-sense of that shift, a dip into a woman-centric history may help. It is not *history* in any scholarly sense, nor will it ever be accorded weight by the majority of human beings who might be willing to engage its propositions. But Judy Grahn's *Blood, Bread, and Roses: How Menstruation Created the World* will offer your mind an immersion in what a woman-centric history *could* be, say, offer.

Her-Story Addendum

I was a couple years into my own F/feminine awakening, allowing myself to peruse things and consider ideas that would have been immediately rejected by everyone in my own worlds of family, faith, academy. *When God Was a Woman*, by Merlin Stone, for instance. Or *Inanna: Lady of Largest Heart*, offering the poetry of a Sumerian High Priestess Enheduanna. But *Blood, Bread and Roses: How Menstruation Created the World* was clearly a step off even the widening path I'd been on. I'd never had an easy relationship with my own bleeding, now coming to its end in my later midlife years. I was incredulous and perhaps even a bit offended. *What in the world . . . ?!?* I felt more than thought. And yet . . . And yet . . . I had been yearning for a *woman-centric* perspective that could hold what I had been experiencing as *womanheart*. The sense of abandonment had only grown within me, accompanied by a deep belly rage directed at this world so clearly hostile to women. The root tradition into which I had poured my life had *never* had my own best interests in view, for me *as a woman*. What if *menstruation* were the woman-centric Archimedes point *for me*?

As an American poet and author affiliated with the California Institute of Integral Studies, author Judy Grahn would never have found welcome or legitimate authority in the institutions and tradition(s) in which I had been formed. Long a butch-lesbian who has faced decades of homophobia and active harassment, she registers her argument in both etymologies and origin stories. Her work found me precisely as I needed it—an unapologetic, uncompromising, and innovative contribution to our understanding of awakening to connections or patterns into consciousness dangerously rooted in separation.

First, the etymologies that led her to her theorizing. *Taboo* recurs again and again in stories of menstrual ritual, she begins. One etymology of the word is the "Polynesian *tapua*, meaning both 'sacred' and 'menstruation,' in the sense as some traditions say, of 'the woman's friend.'"[24] She relays other meanings of this word, beyond "sacred": "forbidden, valuable, wonderful, magic, terrible, frightening, and immutable law."[25] It accompanies the emphatic use of imperatives. It draws attention, strong attention. All of which "reveal the deep power with which believers endowed menstruation, with its close connections to life and death."[26] Even more curious, in her view, is the European etymologies that all connect menstruation with "measure" or "rule": German, *Regel*; French, *regle*; Spanish *las reglas*. Each are cognates with terms regulate, regal, regalia, and *rex*, or king. "These terms thus connect menstruation to orderliness, ceremony, law, leadership, royalty, and measurement."[27] Grahn begins to build a sensibility of how etymological history points to implicit forces in history. *Her-story*, in other words.

Menstruation also distinguishes human beings from other primates, placing it in an originating relationship with an internal-external awakening, or development of consciousness. First of all, from earliest prehistory, menstrual blood was seen as the primary life force, a generative principle. Women could bleed and not die, while when men bled, death was close. Cultures even presumed that the fetus was formed in the womb by the clotting of menstrual blood. Additionally, the human cycle of menstruation, at twenty-nine and a half days, coincides with the cycle of the moon. Humanity is the only species linking this physical cycle with an external, lunar one. Hence the onset of menstruation could be measured by a cycle outside of itself, a cycle visible in the lunar rhythms. Once that connection was made, other patterns could be seen. As Grahn observes, "our capacity to externalize our ideas in language and significant material decoration and objects."[28] Not only did menstrual blood signify the generative principle of life, its entrainment to the lunar cycle drew human awareness into awakening to pattern, connection with a Divine. An awakening of some kind that also thereby *separated* human beings from other species around them.

Origin stories undergird the other aspect of Grahn's argument. "Origin stories remember a time before anything was, a time that consisted entirely of darkness, of water, of endless space, or of flatness without

24. Grahn, *Blood, Bread and Roses*, 5.
25. Grahn, *Blood, Bread and Roses*, 5.
26. Grahn, *Blood, Bread and Roses*, 5.
27. Grahn, *Blood, Bread and Roses*, 5.
28. Grahn, *Blood, Bread and Roses*, 7.

landscape; a time before name, before consciousness; a time described as asleep, or dreaming, or by the Greek word *chaos*, meaning "yawning."[29] Briefly, without too much fanfare, Grahn traces these elements in various origin stories available to us today. "For the Tsimshian Indians of North America, as for many peoples, in the beginning the whole world was darkness." Grahn then notes that the Greeks credit the origin of creation as the separation of Earth and Sky. The ancient Babylonian account of creation focused on *naming* as fount of existence. Then earliest storying—second millennium BCE—names heaven and earth as "'waters' mingling in an undifferentiated state."[30] Tiamat, the original goddess, and her male mate, Apsu, co-mingle. "She herself has been identified as the ocean, as 'bitter waters,' that is salty waters, menstrual fluids. Apsu, the Abyss, is the 'sweet waters,' that is, semen."[31] "Tiamat describes the salty nature of menstrual blood carried to its greatest earthly denominator, the sea. She is the Red Sea . . . . She has been called 'Ocean of Blood.' Tiamat is menstruation externalized," according to Grahn, "a complex metaphor about the nature of the earth and other elements." She then becomes "the original water . . . in the creation story of Genesis, chapter 1, *tehom* or 'the deep.'"[32] Finally, Grahn invites the notion of Chaos as the description of prehuman consciousness *becoming conscious*. What it must have felt like to awaken to light, to become aware of separation from others around you, to move into language, differentiation. Such a powerful yet fragile process within which *chaos* is always within and beyond.

Ultimately, Grahn proposes that the development of human consciousness emerges as an act of separation, grounded in a most primal evolutionary differentiation in *homo sapiens*, first menstruation, or as it is more formally named, *menarche*. Chaos both within and beyond is an inevitable factor in any learning, in any transformation of consciousness. Considering the development of humankind, *homo sapiens*, menstruation is the primal separation and the external-internal link through which consciousness arose. In her own words: "The ancient stories recall a time when our prehuman ancestors could not perceive shape, color, light, depth, distance, as we do, and had no names for them and no fixed sense of their qualities. . . . The act of separating is the act of creation, and

---

29. Grahn, *Blood, Bread and Roses*, 7.
30. Grahn, *Blood, Bread and Roses*, 9.
31. Grahn, *Blood, Bread and Roses*, 9.
32. Grahn, *Blood, Bread and Roses*, 10.

also of consciousness."[33] The challenge, of course, is *disciplined separation*. An orderliness that can become collective. Hence, the menstrual seclusion rites as recorded over centuries in various cultures included (typically) "three basic taboos: the menstruating woman must not see light, she must not touch water, and she must not touch earth."[34] These same elements are differentiated in Genesis and other creation stories. Grahn concludes, "I began to see how menstrual rites might have "created the world" for ancient peoples, and to wonder whether the sleepers who awoke and saw landscape, who named the elements, who separated the above from the below, and darkness from light, were informed by rites of seclusion that specified these very elements, singled them out for attention through *tapua*, sacred law of "the woman's friend."[35] Menstruation and established rites of seclusion therefore provide the embodied foundations for noninstinctual knowledge connected to but outside of our own bodies, as well as an orderly capacity for external measurement and understanding—co-creating—the world(s) around us.

The synchronized collective seclusion of menstruating women *together* opened the door to a new world of consciousness. "Their minds became 'human' through an externalized vision that had as yet and perhaps for millennia to come no other expression than menstrual separation... This separation endowed both menstruation and light with power, the power of memory and first cause, the power of rite to create human mind and culture."[36] By using *tapua*, women were able "to hold the thought still, to capture the perception of the source of light, emphasize its importance, and teach it."[37] Grahn dives deeply here, creating what she has called *metaform theory*, a systematic rendering of all acts or forms of instruction "that make a connection between menstruation and a mental principle."[38] She continues to contend that "the central unit of measurement, the ultimate metaphor to which all metaforms refer, is blood."[39] You can begin to imagine how my establishment-theologically-trained self resisted, initially refused all that Grahn has to say. She mixes the interpretive-analytical with the causal at almost every turn. Her

33. Grahn, *Blood, Bread and Roses*, 10.
34. Grahn, *Blood, Bread and Roses*, 11.
35. Grahn, *Blood, Bread and Roses*, 11.
36. Grahn, *Blood, Bread and Roses*, 15.
37. Grahn, *Blood, Bread and Roses*, 16.
38. Grahn, *Blood, Bread and Roses*, 20.
39. Grahn, *Blood, Bread and Roses*, 22.

argument depends upon supposition and juxtaposition, a pattern out of observable coincidences. Her work was not important to me as a work of *history*, in how I've inherited it.

Grahn's daring work yet opened up entire horizons I had never known could be there. I was beginning to experience *woman-centric* community in my Red Tent and women's writing circles. Grahn's work pointed to possibilities lost, absent, always defended against. But what could her-story have been, had Grahn's argument actually been historical, provable in evidentiary form, analytical?

Today, I'm *so inexplicably grateful* for Judy Grahn's work. Not for the attempt at this menstrual history defining the world, but for the audacity to imagine a woman-centric world, rooted from *her own body*. Just under the wire of my own menopause, I got to experience my own bleeding as the sacred grounding it could have been my entire life, had Grahn's suppositions been historically pervasive. She and her bold work returned something profound to me. She and her bold work gave me something that had previously been imprisoned in shame, for most of my life, by sacred Scripture and Protestant traditioning. *Herstory* may never become accepted history, but its contributions nourish and balance, challenge and ground nonetheless.

A Scriptural-Archaeological Approach

A conscious feminine theologian naturally looks to her disciplinary elders in the theological disciplines, which she is blessed to even have access to these days. This approach centers the women before me who have labored long and hard to re-create women's experience and women's voices in sacred Scripture. Rage nonetheless asks the questions: What is a woman conscious of being a woman, conscious of her own tradition's abandonment and silencing of her as a woman, to do with herself in previous sacred presumptions, proclamations? How does she ground in the sacredness of her own flesh when ancient and contemporary voices refute her dignity, her goodness, her value encased only in the power-over tropes of masculine-gaze, with options as either mother or whore? Does the past hold a future for women?

Earliest voices named these questions then gave preliminary responses. Edited by Carol P. Christ and Judith Plaskow, *Womanspirit Rising: a Feminist Reader in Religion* affirmed the possibilities, offering space for women to challenge traditional abandonment(s) and offer reconstructive perspectives within traditions (reformist perspective). Other women-scholars entirely refused death-dealing traditions for women, arguing instead for creating *new* traditions (a revolutionary perspective). The authors here were largely from Jewish or Christian traditions, though many were moving into Goddess and psychological resources more fulfilling for women's spirituality in second-wave feminist contributions.

I was particularly moved by one of Carol Christ's claims, that a "central feminist experience, the experience of nothingness, is shared by many modern women who begin their life journeys lacking an adequate image of self."[40] This speaks intimately to my own awakening to becoming a woman, being returned to my own body with a terrifying encounter of the Void, nothingness. Christ therefore proposes the pathway to new traditions as a spiritual quest, recognizing that "in a very real sense, women have not experienced their own experience."[41] Women need to engage in their own storytelling, so to have access to their own experience. As she argues, "Men have actively shaped their experiences of self and world by creating the stories they have told. Their deepest stories orient them to what they perceive as the ultimate powers and realities of the universe. We women have not told our own stories. The dialectic between experiencing and shaping experience by storytelling has not been in our own hands."[42] Christ and her companions therefore articulate a woman's encounter with despised aspects of the self in Western culture, specifically the unconscious, the body and nature, and the depth dimension of women's experiences. When quests are "successful," they lead to self-integration and integration with the universe.[43] This reframing speaks to my own experience, my feminist grounding more fully into the conscious feminine in complicated and (un)consciously hostile environments.

Other later scholars then made rigorous critical contributions to the challenges facing women today by wedding traditional theological disciplines with the philosophical strands of hermeneutics—specifically Sandra Schneiders, Elisabeth Schüssler Fiorenza, and Elizabeth Johnson (for my era of scholarship, awakening). Schneiders realized she couldn't really ask the questions *she* wanted to ask within the Roman Catholic doctoral formation, doctrinal habits, of Gregorian University at that

---

40. Christ and Plaskow, *Womanspirit Rising*, 195–96.
41. Christ, "Spiritual Quest and Women's Experience," 228.
42. Christ, "Spiritual Quest and Women's Experience," 229.
43. Christ, "Spiritual Quest and Women's Experience," 196.

time. Eventually, she observes, "It became increasingly clear to me that the dimension of the text that most interested me could not be accessed by the methods I was learning. But there were no other methods that were academically respectable and I was not willing to abandon a serious scholarly approach to the text . . . "[44] Schneiders's work speaks with a primacy here for me because it was her interdisciplinary commitments in spirituality that opened so many doors for my own academic work. She was also a moving force for bringing a focus on *hermeneutics* into Catholic circles, which up to that time had not engaged much with it in either philosophical or Protestant theological discourses.

Other women scholars were articulating their own navigation of hermeneutics and scriptural interpretation as well. Elisabeth Schüssler Fiorenza names the "triple jeopardy" that faces any critical feminist hermeneutics aimed toward liberation within traditional histories and institutions. Making an argument is entering into a minefield, she begins. "One must detect and uncover the contradictions between historical exegesis and systematic theology, between value-free scientific inquiry and "advocacy" scholarship, between universal-objectivist preconceptions of academic theology and the critical partiality of liberation theologies." Once one decides to enter, however, the triple jeopardy pinches and threatens such a scholar. Establishment scholars will "reject such an endeavor as unscientific, biased, and overly conditioned by contemporary questions and therefore unhistorical," or even the question raised cannot be serious because "the issue is raised by a woman."[45] Liberation or political theologians will consider such a feminist theological endeavor as "one problem among others, or at worst label it as middle class and peripheral to the struggle of oppressed people."[46] Why do a middle-class white woman's concerns about power-abuses in society matter when people are starving, being tortured, etc.? Finally, feminist theology simply challenged academic theology to take its own intellectual presuppositions seriously and asked other liberation theologies to specify their option for the oppressed. The third pressure in the triple jeopardy is both integrity and particularity, in other words. Robert McAfee Brown famously observed, "What we see depends on where we are standing."[47] Feminist (and now womanist, mujeristia, queer-

---

44. Schneiders, *Revelatory Text*, 2.
45. Schüssler Fiorenza, *Bread Not Stone*, 43.
46. Schüssler Fiorenza, *Bread Not Stone*, 43.
47. Brown, cited in Schüssler Fiorenza, *Bread Not Stone*, 44.

ing . . .) theology challenges so-called detached objectivity while also pressing for liberation theologians to ground their work with specificity, particularity to human bodies, culture, race, etc. As you can imagine, a lot of energy has been spent over decades refining what a liberating hermeneutics might entail, and for whom.

Without going into intimate detail for each of these versions to come, one can yet bow to the wisdom in the methods or models articulated over the years. First of all, consider the *hermeneutics of suspicion*, as Paul Ricouer famously said, "All hermeneutics involves suspicion; that is, the text presents us with a challenge to believe that the true meaning of the text emerges only through interpretation."[48] Alicia Ostriker offers an excellent summary of this hermeneutics of suspicion, which she defines as "concentrating on issues of power and powerlessness. Insofar as she identifies herself as powerless, the poet mistrusts, resists, and attacks the embodiment of patriarchal power—both the being and the text."[49] Given in the Bucknell Lectures of Literary Theory, Ostriker as a working poet suggests the flattened or flattening power dynamics brought into hermeneutics as a philosophy or an attempted "science." Others aim to stretch and expand understandings of hermeneutics significant for the lived experience of faith.

Elisabeth Schüssler Fiorenza articulates an elegant *hermeneutical circle* relevant to a feminist theological hermeneutics. The circle departs from the traditionally linear habits ingrained in much power-over literature, what Stuhlmacher in historical criticism coined as a *"hermeneutics of consent and affirmation."*[50] Schüssler Fiorenza puts her own spin on this dynamic of consent and affirmation. For her circle, critical interpretation begins with a *hermeneutics of suspicion* as traditionally understood. It then develops a *hermeneutic of proclamation* "rather than a hermeneutics of historical factualness, because the Bible still functions as Holy Scripture in Christian communities today." She then urges an expansive *hermeneutics of remembrance*, so to move from "biblical texts about women" toward the "reconstruction of women's history" that will liberate all humankind. The last movement in her circle is a *hermeneutics of creative actualization* that "involves the church of women in the imaginative articulation of women's biblical story and its

---

48. Ricoeur, cited in Stewart, "Hermeneutics of Suspicion," 297.
49. Ostriker, *Feminist Revision and the Bible*, 66.
50. Stuhlmacher, cited by Schüssler Fiorenza, *Bread Not Stone*, 188n33.

ongoing history and community."[51] In each of these moments of interpretation, Schüssler Fiorenza's commitment is to the liberating impulses for all human beings in an historical wisdom text, woven into centuries of covenantal Christian community. She is not prioritizing feminist experience for women alone, but as a prophetic and integrative witness of truth for all with ears to hear. Much more recently, wearied scholars within contentious disciplines of polarized discourses are beginning to name a *hermeneutics of charity*, or a "humble, relational, and attentional posture toward a person, text, or topic that seeks to understand and so exhibit love to the person, text, or topic in front of one in order to edify the proper end of life, which is to love God."[52]

Elizabeth A. Johnson crafts her own sense of a *hermeneutics of revelation*, which is rooted in Scripture yet more broadly configured with nuances of Wisdom. God's revelations are not only through words, especially not only scriptural words, penned largely by men. She argues,

> Undergirding this kind of appeal to Scripture is a certain idea of revelation, namely, that it is conceptual truth given by God to human beings in verbal form, either directly through the mind of the Evangelist or indirectly through founding historical events. This doctrinal model locates revelation in rational, linguistic statements communicated by God without error that give information about divine mystery and dealings with the world. . . . In this perspective, the church has no option in the light of women's pressing experience but to continue to repeat the pattern of language about God in the metaphor of ruling men.[53]

Yet even a cursory glance of Christian history shows many other models of revelation more viable, among them revelation as *historical event* (the resurrection of Jesus Christ), or as *inner experience*, or as *dialectical presence* (Chalcedonian formulation), or as *new awareness* (Spirit-spirit), or as *symbolic mediation* (the cross, as just one example). Johnson reminds us within the signs and symbols of traditions that a *hermeneutics of revelation* roots our invitation into the sacred underneath and above the words of Scripture written by men.

Poet Alicia Ostriker charts a path resonant with all that is to come in a similar way. She names a *hermeneutics of desire* in which the poet "lets the text stand for pleasure, eroticizing it by inserting herself into the

51. Schüssler Fiorenza, *Bread Not Stone*, 15.
52. Sosler, "Prodigal Love and a Hermeneutic of Charity."
53. Johnson, *She Who Is*, 76–77.

story, by identifying its spiritualities with her own sensualities, and by feminizings of the divine. In contrast with the hermeneutics of suspicion we might call this the hermeneutics of desire: one finds in the text what one desires to find, one bends it to one's wish."[54] More significantly, she also offers what she calls a *hermeneutics of indeterminacy*, taking seriously the rabbinic saying, "There is always another interpretation."[55] In short, Ostriker summarizes, this act of interpretation "is not, cannot ever be a correct interpretation, there can only be another, and another, and another."[56] I love that it takes a working poet to mirror to biblical scholars that no one is *ever* going to land on the sole, only, correct interpretation, which is not a scholarly failing as much as the engine of generativity, confirmed again and again in Spirit. This proposal will land hardest on those focused upon the truth-claims of Christian traditions, but I smile, being a poet myself. Speaking as a woman of faith, I find Ostriker's *hermeneutics of desire* and *indeterminacy* wise, soulful, led.

Yet even Johnson and Ostriker retain a priority for Scripture that can feel like a complicity in the abandonment of women by tradition, at least for an enraged conscious feminine theologian like myself. As Johnson concludes her introductory remarks, setting up her hermeneutics of revelation, "What is not under question is the fact the text must be interpreted."[57] I am finally emboldened enough in my own body to ask, Must it? Really? Must we always drag the history of interpretation behind us while we desperately need to learn new-ancient ways of being human together? Then the words of an elder stateswoman in Pentecostal femininst biblical interpretation came into my life, saying in published prose what I had felt for *years*.

> In regards to the intersections of gender and the Bible, it seems that we have come to the end of ourselves. I am most grateful for those sure-footed individuals who have done the difficult text critical work, helping tease out 'what the Bible meant in the era in which it was written to what it means about women'. But, all their good work never seems enough in convincing people to move beyond their prejudice. To be honest, as of late, all the hermeneutical work regarding the 'biblical view of women' is not enough for me. It is not enough when I open a Bible and find a world in

---

54. Ostriker, *Feminist Revision and the Bible*, 66.
55. Ostriker, *Feminist Revision and the Bible*, 122.
56. Ostriker, *Feminist Revision and the Bible*, 122.
57. Johnson, *Who Is*, 77.

which women are deemed chattel, viewed as unclean, valued for their production of sons, raped and their body parts distributed to others, and on and on. There are days when, listening to the Bible read with its male language and imagery that I cry within my spirit, 'My God, My God, why have you forsaken me?' I need more than 'the right interpretation' to save me from despair. . . . in terms of women, hermeneutics alone cannot save us from the grief of finding little to match the sound of our own cadence.[58]

When these words found me, I simply let the tears come. I sat with them, feeling deeply heard and seen by a sister-in-Christ, which is *not* an experience that happens very often anymore. I am willing to say that Spirit is simply not done with me yet, with respect to Scripture (capital S) or with the irrevocable loss of women's voices *in* writings considered sacred by historic Christian communities. I have innumerable questions, rooted in the pains exacted on human bodies by Scripture and (un)conscious, fearful human beings.

When is Scripture functioning to imprison and confine instead of liberate? When is it used to socialize human beings into their own disempowerment instead of empowering us to transform or transfigure our woundedness? When is our human egoic *use* of Scripture weaponizing our fears against those with whom we disagree? Used violently or aggressively in our grasping need for "our truth" over another? I don't know yet how to reconcile these realities within my own embodied soul, though I know to trust forward as I am, where I am. People around me share their love of Scripture all the time. It still informs, guides, instructs me, though no longer from the written texts. From people, then. Primarily the people whose groundedness in Spirit I can trust.

To be clear, Johns would not follow me here, with her deep commitment to and conviction in the sanctified and sanctifying role of Scripture for healing and restoration. She concludes her introductory observations: "What I wish to offer is a view of the Bible as living subject whose existence is grounded in the economic life of God. As such, the Bible serves as a sanctified, Spirit-filled vessel in service of restoring creation."[59] She begins always with *gratitude*, seemingly without lashing out from the woundedness I know in myself. How can she not rage at the Whirlwind like I have, for years? I wonder sometimes. She names and even seems to welcome the *grief* of it all—unavoidable and overwhelming. So much

---

58. Johns, "Spirit, Word, Transformation," 9.
59. Johns, "Spirit, Word, Transformation," 9.

is rage-worthy, documented here, but she remains steadfastly grounded in a commitment to Scripture. She introduces the scriptural imagery of *brooding* as a place within which women (and others) can wrestle with the brokenness of creation . . . or simply rest in Spirit's invitations, trusting forward. Which returns me to my own earliest experiences of devotion. Active waiting. I have been *brooding*, in her terms, for decades, consciously for over one decade. Trusting such voices, relying on shared experiences to come, I may be able someday to feel into a restored and restoring sense of Scripture.

But for the honoring of rage, its legitimate and valid expressions for accountability for Christians unwilling to see the abandonment of women, these elder women of faith give me courage to name what needs saying, at least for now, for me. In my near six decades of faithful formation, I experience our *use of Scripture* as an idol and a weapon of certainty, defensiveness, exclusion, and refusal. People of faith will always prefer that which they can see, read, hold in their own hands over the unnameable, uncontrollable, unwritten and unspoken Presence of God/de available to them in their own bodies, their own breath (attributed as *ruach* by Scripture). Particularly as these things can be affirmed and confirmed by whatever tribal faction of which we may be a part. Scripture seems to always self-referentially point back to the sensibilities and texts we've memorized, understood in the ways most suited to our certainty's survival. Even worse, biblical studies across the globe retains largely masculinized habits of mind, whether they reside in bodies identified as male or female. *None* of this surely is what God/de intends, as I know H/her now in my own flesh. Each voice in my own scriptural-archeological traditioning has contributed, is so very welcome into my own learning, integration. The embodied dissociations so necessary for analytical scholarly clarity have done great disservice rarely considered or self-implicated within scholarship for community's sake.

Then breathtakingly midrashic text landed into my pile of books, inviting me to breathe, to continue to wait, to listen. As Ostriker tells her own story of coming home to write one night,

> The general idea was that the God of what Christians call the Old Testament and Jews call, simply, the Bible or Torah, seems to like being challenged and called to account, and even rewards those who most boldly interrogate him. As I puzzled over the paradoxical dialogue between Job and God, in which Job's challenge to God's justice is first scorned, then affirmed, my

thoughts were at first recognizably my own. Then something happened. I found myself writing, without forethought and at astonishing speed, as if someone else were directing the pen, about Job's wife, that nameless woman. How would Job's wife feel about having the ten children who have been casually slain in order to test her husband's devotion to his God, replaced by ten new children? And what if Job's wife were to get up the courage to challenge God like her husband? What would she—what would we—say to God if we dared? By the time my pen stopped, I understood that I was on a train I could not get off. *The Nakedness of the Fathers* is the result.[60]

Something about Ostriker's text goaded me deeper, soothing me. I think it was a seed of hope within me, that this raging storyline within me could become something else life-giving. I was found by yet another woman who somehow found the courage to stay within that which wounded her yet would also not release her.

If imitation is a sincere form of flattery, then I model my words after Ostriker, who wrote: "I am and am not a Jew.... To deny my Judaism would be like denying the gift of life, the reality of sorrow, the pleasures of learning and teaching.... But I'm not a Jew, I can't be a Jew, because Judaism repels me as a woman."[61] As the conscious feminine theologian that I am, I say hear hear. *I am and am not a Christian . . . To deny my Christianity would be like denying the gift of life, the reality of sorrow, the pleasures of learning and teaching. . . . But I'm not a Christian, I can't be a Christian, because Christianity repels me as a woman.*

Within non-sectarian wisdom community(ies), in this Body of Humanity that could hold all of me as I am, I began to live my way into a renewing *doxology*, assurance, definitely more expansive questions than those focused on tradition . . . or not. A mentor-elder, Miriam Therese Winter, gifted me with her shamanic sparked word *paradoxology*. She uses it to describe the dance between *paradox* and *paradigm* that goes all the way back to the beginning of Christian origins. "At the very heart of our Christian faith," she writes, "paradox is paradigm." It "rattles the rules of logic, but makes perfect sense in a quantum universe."[62] She recalled how it arrived in her awareness twenty years before she ever wrote further into it. "A shard of the Holy Spirit," she said. "A sacred talisman infused with

---

60. Ostriker, *Nakedness of the Fathers*, xi–xii.
61. Ostriker, *Nakedness of the Fathers*, 5–6.
62. Winter, *Paradoxology*, 15.

shamanic energy."[63] You can almost hear her pausing, caught off-guard by the spirit-of-the-moment, her own F/feminine wisdom becoming articulate in her own cells, voice. This *doxology* was breathing at the center of everything I say I know in my life of faith. Gratitude, praise, even adoration of this Force or Flow that never lets me go. That continues to breathe so deeply within me, I could never part from such Breath. Paraclete. All of which now somehow flows alongside irrevocable loss, the visceral abandonment of women by God and the church.

Winter reminded me, with her energy and smile: *women* have always been eyewitnesses to what has yet been unseen, unheard. "Spirit rising from the remnants of defeat,"[64] in her words. The challenges are always implicit, for all human beings, regardless of gender or the refusal of gender. "Do not cling to the old ways," she urges. "Do not be afraid to witness to what you have seen and heard. Let go of power that overpowers and the need to be believed."[65] Winter also knows about this Body of Humanity, which is the "new community of faith in our evolving universe, flexible and hospitable, with a vision that is big enough to let anybody in."[66] In sum, I don't have any neat reconciliations of the irreconcilable for me here. I don't know how else to hold the anger become conscious, the various lenses within which rage is clearly warranted, legitimate and righteous. I don't know how to hold the sacredness of these ancient texts over generations of human beings alongside the near utter omission of women's voices. My body regularly, viscerally faces the imposition of violence, rooted in these texts. I refuse to be complicit in my own silencing. Yet I too have been blessed now to meet human beings from various traditions and none at all who honor these ancient texts, weaving them into the healing of themselves and those around them, even the Earth. And rage wearies even the strongest of us, becoming heavier and heavier unto hopelessness and despair.

---

63. Winter, *Paradoxology*, 13.
64. Winter, *Paradoxology*, 22.
65. Winter, *Paradoxology*, 22.
66. Winter, *Paradoxology*, 23.

Chapter Three

Awakening to an Unknown Inside—Return to the Body

MY OWN JOURNEY TO this other side that is *inside* opened only in proportion to my awakening to the conscious reality that I was living in a *woman's body*. I realize how incomprehensible this sounds, as I thought for decades I was conscious of being a woman. At some level, I knew that being a woman could be dangerous for me, so I favored what was called (decades ago) the *tomboy* side of myself. I heard my faith community's speech about "those kind of women," usually with derision and disrespect for speaking out or displaying strength, so I learned the indirect use of power. Yes, I became a feminist in seminary simply out of self-defense but it was a feminism that wouldn't offend anyone. My fierceness for women didn't require anything of beloved men in my life, in other words. Some part of me knew that awakening to the F/feminine would make me more vulnerable in my worlds than I could stomach. I found masculinized-ways to be who I was, which opened doors in my worlds, didn't close them.

Fierceness for Women from "Outside"

So many people of faith refuse the gifts of anyone exhibiting a *fierceness for women* because they are already surrounded by women who refuse such wisdom, embedded as it can be in (un)conscious choices to refuse. We've been socialized to push the F/feminine away, repress, suppress, make nice (at least for women). We've learned and accepted these strategies of defensiveness, which keep the wisdom silenced. Until She cannot help but speak, which is when the community usually exiles H/her. The defenses against the F/feminine are endless and infinite, particularly when there is no willingness to even get curious. A beloved seminary mentor taught me that the original sin of men may be pride, but for women? It's self-abdication—the repeated refusal of self and gifts in systems not interested in women's voices *as women*.[1] It takes a remarkable convergence of communities, courage, and compassion for women to come to voice in public, fierce for themselves and others. Blessed in 2019–2020 with the opportunity to work within the Dayton TEDx community, I explained it like this: *I was my father's son for forty-five years, which made coming to voice as a woman quite the surprise. For everyone.... In my family of 'the brothers'—my father and his brothers—you got seen and heard by attuning to what they were interested in, being prepared to achieve and to be right, supported with appropriate authorities.*[2] I then proceeded into an earlier and much more circumspect version of my own coming to voice I had not known was within me . . . yet.

At root here, in this chapter, is the ever-present experience of bewilderment when you learn something you thought you already knew, only to discover you knew only in part or worse, you were completely mistaken. While it was bewildering to find myself deeply in encounter with a part of myself I had never felt before, it was also precisely a kind of awakening I yearn for every human being today: a shift in awareness that leads to *interconnectedness* through *ego-transcendence*, a *timelessness and spaciousness* that comes from being returned to a moment-by-moment attentiveness, in the here-and-now. One is no longer lamenting some perceived past nor fearful of some imagined future. A relaxation or surrender shows up in *acceptance*, a reality free of bondage from and attachment to personal desires, thoughts, feelings. The invitation to unimagined spaces *beyond pleasure and pain* beckons, if accompanied by the *shattering of preconceived notions* and a renewed *clarity* felt deeply in the body.[3] All this rests in the body well attuned, self-regulated, and curious—safe and welcoming—to receive. I was returned fully, finally, to my own flesh, surprised to find it a source of lifelong wisdom, sacred invitation, Spirit-source of intensification of prayer. I awakened to an *inside* I had not known was there, focused so fully on the *outsides*

1. Lakey Hess, *Caretakers of Our Common House*, 54.
2. Hess, "Scarred, Scared and Sacred."
3. Ullman and Reichenberg-Ullman, *Mystics, Masters, Saints and Sages*, xvii–xviii.

traditioned or imposed upon me. When held in a witnessing community, this Body of Humanity, I became reconnected with a juicy, embodied F/feminine I call *womanheart*, though its *energies* are available to each of us beyond gender. A classic voice from second-wave feminism was really significant for me here—Susan Griffin—so her voice may help nuance my own language for the *bewilderment* of *becoming conscious of being in a woman's body*.

Awakening to an Unknown Inside

Griffin's work was just poetic enough to reattune me to a newly visceral awareness landed into me in the Days in the Weeds, often experienced as panic and disarray. Historical and philosophical writings of (mostly) men (or then women writing in the masculine voice so to be heard) had (un)consciously aligned my sense of sacred with the presumed-masculine, an abstracted disembodiment unknown as such. Even my scripturalized love of Wisdom was (un)consciously separated from the physical, earthly body. In contrast, Griffin's now classic work offered a poetic, impassioned *tour de force* of words "written for those of us whose language is not heard, whose words have been stolen or erased, those robbed of language, who are called voiceless or mute, even the earthworms, even the shellfish and the sponges, for those of us who speak our own language . . . "[4] She was the first author I ever read to place any wordlessness of women in the same stream of thought as earthworms, shellfish, sponges. Interconnection. Continuity. Something lit up inside of me, my body.

Yet her work confounded and terrified me at first. It spoke in a poetry and a passion that I recognized, but I also felt such forboding within my affiliations of family, religious community, Protestant Christian tradition. So I guess the invitation here is to listen for your own forboding. Feel it, honor it, but don't let it prevent you from seeing what is here to be seen, and felt. Her text is shaped into four parts—*Matter, Separation, the Separate Rejoined, Matter Revisited*—which chronicle a story of humanity and nature, still emerging. I had a theological story that took me up to the *Separate Rejoined*, all accomplished through one man, Jesus of Nazareth, the focal point of at-one-ment, the Atonement, reuniting God and humanity across the chasm of sin, imputed historically into the bodies of women as well as men. Griffin was placing this sacred story into another

---

4. Griffin, *Woman and Nature*, vii.

sacred story, arguably more ancient than the one I knew. This story had been hidden from me for most of my life—arguably hidden from most faithful people of the Book today, divorced from Nature as ancient texts distract us to be. It was unseen by me until my early thirties, unfelt by me until my mid-forties. Griffin's work found me well before my Days in the Weeds but precisely at the time I was entering what she calls "a labyrinth," women's circles and spirit-friendships able to hold necessary witnessing spaces for me to encounter both sacred stories at once.

The more ancient sacred story had signposts of the story I knew, yet placed within words I had felt (unconsciously) all my life in my body, feelings from which I had ritually, intentionally, dissociated myself. Griffin's words: Matter: *How Man Regards and Makes Use of Woman and Nature.* Separation: *The Separations in His Vision and Under His Rule.* Passage: *Her Journey Through the Labyrinth to the Cave Where She Has Her Vision.* Her Vision: *Now She Sees Through Her Own Eyes.*[5] Griffin got through to me because she didn't give me a linear argument about the rights of women in a world that abuses and silences us across the globe. She wasn't writing primarily to my mind, but to my body. I had been shaped by masculinized traditions to neutralize direct argument. Griffin was offering me poetry in which I began to *recognize myself*, my *own experience*, which I had not been strong enough to claim as my own, for *decades*. At least if I wanted to remain in secure connection with my own family and ecclesial lineages. Intuition could help me, but my own intuition was undeveloped, atrophied in deeply wounded ancestral lineages that cautioned against intuition and any body wisdom.

The entrance into this labyrinth Griffin calls the *room of the dressing*, which gives a felt-sense of things we mostly don't talk about in polite spaces. It's a space of otherizing-mirrors that stand in for the *eyes of men* and the (self-and-otherizing) *judgment of women.* Griffin's poetic writing alludes to the ways mothers teach their daughters to dress, put on makeup so to be pleasing; the ways daughters giggle and whisper with one another, comparing their bodies and excluding the perceivedly-weak; the ways women within power-over environments are conditioned to compare, compete, and abuse one another. It is a room of partial-seeing, or as Simone de Beauvoir describes it, "In woman dressed and adorned, nature is present but under restraint, by human will remolded nearer to man's

---

5. Griffin, *Woman and* Nature, vii.

desire."⁶ I had attempted to resist this room for most of my life, eschewing "feminine norms" for the security of "tomboy" or "masculinized-women" success. Establishment, ecclesial theological education, however, is a particularly cognitive *room of the dressing*, shaped nearly entirely by the masculine gaze.

Then the Days in the Weeds breaking me open in an intersection or perfect storm of women's circles. Consciously, (un)consciously, I chose or was pushed unknowingly to enter *the room of the undressing*: "I go where I love and where I am loved."⁷ Griffin's words eased my conscious mind in, overwhelmed by the numbed pains of the past and the terrifying fears of a disruptive future:

> *Startracks. Spiral nebulae. Craters of the moon.* She lets herself fall. She falls into the room of her wants. The room where the demands of women are endless. Where her voice has endlessly demanded her to go. This room which reveals her. Where she is clumsy again. Where she is awkward in her grown-up clothing. Where she aches. This room of the revelation of all she thought horrible, and of her endlessly demanding body. Of all she shrank from in herself. This room filled with herself. She fell into this room. This room of outcasts. *Where we uncover our bodies. Where we meet our outcast selves.* The room in which she does not mock herself. This room filled with darkness. *Where we go into darkness. Where we embrace darkness. Where we lie close to darkness, breathe when darkness breathes and find darkness inside ourselves.* The room of the darkness of women.

I don't remember *choosing* to enter this room, but my young, embodied self was starved to be there, precisely as she was. Needy. Clumsy. Awkward. Afraid. Vulnerable. Embraced. Little in my own formation up to that point predisposed me to consciously choose anything that felt so uncomfortable, so potentially in confrontation with a well established intellectual, masculine churched environment in which I'd lived most of my life. Which I had loved. Which had nourished my intellect and theological "career." Yet here I found myself, *finally*, as the visceral-infant I was, somehow in a middle-aged woman's body.

---

6. de Beauvoir, *Second Sex*, cited as chapter epigraph by Griffin, *Woman and Nature*, 157.

7. H. D., "The Flowering of the Rod," cited as section epigraph by Griffin, *Woman and Nature*, 159.

In my circles upon circles of women, in my spirit-friendships, I had finally entered into an environment that wanted me as the little girl I was, as the midlife woman I was. *Womancentric* spaces, prioritizing *the needs of women*. I could begin to see horizons in which I could begin to believe anew, a place that allowed me as a woman to exist safely *as a woman*, yet unknowing, uncertain, wounded, unseen. Griffin writes, "Where our words are undressed. And we touch. This room of our touching where the mother teaches her daughter to face her secret feelings. The labyrinth of her knowledge. Where she has her own reasons. *The coral skeleton. The crystals of frost.* Of her knowing. This place of her wandering. *The circles of the tree's growth. The beehive.* The room of her first wandering and of her finding. This place where she finds her way."[8] Nowhere in my familial, ecclesial or civic worlds was I allowed to be as I was, speaking openly and honestly. Nowhere are our little boys growing into body-dissociated men allowed to be fully as they are, could someday yearn in their flesh to be. I was shown something sacred like this when I was six, but it was like I didn't even know it anymore. Out here in the woods with the wilding women of Red Tent, moving then into a circle of women writers celebrating the individual voice in practices of community, I found a way. I could withstand even divine abandonment, the awakening to desire, when I had a community of witnessing to see me, hear me deeply.

I was therefore no longer alone in that place of darkness that had been imposed upon me in my Days in the Weeds. Void, emptiness. Griffin wrote, "We are shaped around emptiness, that we are a voice we do not know."[9] I finally had another context for those Days. In this "nothingness," I began to find, in Griffin's words, "what we could not have known existed. With our hands, we begin to find the sketches of ancient sensations, images, like those etched on cave walls. . . . the once blood and bone, the vanished, shimmering now like an answer from these walls, bright and red. . . . The rectangular shape of his book of knowledge, bending. The shape of our silence . . . "[10] Images from a circular *MotherPeace* deck would find me soon, dancing before my eyes. The remnants of a world in which the F/feminine was revered, at least for the capacity to give birth if yet unseeing of all S/she could offer. The journey of *becoming conscious as a woman* was one of mystery, opening, dreams, ancient rages, then possibility, transformation, clarity. It took nearly ten years,

---

8. Griffin, *Woman and Nature*, 159–60.
9. Griffin, *Woman and Nature*, 161–82.
10. Griffin, *Woman and Nature*, 161–63.

perhaps closer to twenty, for this journey of *sacred bewilderment* to be known as sacred in Spirit for me within my own root tradition, which had previously served largely as obstacle, wound.

Gathering and writing in circle upon circle of women gave me space and time to appreciate all the voices I have had to use, shaped through several decades in which I held space in and for the establishment worlds my family valued—academy, church, family, civic responsibility. The Voice I ultimately wanted to point to in my TEDx talk was not the sense of voice by role, but my *womanhearted*, womancentric F/feminine self I had (un)knowingly killed or hidden away years before. As I spoke it, "Another voice, some unexpected Voice came to me, in my body . . . This Voice happens to you. You don't go outward seeking this One, finding this One. If you're lucky, this Voice finds you. And for so many of us women dancing to the safety tunes of the men in our lives? Our fiercely-gifted Voices may never happen to us at all, much to our world's detriment." The rest of the TED Talk spoke to the rage, to the providence of women's circles, to the power of women's circles to bring women to voice about *their own experience*. Not what we're supposed to say. Not "safe-speech" that won't offend. But truly, what our bodies have experienced throughout the course of our lives.

We call it "catching courage," which is what I learned *happens* when women gather in circle to write, to share their words. [I should also say I now know this power and courage within co-ed, nongendered spaces/persons as well, though a solely woman-identified space was crucial for my own courage.] In my very first public-readaround in 2012, recounted in the TEDx talk, a Voice in me but never *conscious* in me took the lead in my actions. It or She "happened to me." In that readaround, I read one of the most significant pieces I had written to this day (which was eventually incorporated into my last book). Part of the story ended in these words: "Then we sat down, my Voice and me. My body was shaking almost uncontrollably." I was becoming more fully the feminist and conscious feminine theologian I am today, finally able to honor the Voice of H/her speaking without censure or preventative fear. Not insignificantly, the seed of my own awakening was an intense sharing of *erotic power between women*. It was the arising of *desire* that had freed my own *womanheart*. This time, I knew it was Godde's fundamental desire more than my own, as might be misunderstood today. It was coming from the deepest places in me I had not known were there.

Womanheart—the Inside of a F/feminine in the Company of Women

Whenever the *erotic* arises in conversation today, societal assumptions and fears push the conversation deep into the mires of gender, sexual orientation, broader presumptions about sexuality that largely dismiss any other framings of embodied energies. Mostly, without other contexts for hearing or learning, we participate in an enraged (lack of) listening/hearing imposed by identity politics and fearmongering, fears and realities of no longer belonging in our tribes not yet aware of the Body of Humanity. It has taken me so long to integrate my own experiences over decades because of these categories imposed, even as I bow to their importance for political advocacy and the pursuit of human rights, social justice. My stewardship of these realities in my own body is not intended to discount those experiences, nor oppose them. But my own journey wove these ways of thinking about my own sexuality into the much larger theological frames of reference within which I could make sense of my entire body-journey, not just that of my attractions/aversions. I have journeyed through all the identities that could have possibly made sense of my felt-sense, deep-connection with both women and men, and now those who identify as non-binary and/or queer. What can I say? My body is capable of cherishing the unique dignity of most every being I'm privileged to encounter. Sometimes a sense of *eros* arises in the encounter. Most times, *eros* does not arise. But I can say this so freely because of how I was woven into the conscious feminine, into this capacity to nourish with rigor, return to the body, and trust its wisdom. Something that can be done by any human being, regardless of orientation or gender. I can say this so freely today because the gifts of *womanheart* far outweigh the challenges while freeing you to be completely in your *own skin*, without shame. I will invite you into my learning of this *womanheart* before giving a bit of context from the work of Carol Gilligan, whose seeking a *new map of love* was fundamental for me in this larger freedom.

My eyes were opened to *womanheart* as I prepared to enter a conscious feminine leadership training in the summer of 2013. That May, I was also preparing to be installed as Moderator of Presbytery, the governing consortium of local PCUSA churches in the Miami Valley of Ohio (Greater Dayton area). The Conscious Feminine Leadership Academy required the purchase of a *MotherPeace* tarot deck. *Tarot* is like the third rail for conservative Christians, who say it is a sure harbinger of evil and drawing close to Satan. For my part, I trust my body for its warning if or when I am drawing close to evil—I have experienced it viscerally before—and this had none of that. I remember only feeling quietly rebellious and a little curious. The images were stark and discomforting, but there was also something compelling about their circular-form, the fierce intention to honor the world from *women-centric cultures* and symbols. I ordered the deck on the same day as my installation into ecclesial office. "All things in balance," I decided with an impish grin, shared with no one.

One of the first writing-circle prompts the first week of the Academy in June was to pick a card with a question in mind, then write to it. *Motherpeace* was a woman-centric source of intuitive wisdom for this community of becoming-conscious-feminine women. The leader of the training insisted upon its use with an almost liturgical zeal. Other tarot decks were not welcome, in other words, though our circle challenged her. Blessedly, quietly, I got introduced to the *Gaian Tarot* during this week as well, a traditionally-numbered/suited deck created and written by Joanna Powell Colbert honoring the natural world, humans of all ages, both masculine and feminine, creatures, trees, plants, ancient symbology and more.[11] Honoring the circle leader, however, we tended *Motherpeace* as the "central text" of the circle, even as it was a primarily visual work.

I began to sense that there was a communal practice of interpretation, with checks and balances for what the circle of women could and would see as sacred. "Not unlike Scripture," I remember thinking, though my own Protestant tradition eschewed images for receiving faith-wisdom. Too Catholic. (Gasp). It was my Christian community's traditioning of the "text" that gave me entrance, to be honest. I recognized a sacred energy and patterning that could be trusted. Women in our circle honored the F/feminine and one another's lives here, finding our intimate selves validated, legitimated, through the diversity of voices and images in *Motherpeace*, or *MamaP*, as we called her. This contrasts with the popular disdained image of the hanker-chiefed woman behind the curtain, divining the future in some suspect, dangerous way. Most Christians don't stick around long enough to see a community of interpretation forming, to get curious about what images might touch in one's own embodied, intuitive wisdom. One dear spirit-friend in my own seminary context nearly blew a gasket when he learned of my encounters with tarot. He's *still* not ready to discuss it prayerfully, with an open-heart

---

11. Colbert, *Journey through the Gaian Tarot*, 1–8.

to what God/de does in this stream of F/feminine wisdom. Back then, I knew to not tell anyone in my establishment worlds where I was or what I was doing with these circles of women.

Realizing that I'd rarely written about my mother, if ever, I went to *MamaP* with the question, "What do I need to know about my own mother and my relationship with her in order to grow more fully into the Conscious Feminine?" I drew the Three of Cups, whose interpretive description could not have been further from my experience. This card is "an expression of happiness and joyful time shared" between three orgiastically dancing, bare-breasted women. The group in the image embodies vulnerability, safety, security together, even openly reveling in one another. The Three Graces or Muses. Today, I'd even say the Three Norns, doing their thing in close proximity and celebration. Even more incongruous was tarot-artist Vicki Noble's interpretation of the card, suggesting the three women are sharing *pleasure* together, having fun. They celebrate "orgiastically," letting spirits come through their feelings and emotions.[12] Again, the polar opposite of the lived experience I have, made manifest in physical reality as I know it. I can't even imagine having a conversation about pleasure with my mother and sister in the same room, let alone celebrating "orgiastically" with them. Ultimately, this first tarot pull pushed me onto a path I was not aware of choosing.

I imagined, for perhaps the first *conscious* time, that something for which I seemed to yearn deeply could be accessible, possible, different from and *unavailable to me* from within my own family line, my own life. The absence of this *womanheart* became clearer and clearer as I considered my beloved family line shaped around the gifts and graces of four boys, then grown men. It was strangely absent in my family line, beloved as we all are together. The wives are known collectively alongside "the brothers," or left assumed but unnamed at family reunions, organized by the first names of the brothers. I belong to the Mark Hess family. Never have I heard myself referred to as a member of the *Mark and Carol* family at a reunion. Not once. My mother, sister and I share almost no *communal* contact today, for a wide variety of geographical and vocational reasons beyond the lack of *womanheart*. I'm intensely verbal, while they are less so. I was so often in my head, while they were much more attuned to the care of children, their families. My husband and I chose not to have children. My mother, sister and I are indelibly connected, but only

---

12. Noble, *Motherpeace*, 166–67.

individually, each one to only one other at a time. Lack of *womanheart* does not mean lack of love, to be clear. We express our love of one another when we are in communication. But the sensate, juicy, ebullient energies that I now know women-with-women can share are simply not a part of my immediate or extended family experience.

Blessedly, if painfully, it was this complete absence of intimate woman's energy, laughter, ease, and wisdom that pushed me onto the path of awakening to the F/feminine. *Womanheart* became my term for the deep feeling, deeply embodied wisdom that women know intimately with one another, often outside of the masculine gaze, which has nothing to do with sex or sexuality. *Women's mysteries* could be a classical term pointing possibly to similar phenomena, feared by the ancients in my own root tradition. The *conscious feminine* was the phrase in my own leadership circle. I had been starved from who I am for over forty years, which is a sensual, tactile woman coming to know herself loved by women as well as her husband. An incredibly beautiful, chaste, sensual way of being in the world, connected to the Earth, belonging with one another. I came to understand that this was a F/feminine way of being in the world, if previously completely unknown to me in my own body's experiences.

I knew to trust it with spirit-friends from a wide variety of traditions, and none, because three years before, I had been initiated into it before—the first time I ever attended a Red Tent/Temple Circle on the new moon. One night relatively early in my husband's ministry, I wound up at a book-group party, talking with an older woman who I had always assumed didn't like me very much. She was from a progressive part of town and I was a preacher's wife, invited into the book-group by another woman who enjoyed both of us. I asked my non-committal "coffee-hour" question, just to be social: "So what's keepin' you lively these days?" She lit up and began to tell me all about this community of women she was gathering with monthly. "We're calling ourselves a Red Tent, in a Red Tent and Temple movement inspired by Alisa Starkweather," she explained. "You should come! Our next gathering is tomorrow night!" I startled and made some demurring response, but took down the phone number of who to call for directions, if I could come.

That Sunday night, I realized I had had enough of Brian's church for the day. I decided to accept the invitation, surprising even myself. I drove back into a communal wooded property, looking for a yurt. I did not know what a yurt was, really, so I stopped first beside a teepee, unsure how a large circle of women would fit into it. As I quieted, I heard the sound of drums further down the road. I laughed and got back into my car, driving to the end of the lane where the large circular structure was clearly visible. A woman was standing, swaying really, on the small front stoop of the yurt. She had long hair and a dreaminess about her that wafted toward me in her voice of welcome. I smiled, asking if this is where the New Moon circle was gathering. She nodded, waving me closer.

She embraced me in welcome with a stunningly beautiful, embodied *I-frame* hug, startling for a habitually accustomed *A-frame* hugger. I remember gasping, being held so intimately, tactilely, like that. I could feel her entire body, and I realized that meant she could feel *my* entire body. Internalized responses of fear and shame arose in me. It felt like I was doing something forbidden . . . until I remembered a clinical supervisor's teaching on *A-frame* and *I-frame* hugs. Over a decade before, Sr. Shirley Nugent impishly taught us about the dynamics of hugging, particularly amongst "women-religious." Sr. Shirley was inviting us to consider our full embodiment as human beings, illustrating our trained avoidance of bodies.

"Women-religious are famous for A-frame hugs," she laughed. She demonstrated with her teaching colleague, Paula. Arms outstretched, the tips of their shoulders touching, but *bodies not touching at all*, each hugger's feet a good distance apart from the other. Each leaning in for a hug while keeping bodies below the shoulders completely separate. An *A-frame hug*. An *I-frame hug*, on the other hand, was two bodies in full contact, in an embrace of embodiment in one another. Arms outstretched, drawing close, shoulders touching shoulders, bellies touching bellies, legs touching legs. An I-frame hug. Nothing sexual about it, but intensely connectional, even sensual. Visceral sense of belonging together in a tactile way. Red Tent was deliciously all about I-frame hugs. Embodiment. Embrace of one another, just as we arrived. Learning/teaching how to offer gifts toward communal and individual well-being, and how to receive gifts for well-being, our own and that of the community gathering.

The community of women in this Red Tent/Temple welcomed me in as they would an infant girl, surrounded by a village of mothers, grandmothers, and aunties.[13] The internal experience of it, however, was befuddling, even embarrassing. It was like one aspect of my own consciousness came into its infancy only in 2014. In the years that followed, whenever I did not have ready visceral access to this F/feminine—in

---

13. I recount this in my previous book as "Rebirthing," Hess, *Companionable Way*, 93–95.

spirit-friendship or in women's circles—I would literally slip into a panic attack. Today, when someone asks how old I am, it's most honest to name the expected chronological age, then to add the age of my own *womanheart*, however old this "painfully-retrieved" part of me is. As of this writing, I am both fifty-five and ten years of age.

A glimpse from some of my own writing of that time may help give the feeling of the experience.

> ... I don't know what to do with my body, as an awakened woman. Awakened to a purity of flesh my religious tradition never offered me. Awakened to a beauty I was never allowed to call my own. Awakened to a love that liberates and does not bind. I am learning that this love has a Flow, even an order, but none like I have been traditioned to know from the outside, from the experiences of others I have prioritized for decades. And yet I struggle so to witness to my own experience, without reference to anyone else, anything else. Particularly without reference to those who would judge me, compare, assess my own journey of spirit . . . (read: husband, family, faith community, school, and more). Constancy and vulnerability are both a part of this Flow, I know, if again not primarily in conceptual terms. As I draw near within my body, as I attempt to (habitually, trained to) shame it and pull away, this Flow calls me to a constancy of trust and vulnerability. Stay with my sensation. Trust that the shame is leaving and will have no power over me. Allow myself to be touched, to reach out to touch. All of this arises within me as so ancient, yet it is so new to me.

This journey of becoming conscious of being the woman I am was one of integration, unification. A reborn part of me was finding her place in my physiology, my own flesh and bones. And Godde was doing what only Godde could do: bringing the community of witnessing and healing that could hold me precisely at the moment my own desire and embodied learning needed re-attunement, an alignment with holy purpose beyond what the congregational over-culture could offer a woman of faith like myself.

For a period of nearly ten years—four years before my Days in the Weeds, then six years afterward—I attended Red Tent circle gatherings so to become more *consciously a woman*, attuned to my own body, able to more healthily self-regulate and attune with others, viscerally.[14] I wouldn't have described it that way then, of course. I was going to be

---

14. Haines, *Politics of Trauma*, 217. See also Hemphill, *What It Takes to Heal*.

with sisters and friends, tactile women and complete strangers, with whom—when we sat in formal circle time—we became the *ecclesia* that could hold my experience—my pains, my joys, my delights. We learned new gathering practices, new ways of simply being-with one another. We learned how to listen deeply to another, even if/when she spoke things that made us afraid or sad. We laughed uproariously together, when a story instigated it. We sang together while another woman needed to weep. I came to understand this tactile way of being a woman was sacred, holy, healing. For me and for others. It may have been (un)consciously shamed and condemned in my family of origin, with our ancestral woundings, but I was growing stronger in my own F/feminine, feeling my essential Self solidifying the more I allowed touch—touching others, being touched, by women especially.

My own journey could be called *learning to re-mother myself*, to provide my youngest self-awareness also named Lisa the nourishment and safety she needs. *Lisa-Lisa* was born here, a strangely dual-yet-unified personhood I knew I could trust because my root tradition understands the unity of the irreconcilables like this. This Lisa-Lisa-ness was (and is) incredibly grace-filled *and* terrifying, threatening of my various status quos, whether in church or in academy, or even in women's circle community. No one in my family recognized this journey, nor was it to be their own, for themselves. Ruptures resulted, with deep betrayals and grief on all sides. Communities exist to protect us as we grow, but when we outgrow them, they can wound us deeply. Families especially. Without the spirit-friendships and non-traditional community-of-witnessing—without the Body of Humanity—I could never have grown into the increasingly whole and healing woman that I am. I could never have understood in my own body the juiciness of the F/feminine, what I call *womanheart*.

Some Clarifying Glimpses, Pleasure and *Eros*—Carol Gilligan

A word about *pleasure* and *eros* may help refine the senses I intend here, as well as honor how beautifully Godde prepared me for this abandonment and renewed awakening to desire as sacred, a holy way to receive what I will call a *renewed and renewing Trinitarianism*. A good place to begin is in Carol Gilligan's recollection of one of her dreams in which she removed glasses she no longer needed: "Once I removed the second set of corrective lenses, my desire lost its overlay of shame—I wanted what I had wanted with my mother and my women teachers, I wanted the woman in the dream to be herself."[15] An ancient echo resounded in my flesh and bones when I read these words. *My desire. Overlay of shame. I wanted what I had wanted. With my mother and my women teachers. I wanted the woman to be herself.* These words touched and continue to touch the loss of this F/feminine for most of my life, condoned by historic tradition, if (un)consciously so. I had read Gilligan's book years before, reminded only by the highlighter evidence. I honestly don't remember reading it before. Something drew me back to it, both in my own writing and in Spirit nudges in my workaday life. *The Birth of Pleasure.* I both don't know and now deeply know why this title brought me such forboding, which is precisely the seed of Gilligan's argument. She looks to the forgetting, dissociative, repressed voices we live with constantly, so we might map out a more radical geography of love. She unearths something more hopeful underneath and beyond our seemingly inevitable fascination with tragedies, love stories requiring dissociation, loss, sacrifice, self-deception. She dares to mark a pathway maybe, finally, into vulnerable self-revelation and a rebirth of *pleasure* as mark of this sacred.

In my abandonment back to awakening, or chronologically, my awakening unto abandonment, I've come to see the deep knowing that I had to forget in order to survive in the unhealed ancestral wounds of my lineages. The remembering—an awakening to the F/feminine when it was just on the midlife cusp of *time* to retrieve this knowing—instigated in me the very human work of integrating a deep knowing *in desire* that most everyone in my communities did *not* want to know or face. Still do not. There had to be a forgetting and dissociation, which then required in me a return and remembering. All while attempting to remain in connection, communion or belonging with those who refuse to see what you now see, know what you are coming to know. Such is the conundrum of conscious feminine wisdom, refusal, rage, and ultimately the invitation into a beyond for the world today.

While Gilligan's work points to only half of a constructive response to what will surely arise in later chapters, it does help us to see our propensity for familiar-tragic stories over new possibilities. Gilligan's work proposes a hope into which we actually *can* choose new pathways *together*. What she daringly calls a new map of love. She invites us in by naming three central "characters" in our current human storying never

---

15. Gilligan, *Birth of Pleasure*, 25.

considered in theological formulations today: "the girl who sees and says what she knows, the woman who breaks the taboo on seeing and speaking about love, the man who hides and then reveals his love."[16] Safe to say few to no theologians have been interested enough in what little girls know to consider weaving it into their historic wisdom. More today, but still very few find women's willingness to "break the taboo on seeing and speaking about love" welcome in traditional theological formulations. "The man who hides then reveals his love"? Time will tell.

Over the course of her research, Gilligan notes that boys younger than five also see and say what they know, so *every human being* comes in with a knowing in connection, irrespective of gender. The loss or forgetting happens for boys around age five, and for girls as they enter adolescence. Gilligan began to listen in her work for this new map, based on the intuitive, knowing younger voices that speak so accurately of love in belonging before the loss of voice and knowing, both becoming forgotten. She traces the forgettings through the dissociative language that begins "I don't know," which will become instructive for us as we deepen our understandings here. Similar phrases she watched for: "I mean . . ." "I think." "I can think." "I can't feel." "I have to be careful." "They said." "You should." Gilligan trained herself to look for the doubling of thoughts and feelings, and the conditions under which we will reveal to others and to ourselves what we know. "Do you want to know what I think? Or do you want to know what I *really* think?"[17]

How many times in congregational settings today do we hear these phrases? This doubling and self-doubt? *Constantly.* Particularly with women. Over decades of research, Gilligan tracked this doubling, fragmented voice in both young women and young boys. "This is the voice that catches my attention," she says. "The voice of the self speaking to itself in the midst of oppression, beset by the voices of what 'They said to me' and what 'you must' do—voices that confuse and confound the psyche in its search for love and friendship and attention and freedom."[18] She describes it as "the 'I' coming out of dissociation, seeking to orient itself by returning to the rhythms of the body, of nature."[19] I suggest for us here that these phrases, this becoming sensitized to doubling-thoughts within historic wisdom communities, could be illuminating. Instructive for how

---

16. Gilligan, *Birth of Pleasure*, 9.
17. Gilligan, *Birth of Pleasure*, 22.
18. Gilligan, *Birth of Pleasure*, 9.
19. Gilligan, *Birth of Pleasure*, 10.

to return to the body, to begin to trust the body and desire as spark of the sacred, with invitations to communion marked in pleasure.

"Pleasure will become a marker," Gilligan argues, "a compass point to emotional true north."[20] She links this because we come into the world knowing when love is real and when it is not. "As babies, we know the rhythm of relationship—turning to, turning away, turning back again; know without knowing we know it the pleasure of moving in synchrony with another person."[21] Pleasure in this grounding sense is synchrony, belonging, resonance. It doesn't have solely sexual overtones at all. "We come in expecting the communion of the village,"[22] says Francis Weller. "We come into this world from community, so we arrive expecting community,"[23] says Quanita Roberson. Such deep knowing depends, of course, on staying connected with our bodies. Yet rarely have we seen a time in history with such *disconnection* and *disembodiment* as today, amidst an array of forces named and unnamed. Intergenerational trauma is one interpretive phrase. Collective trauma is another, made more relevant and obvious post-COVID.[24] Tragic love stories is Gilligan's lens. Wounded ancestral lineages conditioned *not to feel* is my own language, experience. "Thus we come to the question of choosing pleasure. Choosing, so to speak, to give birth to pleasure,"[25] says Gilligan, in a world quite dissociated from it. In a world that imagines *pleasure* to be primarily about sexual gratification.[26]

I was primed to find myself *eventually* on this *inside* of my woman's body, attentive to desire, because the journey to understanding a *companionable way* had already been charged with an intense energy of the body felt between me and spirit-friends of all kinds, genders, orientations, traditions. I'd already had to do some of the work, in other words, to name this energy of the body in a way others in historic traditions could hear it. At that time, I named this Force or Flow *devotion*. I still stand by that writing, even as I would nuance it more now. The first teaching I received on this was this energy as "the river that cannot be

---

20. Gilligan, *Birth of Pleasure*, 161.
21. Gilligan, *Birth of Pleasure*, 162.
22. Weller, *Wild Edge of Sorrow*, 54.
23. Quanita Roberson, personal conversation.
24. Sancken, *All Our Griefs to Bear*, 21–53.
25. Gilligan, *Birth of Pleasure*, 164.
26. adrienne marie brown's *Pleasure Activism* brings a more expansive engagement with pleasure, including sexual pleasure. Both/and.

frozen." I had already been invited into a "life of curiosity and practical investigation of a force of love felt in my bones, lived in any community intent upon lovingkindness, what I will name with Jean-Luc Marion a *love without being*."[27] I even called it "the center of a companionable way—both drive and destination, invitation and sanctuary amidst all that the world pours into us today."[28]

Perhaps *pleasure*, in this context, is the positive or *desired* subset to devotion, which is the *theo*-logical container I've attempted to name for decades. Well before *A Companionable Way* was published, Lisa Isherwood's work had given me a framework within which I could understand this energy of devotion outside of the sexual compulsions so prevalent today. *The Power of Erotic Celibacy* created a container "to be an erotic people empowered by an erotic Christ, and how these passionate people may live more abundantly."[29] I devoured and digested her work, which was crucial for me in understanding my own body's experience of intense devotion within my covenantally committed marriage *and* the spirit-friendships unfolding in my life across gender, across religious tradition, across expectation. She startled me, as the offhand comment from a nun had startled her: "It's not about whether we have sex or not is it? We are passionate people. It's about how powerful we are."[30] I was being shown an energetics of the human body that was fundamentally sacred, which will eventually become God/de's *ontology of desire* in the next chapter—intensifying, refining, sanctifying our flesh. Non-Christian resourcing found me too, aligning and resonating with Isherwood's work. Stuart Sovatsky, for instance, exploring tantric celibacy and spiritual intimacy: "Possibilities begin to unfold," he observes. " . . . what I had previously *called* sexual feelings began to change in a radical way. I knew that I could never have caused such changes to occur by an act of will or choice. Why would I have wanted to? [i.e., why give up physical pleasure in *sex*?] But now that they were happening, I could see why: increased emotionality, stronger bodily coursings of the life force, and a boost of creativity were some initial results."[31] Sovatsky's contribution spoke to me of what I already knew within my Christian christological world: a philosophy of paradox—*tantra*—which "fosters individual development through the

---

27. Deep bow to Garchen Rinpoche. Hess, *Companionable Way*, 70.
28. Hess, *Companionable Way*, 71.
29. Isherwood, *Power of Erotic Celibacy*, 2.
30. Isherwood, *Power of Erotic Celibacy*, 2.
31. Sovatsky, *Eros, Consciousness, and Kundalini*, 2–3.

integration of seemingly opposite aspects of life. It describes a mundane world, which is at the same time a sacred world." This requires a body-affirming, sex-positive attitude, not one of evasion, escape, or shame. Sovatsky's ultimate interest is to witness to and invite others into an *erotic ecology*,[32] which is an aim I ultimately share. Passion, not necessarily sex. Mundane, also sacred—within an incarnational theological commitment to Spirit as guest within human flesh.

Innumerable voices within Christian traditions speak to this unifying human experience, long-fragmented by the church's bastardizing relationship to the human body, projected often onto the F/feminine or our bodies as shame, sin. Mary Anne McPherson Oliver dives deeply into these traditions to confront the assumption that spirituality is not primarily celibate but conjugal. *Conjugal spirituality* "takes seriously the fact that humans can exist only in more or less intimate relation to that which is outside of themselves, and that they are always acting to a greater or lesser degree in conjunction with realities other than their own. . . . [it] points to the possibility of a shift of the center of spiritual attention from within individuals to the spaces between them, to their encounters and to the interpenetration which sometimes results."[33] She is arguing to free our focus so we may discern Godde's presence and action in relationships, yes, but most significantly in the *spaces in between*, "relevant to everyone, since 'no one is an island,'"[34] in her words. For her, as well as for both Isherwood and Sovatsky, the focal point is not sex nor sexual relations but the body's energetic-relational capacity for connection. There is an energetics of connection we have flattened into sexualities alone, in our collective losses, fears and grief.

Oliver's aim is on a dyadic way, focused ultimately on creating a healthier spiritual container for living in intentional spiritual practices for committed covenantal partnerships traditionalists would call marriage. This language becomes significant for me beyond our notions of marital roles because she focuses upon proximity to emphasize connectedness of the whole. This can broaden energetically into awarenesses about shared *capacities for connectedness* in the community able to hold dyadic connections in larger contexts. *Conjugal* emerges with root words *con-* and *jugium* meaning "yoked together."[35] Oliver contrasts it with "sexual"

32. Sovatsky, *Eros, Consciousness, and Kundalini*, 7.
33. Oliver, *Conjugal Spirituality*, 21.
34. Oliver, *Conjugal Spirituality*, 21.
35. Oliver, *Conjugal Spirituality*, 22.

and "marital," noting the physical focus for the former, the institutional focus for the latter. The bulk of her work gave practices for decentering oneself amidst relational connections, becoming part of something alive and more whole than the sum of its parts. This *connection between* honors that every dyadic couple is rooted *in some form of broader community* as well. In her words, "It is perhaps only in our day that a fully developed conjugal spirituality—a spirituality which recognizes that whenever relationship occurs, something radically new comes into being—has become a real possibility. To speak of radical proximity as spiritual journey is to explore as yet uncharted territory."[36] Her overview offers some practical background and guidance for living directly and unequivocally into the connections between us, as committed dyads or partnerships *and* as communities that hold our partnerships in contexts.

Eros and pleasure are integral, intimate parts of this capacity to connect, even as we have co-created a world increasingly divided and polarized precisely around desire, pleasure and eros. We have travelled a far piece from Gilligan's three characters in our trinitarian reconsiderations: "the girl who sees and says what she knows, the woman who breaks the taboo on seeing and speaking about love, the man who hides and then reveals his love."[37] Gilligan's exploration brings renewed attention to our fascination with tragic love stories, reified again and again in Scripture quite damning of women and women's bodies. These longstanding narratives have required dissociation, loss, sacrifice, and self-deception for centuries, simply to belong in communities shaped in a power-over way imprisoning all of us in these stories. At least when they are left untended and (un)critically understood. Gilligan trained herself to look for the doubling of thoughts and feelings, and the conditions under which we will reveal to others and to ourselves what we know. Her work can bring us back to *pleasure* as a sacred calling. Its (re)birth pulls us back to our deepest knowings of belonging, synchrony, resonance. *Communion.* One-ing with God/de, always accessible to us, Godde *in the body*.

What Gilligan's work does *not* help us with is what I've attempted to recreate from within my own experience and covenantal commitments, with the help of authors' wisdom finding me along the way: the Body of Humanity beyond any tribal identity. Gilligan's work leaves us as individuals mapping out a new form of love with all communal-collective

---

36. Oliver, *Conjugal Spirituality*, 23.
37. Gilligan, *Birth of Pleasure*, 9.

realities left strangely absent, silent. Any map of love necessarily requires a healing, integrative personal journey *held within webs of communities* ever evolving, declining, changing. My own integrative journey was impossible but for the forming and reforming community able to witness my pain, hold me as I healed, trust me to return with my gifts for the Whole. Years of forming and unforming circles, in-person and then accessed virtually. Diverse participants and communities. Isherwood can remind us that the ascetic path so long vowed in our Christian traditions is not the weak path of escape from the world but an incredibly powerful pathway for getting in touch with our own bodies' energies, passions, power. *It's the community that holds the context*, in both attraction and accountability, possibility for healing and the everpresent woundings too. How may we better focus our attentions on the *connectional spaces between* where we potentially sublimate and channel our own spirit energies made conscious, in the power of the Spirit, trusting the intensifications to come in our bodies for sacred purpose? There's impassioned, devotional energy in the body, for holding, discerning, perhaps intensification in the Spirit, perhaps for purgation and refinement. There certainly can be *pleasure* in this connection without it needing to be about sexual gratification.

Christians by and large need an entire reorientation in the sacred power of the erotic and the centuries of entanglement that have landed congregational churches in the polarizations and ugly divisions driven by fear and dissociation from the body that we see so fully today. More of us need to experience the interconnectedness of all things if and when we begin to steward reconnecting human beings with their own bodies from the inside. The most compelling pathway for me has been *deeply embodied prayer*, the practices of proximity within a Body of Humanity able to return me to my own body, its sacred beauty, its impassioned power for connection with self, other, in God/de's desire.

_____ Chapter Four

Problem of Prayer Well Met in a Trinitarian Möbius

A RENEWED AND RENEWING TRINITARIANISM emerged as the proverbial center of this work only at the very end of the story of awakening desire and divine abandonment. No one was more surprised than I, in other words. The surprising phrase refers to deeply embodied prayer that gifts us with an awakening to desire, palpable in pleasure, back into prayer, forever in an infinitely flowing Möbius pattern. It also prioritizes cocreative participation and movement that brings new life, that *renews*. It speaks to our invitation into this Force or Flow Who never lets us go, proclaimed within historic Christian tradition but equally available to the Body of Humanity within and beyond our sectarian language for it. What I hope to point to here emerges only with deeply embodied prayer, contemplative practice in community within which our own rationalities and assumptions are transfigured beyond our control or imagination. What my elder-mentor Loder would refer to as transformation-transformed, or the logic of the Spirit within Whom our spirits are posited in the first place. Though I have had a love-hate relationship with both church and academy for most of my life, the theory-practice divide within university discourse theology *was* the perfect place for all this to unfold.

I think I was always slated for educational fascinations—educational ministries, as a subset of the discipline of practical theology, in my day—but this two-in-oneness of prayer-into-God/de-back-into-prayer arises out of the fragmentations of wholeness within university habits of mind. Can you hear here the whiff of the age-old theological chicken-and-egg:

theory first or practice? Practice first, then theorizing? Elders and colleagues have been plagued with this analytical fragmentation for decades, centuries really. Precision of understanding at the expense of the whole. The whole disdained and refused, because analytical understanding was more palatable to scholarship. My approach inherited from James Loder here is paradoxical, non-correlational[1] to use the more formal-practical-theological term. Differentiating, sometimes opposing, sometimes aligning forces are placed into an infinity loop, a Möbius band of two-yet-one flow: deeply embodied prayer within which a renewed and renewing Flow gifts us, awakening to desire concentrated, intensified, refined, shaped in God/de's Heart, returning our awarenesses back into prayer, always held in Spirit/spirit intimacies. Needless to say, the heart of Christian doctrine, the Trinity that I will offer here, will be arguably inconceivable, even accused as incoherent. So be it. All that follows *does* incorporate such doctrinal understandings at the root—historical and coherent with what has been—even as my experiences as a woman, in a woman's body, require an openness to what can be today and tomorrow. The Christian Orthodoxy crafted over centuries—largely through the voices and body-fears of the men who loved God fiercely in the best if limited ways they knew how—is simply no longer sufficient for the expansiveness and grace-filled spaciousness Spirit invites, even demands within a Creation groaning under humanity's mismanaged dominion. I begin here with the problem of prayer in a woman's body, enraged at abandonment yet covenantally committed to remain in academic and ecclesial environments (un)consciously hostile to H/her. Trinitarian language was not remotely in my best interest, and I had *no intention* of using it.

The Problem of Prayer in (This) Woman's Economic Trinity

When the One you love most, the One Whom your family and church community has promised *will never leave you*, repeatedly claimed and supported by their memorized sacred Scriptures, *leaves you bereft* as if you were created to be that way, what can it possibly mean to *pray to* or *with* this One? Or have this One pray *through* you? Wounded deeply in my Days in the Weeds, clearly bereft in my abandonment as a woman by God and the church, I eventually became plagued with the problem of *prayer*, conceivably untenable yet viscerally palpable in yearning all the

---

1. Tracy in Marion, *God without Being*, xi.

same. My problem was that the renewed sacred Beauty within me was speaking more loudly than the stale collective of the church, abusive and silencing of women as women, denying any of my own experience as worthy of hearing. I was finally returned to my *woman's body*, but only non-sectarian, non-traditional communities were willing and able to hold my woundedness, my pain, until a time when healing might emerge. Why would I ever return to the stale, doctrinal assertions of my root tradition, of those "people of faith" who persistently refused to listen to me? I seriously doubted that *prayer* could come to mean anything valuable when a woman was finally, righteously, enraged and advocating for redress of the loss of the F/feminine, in our world, for decades in my own body.

My conscious feminine theologian could name the theological arguments within theodicy streams of wisdom traditions that try to unravel in Job-like fashion the Gordian knot of human suffering and God as Good. This was the strategy of my earliest scholarly formation. Those arguments can satisfy only when they do, then really *not* when they don't. None could satisfy me after my Days in the Weeds. My feminist with her forgiveness problem had awakened to the divine spark within, the woman's body as the repository of the Divine Feminine. This made prayer as I had learned it incredibly confusing, inaccessible. For decades, I had been trained to disdain my own body, my flesh, to use Pauline terms, yet *now* I'm learning of its sacredness in the F/feminine? Its goodness is proclaimed in my own root tradition, yet immediately overrun by the Fall, Eve's story we never recover from (to quote Dar Williams). I'd long been trained in the practices of praying to a wholly Other God—Father Son and Holy Spirit—creature to Creator, sin-ridden to Redeemer, enfleshed to Sanctifier (if we want to go modally heretical). Not anymore. None of those Persons helped a woman abandoned and enraged. My preacher's wife voice for most of these years knew it was best to keep quiet about the overwhelming masculine-imbalances and the increasingly triumphalistic, fear-ridden liturgies she was hearing in seminary and ecclesial contexts. She distanced herself well after years of not feeling welcomed within her husband's callings anyway. With an impish smile, I would think, "Not my circus, not my monkeys." I relinquished all sense of responsibility for them as they refused any willingness to listen to or hear me. I absented myself from seminary worship as often as possible. I learned to remain present if quiet in my husband's congregation, mostly because his ministry became more vulnerable when I was absent. In both settings, academic and ecclesial, I would bring my own F/feminine presence without participation or voice, so to honor the silencing of the F/feminine in congregational practices. I became less and less able to sit in "communities" that were not nourishing or challenging for my well-being as a woman. It seemed I lost all access to "direct-address" or "spoken" prayer. Then came the question from a spiritual director I had visited, years into my awakening to feminine rage:

"Do you pray?"

She and I had lain down, stretched out on our stomachs, on a clean patch of the pasture. I had come to her barn and home spaces, *Divine Equines*, to explore the felt sense of deepening presence with horses, these Zen-like equine-teachers being a lifelong yearning in me. When she invited me to approach the herd in the pasture, I had become deeply in touch with my own grief, sadness, about . . . well, *everything*, it seemed. My body was weary with rage and injury. I was sad and angry with how so many human beings treat horses, our world. I yearned for connection, interconnection, always feeling refused, denied, abandoned. One mare approached me when I walked slowly into her pasture. She bent her front legs, lowering herself to rest on the ground a short distance from where I stood still, rather in awe of her, her eyes, her gentleness, the sound of her breath. Then another mare drew close, doing the same. Then another and another until I was surrounded by four mares, each choosing to lie down in almost a four-cornered space that felt like a circle of care. Of *me*. The holder of women's circles *for years* was *being held* by these gentlest creatures of prey. The human being who had accompanied me asked quietly, "Do you pray?"

Tears came, unbidden. After some silence, I said quietly, "Yes and no." My pause allowed me to feel my way into the surprise at the question, the gift of being completely honest as a seminary professor and clergywoman long wounded by a congregational Christianity that denies its shadow. "I no longer pray as I was taught," I began. "Nor can I pray in most of the corporate expressions of Christian prayer that surround me today, in my woman's body." I paused again, feeling the familiar bittersweet sadness of being a woman in a religious tradition (un)consciously hostile to the F/feminine. "I do consider my entire life to be a *prayer without ceasing*, as Thessalonians might name it," I finished. The silence surrounded us again, we human beings and we mares. I felt the familiar P/presence that can arise for me *in prayer, as prayer*: largely wordless P/presence, deeply embodied, often accompanied by unbidden tears. My human companion smiled, nodding. We breathed against the earth, surrounded by mares.

Some words of Thomas Merton eventually found me, so to bless me in my problem of prayer. "Pure love and prayer are learned in the hour when prayer has become impossible and your heart has turned to stone."[2] Prayer as I had been taught vanished in the years after my Days in the Weeds. I would describe it eventually as losing access to *direct-address* or *spoken-intimate* prayer. If my relationship with God had truly ruptured, speaking into the silences around me felt foolish. To Whom? To No One in Particular? It didn't feel like prayer had ceased, however. My body was daily newly *alive,* just in ways my traditional faith community refused or denied. I felt this new aliveness in communities that *could* hold my experience—circles of women, spirit-friendships utterly devoted to tradition and observance. It was not a solitary religious experience at all, though it was in contrast to all into which I had been previously formed.

I could still see, sense and honor the more traditionally prayer-filled lives of others in my own callings. My decades of Christian formation had taught me to hold spaces for students, directees, Brian and his congregants. Honoring others' connections to the Sacred has rarely been a conflict for me, given my propensity to know myself best and safest in relation to those around me, their sacred sensibilities. I *would* get envious sometimes, wishing I could find my way back to such an easy practice as praying for myself and others, speaking to God in familiar ways. But my own felt sense of integrity and outrage disallowed it. I was no longer going to be complicit in my own abandonment as a woman, even if all around me continued to deny what my body knew. I would not unsee what I had been shown, at least if I could help it. So I had a prayer problem while still feeling irreconcilably drawn to a Force of Flow who would not let me go, Someone or Something breathing so deeply within me.

Early Strategies: The Silent Treatment

I can say today that *embodied prayer itself* was driving me to heal, to feel the hurt of it all, ultimately even to *forgive,* though I was nowhere near ready to hear that yet. One day, I found myself writing a poem, *The Silent Treatment,* inspired by my mother, though she's shy and embarrassed by it. Honoring the embarrassment, I yet offer it here, bowing to her wisdom,

---

2. Merton, cited in Chittister, *Breath of the Soul,* 92.

her tenacity to do what she did with what she had. She's agreed with a description I sometimes offer when people ask me about my mother: she's a survivor, though she's never spoken openly of anything or all she survived. Her quiet wisdom made a difference for me here, continues to make a difference for me in this problem of prayer, particularly as I remain in communities of faith that disregard my experience(s).

The Silent Treatment

When my mother so decided,
when she *needed* to decide,
she would give my father
the Silent Treatment.

Sometimes for hours.
Sometimes for days.
In the deadly, deafening quiet
the house would shimmer, shake.
My sister and I never knew
what he had done,
why she was so angry.
No one would speak.
Neither did anyone know
what would break the cycle.

There was simply nothingness.
No smile. Especially
no looking into the eyes.
Nothing that could suggest
connection, belonging, love.
Curt words were allowed
in proximate spaces,
unavoidable in such proximity.

Terse body language
screamed her rage.
Without sound
everyone could hear.

I used to think
my own dance with anger
was anything but silent.
Lots and lots of words
or an F-bomb in quiet prose
was more my style.

A measured tone
with surgically precise language
describing the offense,
the affront to my world, my body.
I had long ago learned
the verbal choreography of anger
necessary in the worlds of men.

But then I woke up
to a reality I had resisted:
the centuries-long
historic abandonment,
the irreparable
silencing and omission
of women, girls, all of creation.
Silenced. Shoved aside.
Raped. Pillaged. Dismembered.

God protects us from nothing,
even if He sustains us in all things
(says James Finley).
Goddess seems to have lost
the battle, if not yet the war
(I say).
S/she came too late, really,
for this little girl in me
abandoned as a woman.

A rupture of "faith"
departure from the "faith community"
errant in its ignorance
culpable in its persistent choice

to neglect, to see, to hear.
Pointing to scriptures
long gone stale in the
crucifixion of women.

And yet . . .

How do you leave something
six decades embedded
into your very cells?

You don't.
Not without spending
the rest of your precious years
fighting yourself.

What can a woman do
disempowered in a dangerous world?
Filled with righteous anger,
emptied of herself
in God's abandonment of Her
as an infant
a young woman
a clergywoman
a feminist
a theologian?
Mom was *onto something*.

She gives
All That Is Holy
the Silent Treatment

    My inability to pray as I had been taught, my lack of access to direct-address prayer, was made bearable for me because of this gift to me from my mother. One she would never consider a gift in her own journey of faith. I was finally *consciously* seeing the silent treatment as one of the few indirect-power-strategies for myself as a woman disempowered by all around me. Remember Carol Gilligan's words from her dream? *Desire. Overlay of shame. I wanted what I had wanted. With my mother and my women teachers. I wanted the woman to be herself.* In the world(s) that my mother inherited, she was being herself in the only way to which she had access and security at the same time. My paternal grandfather gave me precedent for this as well, if not the poetry. He long confessed the creeds of the church in congregational worship, simply *going quiet* on all the phrases he could not say with integrity. *Descended into Hell*, for instance. He was glad the church said them, so the story goes, but some things he simply could *not* speak with integrity. Not surprisingly, he held the F/feminine for that generation of our lineage, *not* my grandmother.

The Silent Treatment's wisdom is in creating a holding pattern in which neither party in the relationship—then, me and the God of the church—gets too close to the rupture, the anger. It bought me a sense of security or safety that was necessary for a time. It could last for shorter or longer periods of time, depending upon the boundary transgressed. The strategy also limits someone to largely one aspect of consciousness, however—being right, at almost all costs. Rage requires this righteousness, weaponized by the wound to protect, to defend. This is also necessary, for as long as it's necessary. Yet *this* kind of righteousness refuses other aspects of consciousness, such as being curious, being willing to see all things as interconnected, interdependent. In these years, praying in any direct address to either God/Goddess who abandoned me/us felt like complicity in my own and all women's abandonment. Offering up anything of my own intimate life in devotion to this One? Sawdust in the mouth and airways.

Finally, however, I woke up to the parallel of anger behaviors and their limitation for what I was becoming ready to reconsider. I was doing precisely what I had witnessed for years growing up, the only thing I knew as a woman to do when she's angry in a world that is dangerous for women. You refuse to speak to the one who has transgressed the boundary. You deny access to your eyes, and you neglect their needs/desires as much as you can get away with. For a while, you can pretend that you control the space and you'll be able to protect yourself from the pain that happened . . .

For a while . . .

Strategies Unknowingly Seeded in the Crucible: the Gaze

Years before my Days in the Weeds, before any of my overt F/feminine awakening, a most powerful practice became an integral part of my life, my spiritual disciplines: the *gaze*. I first stumbled into it in my early thirties, as a spirit-friend relationship began to blossom in my husband's and my new life in southwestern Ohio. She and I found ourselves praying together, entering in meditation practices together, side-by-side. As we grew more comfortable with the shared silence, we found ourselves drawn into a gaze. Seeing one another for long periods of time. Not looking away. Being seen, just as I was, just as she was. A spaciousness would open between us somehow, which a Rumi scholar, Will Johnson, calls *beholding the divine*.[3] As I would describe it today: Godde's energies became palpable, felt in the spaces in between us yet also deeply throughout my entire body. Unbeknownst to me, I was allowing access to my eyes in deeply intimate spaces, with another human being who was curious to do the same. Utterly chaste. Deeply sensate. Visceral connection. I was being shaped in a deeply embodied prayer life that had no words. A prayer life long traditioned in my own Christian tradition with icons.

In that root-traditional sense, my formation with the gaze began even earlier, on a sleepless night in grad school. I had been invited to interview for an administrative-director job at a seminary some distance from where I lived. I knew it was past time for me to leave my then-current seminary-ecclesial home, so this was *very* attractive to me. I was also terrified. I was to give a presentation to a roomful of seminary administrators and faculty. I felt paralyzed, like a rabbit in the headlights of an oncoming car. Unable to sleep, I eased out of the bed. Unsure what to do, I set up a chair and a candle before the Sinai Jesus icon we had resting on the buffet table in our apartment. I lit the candle, which lit up Jesus's face.

Feeling trapped and afraid, I glared at Jesus, more than gazed. Being faithful to this One was what had gotten me into this *mess*. I don't know how long I sat there, accusatorially staring, fuming, fearing. Startled, I heard the words: *Begin with what you know*... My voice, in my head, but also *not* from me somehow. Not from a sense of Self I knew in the daylight. Relief poured into me. I began to jot down things I knew, pieces of my intellectual work that I felt had energy, contribution. I grew sleepy again, heading back to bed. The presentation literally fell into place in the next days. I entered into the interview and presentation with a sense of holy

---

3. Johnson, *Spiritual Practices of Rumi*, 2.

guidance, even assurance that this *must* be what God intended for me. Of course, I did *not* get the job, which sent me into a paroxysm of anger and grief. I felt foolish in my assumptions, presumption, even raging at God for weeks. Weeks lovingly held by a wise spiritual director who directed me to walk every day, "at least forty minutes each day." He was right, and it was a blessing I did *not* receive the job. As I see today, had I landed there, I would not have met the women, nor the perfect storm of circling that brought me *here*.

Yet traditionally ecclesially located icons cloak most of the F/feminine I would eventually come to know. The *women's mysteries* or *womanheart* I now know in much more detail could not have landed as they did without signposts or creative icons in addition to the classical ones. The summer of 2012, I met an artist-painter and her daughter while attending a conference in Loveland, Colorado. Artist Jean Jensen and I connected in laughter, in wonder, in deepening curiosity for spiritual awakenings. A couple months after the conference, I received an 8x11 drawing from Jean, "just because," she said. I found it most peculiar at the time, but appreciated receiving it. I love gifts from artist friends, even when I don't "understand" them.

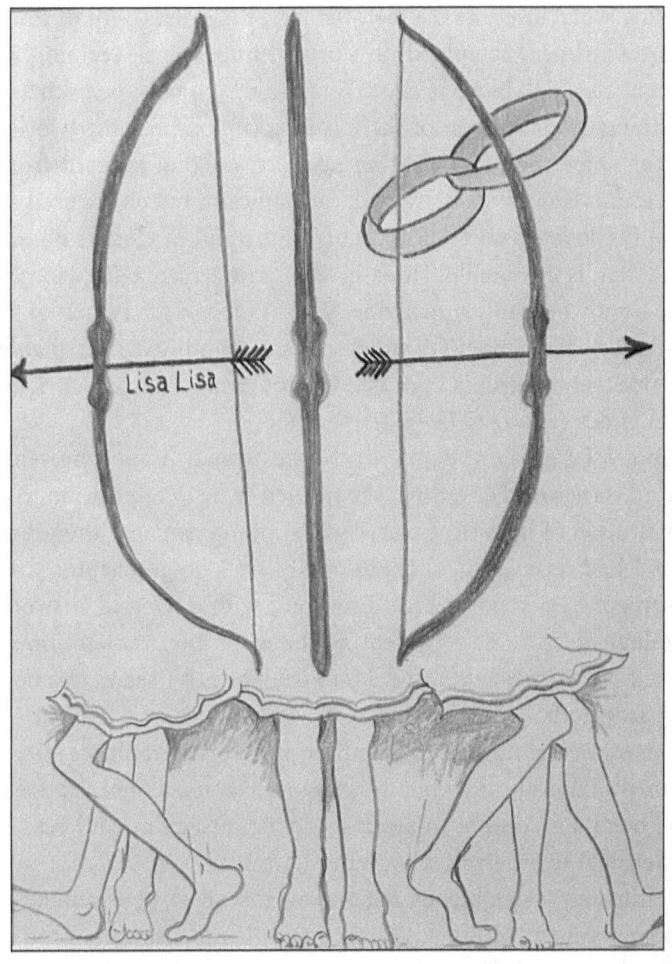

Jean Jensen, image used with permission. http://www.jeanjensenart.com/

What is stunning to me today is how much of an icon it became. I didn't understand the "Lisa Lisa" bit on the left-side arrow at first. I remember asking Jean about it, but she demurred. She didn't know either. "I simply heard it as I drew," she said. Three bows-and-arrows, with one facing directly forward, toward the viewer. The left with Lisa-Lisa holds an arrow to be sprung in that direction. The right bow holds either two linked wedding rings, or an infinity loop. I mostly saw linked wedding rings in the beginning. The bow facing forward does not seem to have an arrow in its unseen, tensive-string.

Now look closely at the feet, the legs, the skirt(s). All of this bow-and-arrow imagery is upheld on skirted human legs—seemingly three skirts that also look like one skirt. This strange three-in-one skirt(s) covers a strange combination of three beings (if you presume two-leggedness) somehow moving or sitting upon or walking forward from one being. Jean is not formally trained, theologically, but she offered a mysterious, intuitive artistic rendition of Trinity and of Christ's nature that to me, today, is irrefutable. Three-in-One. Two irreconcilable forces held as One—truly human, truly divine, held as One in the Person of Christ. Dancing feet. Movement yet stillness. One, seen in two legs planted on either side, yet three-ness in directions, movement. *So very curious.* Palpable energies yet sacred bewilderment too.

Today, I can see the now dual-aged woman I am represented in the Lisa Lisa arrow. For a time, she needed to be in opposition to either the institution of historical marriage (wedding rings) *or* the infinity of God as I had received God traditionally. As I say in chapter 3, whenever someone asks me my age, I respond with a twofold answer—one chronological, and one representing the most internal-feminine sense of myself not borne until 2014. *Lisa Lisa.* The gift I see in this contemporary icon today is the *arrowless bow* facing us—you and me—as all is centered and grounded in the three-in-one and multiple-directions movement. I don't know what the image will come to mean to me in the future, but I am content to await in my bemusement, and yes, sacred bewilderment to receive such a timely gift.

Ultimately, as righteous rage and a refusal to be complicit in my own abandonment within ecclesial and academic institutions took hold, so the gaze—historically traditioned and in an unexpectedly newly gifted fashion—was the already-created, significant "container" for the embodied yet silent-treatment prayer life that was beginning to shape in me, my own life. The gaze was a portal to my own deepest embodied sensations, into Whom I came to know as F/feminine in my own flesh, received viscerally when mirrored regularly to me in practice with spirit-friends, with a community able to witness me in my experience. Over a period of years, one could say my own limbic system was literally, viscerally, *rewired* by Godde, in the M/maternal presence and wisdom of women *deeply* in touch with their own bodies, our own tactile way of being in the world. I had had no access to such women, to the F/feminine, until then. I had been starved for Her, terrified yet drawn with such *desire* to this Sacred Force or Flow, viscerally, intimately. Whenever I could not be in physical proximity with a women's circle, it literally felt like I was being dragged back into the Weeds. I was being abandoned again, this time I feared, forever. As it had been before, it seemed there was nothing I could do from the outside to prevent the panic. But slowly, week by week, year by year, I grew stronger in this visceral consciousness. And I soon began to marvel at an undeniable sacred abundance from *within*, a completely unfamiliar but achy humanness that was my F/feminine purity, beauty, *in my own body*. Both the Silent Treatment—my own integrity and capacity—and the Gaze—a visceral portal to interconnectedness—were necessary to heal, to land here on the other side.

A Renewing Trinitarianism?

Yet I was still not prepared for the deepening of the Spirit, for the returning to wholeness in my own root tradition. My feminist, steeped in rage, made sure of it. My conscious feminine theologian remained rooted where she'd been planted, but it was exhausting and persistently dehumanizing to persistently be unseen, unheard in my own voice awakened. Certainly, by 2017, I had had no theologically authorized re-framing readily available. In hindsight, I can of course see the breadcrumbs planted *every step of the way*. "Life can only be understood backwards; it must be lived forward,"[4] quips Søren Kierkegaard.

It was the deeply embodied prayer, held over years by the Body of Humanity, that opened the doorway to what I now know is a *renewed and renewing Trinitarianism*, begun in a *concentration of desire*, grounded in an *ontology of God/de's desire*, coursing through our world(s) and bodies as a process of becoming fully alive. *The glory of God is a human being fully alive.* "Trinity" here is prioritized less as doctrinal belief and more as a means of participation, even scandalously incarnate cocreation into which we are invited, in all our fragilities and ignorance. It does not oppose nor refute the historical-doctrinal sense of the word, but it does place such doctrinal center in a broader, more ancient and more anticipatory context of the *restoration of all things*. This renewing sense of the word is one that makes sense of sacred tradition for me. I am finally able to shape a *theological* Center that could be life-giving in

---

4. Søren Kierkegaard, *Journals and Papers*, 1:1030, cited in Lloyd, "Politicizing Kierkegaardian Repetition," *Kierkegaard and Political Theology*, 220. Precisely stated: "Philosophy is perfectly right in saying that life must be understood backwards. But then one forgets the other clause—that it must be lived forwards."

the *body of a 6-year-old girl*. Why do our theologies not give life to our youngest humans? I began to wonder . . .

The obstacles for being heard within ecclesial or seminary communities are legion, of course. Refusal and derision of the body. The shaming of desire, splitting all of us into splinters and fragments increasingly sharp and violent. I was reared on the ecclesial proclamations of God's love for me, deeply socialized into today's congregational expressions of that proclamation. Unconsciously, for the most part, this vehicle of formation has created the institutional structures within which a faith tradition is to be practiced, to live into the world, all of which becomes synonymous with faith itself. Faith is a cognitive assent to propositions and their applications in the world around us. Faith was not about feeling, or if it was, it was fallen. Our household purred along in duty. Obligation. Belief. Service. On the crafted cross of these historical institutional-familial structures, the F/feminine and women-identified bodies were surely crucified. Shamed. Derided. *Trinity* is the conciliar authoritative language within which Christian proclamation was recognized as faithful and heretics were murdered. Propositional assent. No place for human bodies, desire, becoming conscious as a woman in a woman's body, except as an object in the masculine gaze, except as an objectified other. What might be lifegiving for a six-year-old child?

Reliant upon the traditionally rooted yet woman-handled theological work of Cynthia Bourgeault and Sarah Coakley, a renewing Trinitarianism breathes as an incorporative Trinity, inspired by Romans 8, willing to dance alongside the ecclesially orthodox Trinity of Father-Son-Spirit in today's church so in need of renewal. I argue Godde's desire is fundamental here, known as the divine spark in each of us, palpable in pleasure created, refined, and shaped into a Christlike self-offering amidst an expressive delight and abundance intended for all.

The Throne of Wisdom

Weeks after the 2013 Conscious Feminine Leadership Academy, my husband Brian and I went to St. John's Monastery in Collegeville, Minnesota, for a week of retreat together. It's a Benedictine men's college, formally affiliated with the women's College of St. Benedict, housed on a campus not too far away. Six months before my Days in the Weeds, a preliminary question was beginning to take root in my own body.

How does a Christian theological woman awakened to the conscious feminine hold her own Christianity as life-giving? How is a woman to hold, even love, persons and their communities who do not value what is becoming most essentially true about her own life?

I remember walking into the huge sanctuary at St. John's, stunned by all the concrete, shadowed light, with a cold but lively acoustics. It felt familiar, but it was becoming dissonant for me now. Something was not coherent any longer, though I could not articulate clearly yet just *what*. On a whim, I took the shuttle bus over to the women's campus, the sanctuary at St. Benedict's: warmly lit, plants everywhere, large airy spaces inviting deep breaths and welcome tears. I knew where I belonged, but that was not where we were staying that week. At St. John's, I *had* stumbled across a wilderness chapel, Stella Maris Chapel, after a long run away from campus. "In 1872 a romantic and picturesque chapel was built across Lake Sagatagan to honor Mary, the Mother of God, under the title of Stella Maris (meaning 'Star of the Sea')," reads the website.[5] It was significant to me that you had to take a shuttle-bus or walk a long ways from campus into the woods to even get to a F/feminine space. Heavy in my awareness was this question of how to hold my beloved Christian wisdom amidst a conscious feminine awakening in which religious traditions kept the F/feminine at such distance, beyond arm's length. How was I to be who I had been while becoming consciously a woman irrevocably steeped in a tradition that abandoned and so abused the F/feminine?

I found myself reading a book by Cynthia Bourgeault that had arrived in the mail before we left home: *The Holy Trinity and the Law of Three*. I took notes in a small journal, decorated with a butterfly. Brian implored me to join him in the order of prayers, but I refused. I didn't know how to be there in that cold, masculine sanctuary. He wouldn't come with me to the warmly lit sanctuary. Too far. But on the last afternoon, I caved. I accompanied him to Evening Prayer with the brothers. I figured I could hold my breath, withstand the cold refusals, for at least that long. Walking down the side aisle to the choral loft, where the brothers sat for prayer, I passed a side prayer chapel I had not known was there. A soft lighting drew my attention and I gasped.

Sitting there, a figure well over six-feet tall, *sitting*, was this F/feminine, holding a much smaller masculine figure on her lap. I entered the prayer chapel to learn more. *The Throne of Wisdom*, said a plaque on the

---

5 College of Saint Benedict, "Stella Maris Chapel."

side. She had a wooden patina of some kind, an earthiness that was immoveable. I was drawn to her hands—one open-palmed, creating a spacious holding of the small figure on her lap; the other palm-down, resting gently on the small boy's leg. Her robe was a sculpted pattern, hanging gently from her form, clasped below her neck, close to her heart. Her face tilted downward but not downtrodden. Almost like she was gazing in love at the figure on her lap, even as there was a sadness to her expression as well. Her feet were protected by pointed, ecclesially garmented slippers, like a bishop of the twelfth-century Spanish church might wear. This larger-than-life, huge but gentle presence sat on a wooden throne that her own figure simply towered over. Filled completely.

An altar-size replica of the *Throne of Wisdom*

The tiny childlike man rested on her lap, sitting slightly to one side, one hand holding a book, the other hand raised in the two-fingered, open-palm blessing common to Byzantine or Eastern Orthodox custom. Clearly not a child, but also quite diminutive for a man being honored in sculpted form. She appears well over twice his size. As my breath returned and tears arose, I heard myself say, "*Oh . . . the Throne.*" *She is his throne.* There was no *him* without *her*. After a bow, a smile, I left the prayer chapel and joined the brothers in their choral loft. I sat with reverence, silent but present, just like H/her. I experimented with how I was holding my hands, holding the prayerbook. At the precise moment I was articulating a question of how to hold my own Christian heritage, deeply steeped but now dissonant somehow in my cells, I was being shown.

Driveshaft of All Creation

Bourgeault's *The Holy Trinity and the Law of Three: Discovering the Radical Truth at the Heart of Christianity* traces the origin and theological-historical-material development of the Trinity within orthodox Christian terms, if prior to and beyond them as well. Honoring Trinity as the Heart of Christian proclamation, she plants the seed of Trinity as *process*, as *participation*. Not in contradiction or opposition, but in utter alignment and resonance, with greater reach and perspective, imaginable within contemplative prayer and the *ora-labora* rhythms of a life of discipleship. In addition to the ever familiar Trinity—Father, Son, and Holy Spirit, which she names "the Pentecostal Trinity"[6]—she insists our perceptions expand exponentially inward, prior, and outward, from arguable Origins unto the Divine Plan, all within a *pattern that is trustworthy* toward the *restoration of all things*. She names a Trinitarian flow in which the alchemy of love originates and continues to create new life, bridging inaccessible and accessible light. In devotion to historic Christian traditioning, then, she calls Love the *driveshaft of all creation*. Not a metaphysical character of God that we must attain or toward which we must strive. As I would name it today, it is the flow and energetic fruit of God/de becoming Godde's desire within us, around us, if and when we allow it.

Bourgeault's work entranced me, whether it was her daring esoteric innovations with clearly traditional integrity, or the awareness that I could be companioned by this traditional integrity while none of my seminary colleagues would ever read a book on the Trinity published by Shambhala Press, a more Buddhist-oriented publisher. Regardless, this work seemed

---

6. Bourgeault, *Holy Trinity and the Law of Three*, 170ff.

to invite a commitment to tradition with a breath of fresh air, which I desperately needed. Bourgeault's words: Trinity is "how God moves and flows, how God changes from one form (or 'state') into another within the domain of manifestation and interpenetrates the mutability of creation with the wholeness of divine being. The idea that the Trinity might be about process rather than persons seems to be a radical notion . . . "[7] She draws a contrast, yes, but ultimately points to a complementary Force amidst-among-between our traditional "Persons." She begins to enflesh an apophatic horizon often neglected in doctrinal certainties but necessary when pointing to the mysteries of God. Demonstrating what she inherits from Gurdjieff's thought as "third force," she points the way to making opposition into opportunity. Bourgeault invites consideration of the *pattern* that can be trusted in a Trinity more subtle in movement bridging inaccessible and accessible light in material form. Trinity is emphasized here as the movement of God/de, more important (here) than the being or substance of God argued in power-over masculinized terms.

Love is the *driveshaft of all creation*,[8] so its movement? Its drive? Bourgeault relies on a medieval mystic elder for this wisdom teaching, Jacob Boehme, who suggests "the impressure of nothing into something" for understanding the movement of God in his own life. "How does one move from God at rest, from the eternal, immense, incomprehensible Unity of God," she asks within his work, "to God the author of multiplicity and diversity that is our created universe?"[9] A first principle, the *concentration of desire*.[10] God/de as origin and Force moves in desire, intensifying, agitating, unrequited as One, opening in and through the "very insatiability of desire . . . "[11] Bourgeault through Boehme posits *sensibility*, the capacity for self-reflective awareness or Boehme's term, *anguish*, arising out of this desire, its aching.[12] Originating the pattern that embodies all of Trinity's subtle movement, "the divine nature becomes perceptible to itself. It goes "into that out of which it originally came," and knows itself from within. . . . The divine must undergo *a compression into somethingness* . . . which entails a passage through the fiery matrix of desire and its frustration, flow into light, new dimension,

---

7. Bourgeault, *Holy Trinity and the Law of Three*, 15.
8. Bourgeault, *Holy Trinity and the Law of Three*, 17.
9. Bourgeault, *Holy Trinity and the Law of Three*, 96ff.
10. Bourgeault, *Holy Trinity and the Law of Three*, 97.
11. Bourgeault, *Holy Trinity and the Law of Three*, 98.
12. Bourgeault, *Holy Trinity and the Law of Three*, 98.

accessible light."[13] Here we see the originating and culminating pattern—perichoresis, one might eventually say—of the Trinity, Love becoming, Love originating all creation to come.

Bourgeault observes the flowing nature of love—driveshaft of creation—which means it is less metaphysical substance and more alchemical process. Love "is not a preexistent divine attribute, but more like a new alchemical compound that arises out of the originating movements of God."[14] In Boehme's words, "The eternal delight becomes perceivable, and this perceiving of the Unity is called love."[15] Jean-Luc Marion's *love without being* has similar fruit here for liberating the movement of God/de amidst the the*ologies* of God we proclaim today.[16] It may be as simple as God not having a "being" that anyone can define or delimit with words, even as this movement of Godde does not falsify the conciliar tradition of the historic faith, which is also important to me. Bold, yes. Audacious to presume esoteric language for the patterning of God/de, yes. But if it is life-giving while in alignment with its historic traditions? Win-win, seems to me.

Being shaped in my own root tradition's conciliar history—Trinitarian thought, Chalcedonian pattern, a logic of the Spirit—I could *feel* tradition beginning to sing in a new direction while grounded in its roots. The threefold "dance" of the Trinity, *perichoresis*. The integration of irreconcilable opposites—fully human, fully God—in the personhood of the Son. Time and again I've witnessed the either/or conflict in a community, a both/and perspective or third-force coming in, transforming or transfiguring the conflict in context into a wholly unexpected new frame of reference, larger pattern of more. As Bourgeault pursues this trinitarian flow from its esoteric origins (the audacity of articulating how the Trinity came into being?) through to the fulfillment of the Divine Plan, we see orthodox Christian thought in a *movement*, a flow, confirming its historical proclamation *and* pushing us into *participating in it*, a process or practice in which we are invited to co-create, *participate*. Bourgeault spells out this Trinitarian flow in Orthodox Christian thought, the unfolding of what would be called *salvation history*. She spells out how this way of diving into trinitarian thought resolves the "problem of the missing feminine,"

13. Bourgeault, *Holy Trinity and the Law of Three*, 99.
14. Bourgeault, *Holy Trinity and the Law of Three*, 100.
15. Boehme, *Clavis*, 22–23, cited in Bourgeault, *Holy Trinity and the Law of Three*, 100.
16. Marion, *Erotic Phenomenon*, 6.

remythologizes Christianity in a much more spacious container, reclaims the primacy of Christ, and integrates theory and practice in one fell swoop.[17] That is crucial for Christians committed to the roots of our own tradition. Therefore, for me, today. Yet her enfleshment of it all within the subtle energetics of the human body—for our era—is what opens her wisdom for traditional and non-sectarian beloveds alike.

Bourgeault charts both a task and a visceral-sensate invitation I can recognize in my own woman's body. The work of this stage, ongoing now for centuries in our traditional "Pentecostal Trinity," seems to be a "more subtle embodiment, the discovery of an essential quality of aliveness that lives within all things as their animating principle and purpose."[18] Bourgeault suggests this work is actually a radical transformation of consciousness in which we can engage with this aliveness directly. Mediation has been required, so to participate and begin to imagine further into this realm—what can be called the *imaginal* realm[19]—but pathways are beckoning for the engagement of this aliveness more and more directly. With the Holy Spirit, dancing in the Unity of God, encountering the Kingdom of Heaven, the final new arising is "the divine plan," the "restoration of all things." *Oikonomia*, in the Greek.

The esoteric arguments and the audacity of Bourgeault's work can be off-putting to many, particularly those most defined by solely Christianizing language. But her work, finding me at just the right *when* time I needed it,[20] soothed the fiery rage, my felt sense of abandonment I know as a woman in my own root tradition of Christianity. The Pentecostal Trinity, as wielded by most of the theological academics I know today, refuses the experiences of those wounded by it, by sacred authority of the ecclesia, intent upon its own grasping survival. Trinity in this Christian community is a believe-and-conform doctrine, demonstrating a likely fear-mongering expression of Christianity today. Bourgeault's daring innovations with clear traditional integrity, however, honor the historic evolution of Christian thought while pushing us to grow up, to mature more fully, to actually participate in the cosmic vision of God/de, testified to in our holy historic traditions. Risking into a more resonant, participatory invitation, the Trinity now can serve as a radically renewing journey into

---

17. Bourgeault, *Holy Trinity and the Law of Three*, 199–205.

18. Bourgeault, *Holy Trinity and the Law of Three*, 171.

19. Bourgeault, *Holy Trinity and the Law of Three*, 189. See also *Eye of the Heart*, 13–41.

20. Smith, *How to Inhabit Time*.

repeated surrenders, into obstacles that become opportunities, growing savvy to the wisdom of third force(s) in hope of new arisings.

Renewing What Has Been

So how does all this theologizing help the abandoned and forgotten little six-year-old girl? If we posit that desire is truly the spark of God/de within us, then the undercurrents of desire she feels so fully in her very body become sacred invitations, gifts, mysteries to be held in beauty, awe, wonder. When she gets curious, she gets to know more, gently, playfully, without shame. She becomes grounded and assured, knowing who and Whose she is, in her body, in a world more mysterious than humans can imagine. There is no double-checking or forgetting what she knows so to belong,[21] trying to find safety in her community. When she begins her bleeding times, she gets to learn of the depth-orientation her body can offer her—an intuitive, deepening, even mystical connection across visible and invisible worlds. If love is the driveshaft of all creation, moving through a *concentration of desire*, then the intensifying of desire in her flesh and bones becomes a pathway, a way to develop deeper and deeper attunement to what is sacred, life-giving, gifted holiness deep within any human body, hers included.

If a community were to accord this understanding of Trinity as co-creative participation in the energies of God/de, her life of earliest formation could have been different. When she felt this desire intensifying to such a degree that she grew scared, *this* Body of Humanity deeply grounded in the body as gift, as source of wisdom, could *assist her to discern her own experiences* in safety. They could provide a context for sacred meanings *she* and *they* could ascribe to her body's wisdom. This community could then welcome how these experiences could become signs of wisdom for the whole community. And in those desires that drew her away from herself somehow, that drew her into the violences around her, she'd have a faith community wise enough to discern the Spirit undergirding her own spirit. To help hold her accountable to higher frequencies of mercy, forgiveness, love. A faithful container of community and body, surrendered to God/de, would hold gently while she allowed some of her desires to be refined, contained, surrendering them into a purgation of form, an alchemical process of shaping herself

---

21. Gilligan, *Birth of Pleasure*, 4.

most wholly and in a most giving-receiving wisdom she'd know because she felt it assured from within and around her.

For so many of us wounded by established wisdom traditions, this reconfiguring and renewing Trinitarianism could feel like a utopian flight of fancy, a new-agey refusal of the "sacrifice and submit" bastardizations of love proclaimed in the power-over histories we've known. Those who have proposed this incorporative, beautifully grounded, earthy-holy way of being human have long been marginalized, refused, imprisoned and killed by civil authorities, whether with religious rationales or not. As the enraged woman I was, I certainly did not expect Trinity to approach *alignment with* ecclesially regulatory traditions. You could imagine how I would not have looked here for an intellectual-embodied key to freedom, forgiveness, love and hope. Ten years after Bourgeault's work seeded and blossomed into my theological teaching, another established, tradition-committed woman-scholar poked into my world. Unsought by my wounded embodied-soul, "An Essay on the Trinity" was about to find me, on a cruise ship across the Caribbean.

Falling Asleep into Praying the Trinity

Beautifully bored, entering into the spacious silences of the deep blue ocean, I stumbled into an unexpected volume purchased on my Kindle years before. "[T]his book is written in the fundamental conviction that no cogent answer to the contemporary Christian question of the trinitarian God can be given without charting the necessary and *intrinsic* entanglement of human sexuality and spirituality in such a quest: the questions of right contemplation of God, right speech about God, and right ordering of desire all hang together. They emerge in primary interaction with Scripture, become intensified and contested in early Christian tradition, and are purified in the crucible of prayer."[22] I had been mildly interested in Sarah Coakley's work over the years, but saw her well within the hallowed halls of a narrow theological orthodoxy I'd long since departed, even if I still grieved it from time to time. Why spend any time listening to those who adamantly refuse to listen to you as the woman you are becoming? Yet I read the entire volume on that cruise, cyber-cover to cyber-cover, not quite sure why I was reading it. The waters were bluest blues. The ocean was vast. It was restful to rest in her words, for some

22. Coakley, *God, Sexuality, and the Self*, 1–2.

reason. Shortly upon arrival home, I decided to use the text for a spring semester Masters degree elective on deepening Christian leaders' embodiment, resourced by body-positive resourcing in Christian traditions. I'd already read it, after all.

Coakley's first volume of systematics is a re-read of formative, patristic sources for the origins of the doctrine of the Trinity. Alongside the predictable "textbook" renditions of this history, she points us to "the crucial prayer-based logic of emergent Trinitarianism, and the related and complicated entanglements . . . "[23] I recognized and resonated with her narrative "of an explicitly prayer-based access to the workings of the divine," its simultaneous "insistent questions about the relation of sexual desire and desire for God."[24] The most recent decades in my life were recognizable there. These were the reasons I assigned the text to my students.

Then I was rereading her Introduction for the third or fourth time, preparing lecture notes for class one morning, when I grew inordinately sleepy. I couldn't keep my eyes open. *This* is a body-response I know, have long known as a signal of resistance and fear in me. Utterly predictable, recognized in years of clinical training and spiritual friendships as containers for deepening maturity: when Godde is bringing something new or tender for me to learn, I first fear it, then I resist it by becoming so weary I can hardly keep my eyes open to see/hear it. My mind rarely knows why or what or how. It simply shuts down, stops functioning.

This "narrative of an explicitly prayer-based access to the workings of the divine" was something I could recognize in my by-then decades of awakening. Coakley was speaking my body's language, comfortable enough in the Silent Treatment for now. But she was arguing this access to the divine "begged trinitarian shape from its inception."[25] She was making *Trinitarian* that which had been nothing for me but *traditionally imposed shames*. Human desires of most any kind, inherited from my ancestral lineage's woundedness about the body. Desires and experiences of pleasure long-submerged because they were dangerous or sinful. My *awakening as a woman* was what had offered me a pathway to my own body's beauty, goodness, wisdom, even purpose. And now some woman from Cambridge was beginning to build an argument for the wonders and refinements of human desire rooted in *God's desire, in the Trinity*? Coakley continues, this "[prayer-based access to the workings of the

23. Coakley, *God, Sexuality, and the Self*, 4.
24. Coakley, *God, Sexuality, and the Self*, 6.
25. Coakley, *God, Sexuality, and the Self*, 6.

divine] provides the resources for the presentation of a contemporary trinitarian *ontology of desire*—a vision of God's trinitarian nature as both the source and goal of human desires, as God intends them. It indicates how God the 'Father,' in and through the Spirit, both stirs up, and progressively chastens and purges, the frailer and often misdirected desires of humans, and so forges them, by stages of sometimes painful growth, into the likeness of his Son. . . . here divine desire can be seen as the ultimate progenitor of human desire, and the very means of its transformation."[26] Overwhelmed, I lapsed into a sound sleep.

The previously inconceivable collusion of my own shame-filled desires with fundamentally God's desire within my body imploded my cognitive functions. Yes, I awakened to my own sensuality at age six, but I had spent nearly every decade after that numbing, sublimating, repressing, forgetting. Some wise part of me at age six knew to keep the experience to myself, even as my entire reawakening journey beginning with CPE had been about the reclamation of healthy desire. But there is little to no more conflicted area of inquiry or awareness in my ancestral lineages than desire in the human body. My Days in the Weeds had conditioned me to fear visceral sensation, unless held in the strong gaze of a spirit-friend or the mothering energies of a circle of women or non-sectarian friends. Coakley's work, unsought and even undesired at the time, broke me open to see a "red-thread" of desiring connection. God/de's desire had always been underneath my own, within my own? How is it that what had brought me such shame was now becoming a sacred path? Of course I short-circuited. Nothing in my theological traditioning had prepared me for *this* ontology of desire. And yet everything in my life had prepared me to receive it *when it was time*.

Coakley's Ontology of Desire Clarified

Coakley clarifies the use of the word *desire* across American and British contexts to prevent misunderstandings—cross-Atlantic but also analytical or psychological. She observes—particularly in the American context, if less so in the British one—that *physiological* desires and urges are often presumed as basic and fundamental to the *sexual* realm. Unsatisfied (physical) sexual desire is considered necessarily harmful, even an "unnatural" state. As such, desire instigates a fear and confusion around traditional

---

26. Coakley, *God, Sexuality, and the Self*, 6.

practices of celibacy or even the use of sublimation in any collective setting. Considering desire in this primarily sexual nuance *does* make both celibacy and sublimation "monstrous," as Coakley says, or "a veritable charade."[27] Contrary to previous understandings of Freud, he actually *did* observe the necessity of sublimation, for civilization's sake, she observes. Coakley's aim, in some contrast to all this, is to offer classical wisdom as applicable to those who are sexually active as to those who are not. Desire is not about sex, in the end. Much like the clarifications of *pleasure* and *eros* provided by Carol Gilligan in the last chapter, *desire* here points more to *eros*, passion for Life, capacity for connectedness than something as secularly flattening as sexual intercourse. Even sexual relations are boring unless there is this transcendent connectedness, I say.

For Coakley—and what I have learned over the years that draws me to her work— "It is not that physical 'sex' is basic and 'God' ephemeral; rather, it is God who is basic, and 'desire' the precious clue that ever tugs at the heart, reminding the human soul—however dimly—of its created source."[28] It is the tug at the heart. The clue to something on the horizon and intimately within. Coakley offers *desire* as an "ontological category belonging primarily to God, and only secondarily to humans as a token of their createdness 'in the image.'"[29] It is also not a signal of "lack" therefore, but of a "plenitude of longing love that God has for God's own creation and for its full and ecstatic participation in the divine, trinitarian, life."[30]

Today, as I have crawled into her argument to see how it fits, stretches, warms to a woman's body, I find myself curious and hopeful. I already know in my bones that when you allow Godde to be at the center, finally, without resistance, surrendering into What Is, hope is planted and possibility is born. And while so many in our world focus upon the sanctification (my word, not theirs) of gender and/or orientation, my own concerns simmer underneath that entire discourse. I've never found those discourses/debates to be life-giving, though I strive to honor how they are for others. Coakley's work aims to support all able and willing to entertain her grounded, radically renewing proposal, in the end. "From 'sexuality' and the 'self' to participation in the trinitarian God: this way lies a long haul of erotic purgation, but

27. Coakley, *God, Sexuality, and the Self*, 7.
28. Coakley, *God, Sexuality, and the Self*, 10.
29. Coakley, *God, Sexuality, and the Self*, 10.
30. Coakley, *God, Sexuality, and the Self*, 10.

its goal is one of infinite delight."[31] This was an accurate and viscerally recognizable description of my entire journey, rupture of faith in God, participation in some Force or Flow that would not let me go, One so deeply within me I could never be apart if I tried. Godde. Eventually, God/de. A companionable way into an expressive delight, able to companion the suffering of self and others. A pathway and practice that made sense of excruciating suffering becoming abundant delight, somehow underneath and beyond my capacity for either.

Coakley's *théologie totale* into a "Dance of Orthodoxies"

A couple of the main features of Coakley's *theologie totale* are worth highlighting before we land into her invitation to what Christians could call *praying the Trinity*.[32] First of all, her work privileges *contemplation*, a lived devotion and active waiting receptive to God's fundamental desire, Presence. This offers a counterpoint to much of the modern and postmodern philosophical and scientific senses of *reason*. "Theology does not claim to *subsume* or 'overcome' secular philosophy and science . . . It is the Spirit's interruption that finally enables full human participation in God. . . . Theology's 'reason,' however in comparison to all secular reasons, is both purified and *expanded* by the dark purgation of contemplation. So theology's reason, at a profound level, is in ongoing contrapuntal relation to revelation and grace, and continues to be transformed by it."[33] Coakley's work invites a lived theology *in via*. It privileges contemplation not for "authenticating 'religious experience'" but as "an attentive openness to the whole self (intellect, will, memory, imagination, feeling, bodiliness) to the reality of God and creation."[34] Orthodoxy remains valued, but understood as "a project, the longed-for horizon of personal transformation in response to divine truth."[35] Not creedal correctness. Not imposed ecclesiastical regulation. All this is socially located, of course, but not socially reductionistic. *Desire* is the constellating theological category, at the heart, inviting an examination of the relation of divine and human desires. The bulk of Coakley's first systematics volume, therefore,

31. Coakley *God, Sexuality, and the Self*, 11.
32. Coakley, *God, Sexuality, and the Self*, 88–92.
33. Coakley, *God, Sexuality, and the Self*, 89.
34. Coakley, *God, Sexuality, and the Self*, 88.
35. Coakley, *God, Sexuality, and the Self*, 89–90.

is an argument for *praying the Trinity*, which she demonstrates is *a neglected but traceable patristic tradition*.

Woven throughout Christian patristic traditions is a Spirit-leading approach to the trinitarian life of God, though it also faced great centralized ecclesial opposition in the early centuries. In Origen, Augustine, Gregory of Nyssa and others, one learns of this devotion to God as Triune guided by Romans 8, led first by the Spirit. The presence and authority of this approach can be gleaned by the extensive ecclesial arguments against it. "It could lead to 'sectarian' or purist tendencies on the part of those seeking a life of special abandonment to the Spirit, increasingly frowned upon by Rome from the second century onwards."[36] Others spoke against the "dangers of erotic power, its intensification and the problematic entanglement of human spiritual and sexual desires"[37] (often instigated by a special commitment to deep prayer in the Spirit). Forms of prayer that ostensibly released the pray-er from rational means of control were to be condemned. Yet a Spirit-led approach to the Trinity "links trinitarian thought more directly to its true matrix in prayer and worship,"[38] comes the rebuttal, in both patristic voice and Coakley's argument.

This resists mere cognitive approaches to the trinitarian life of God. It mirrors how the Trinity has historically been abused and used in the (un)conscious challenges of desire, power, and gender in ecclesial community(ies). Ultimately, Coakley presents the inevitable conundrum facing ecclesial life today. "[I]f the most fruitful *spiritual* contexts for a vibrant Trinitarianism tend to be marginalized institutionally, how can the churches today regenerate themselves doctrinally, and especially in relation to the deeply connected issues of prayer and desire?"[39] Here she argues for two sorts of orthodoxy at play: one, a transformative spiritual process, which constantly risks the charge against it of "unorthodoxy" and two, another sort of orthodoxy "primarily concerned to protect and sustain ecclesiastical and political order through doctrinal rectitude, creedal assent as well as churchly obedience"—all of which "runs the risk of an effective subordination or taming of the Spirit, even as the creed it proclaims explicitly denies this."[40] Unbeknownst to me, a *renewed and renewing Trinitarianism* emerged here as whole, holy felt, viscerally

36. Coakley, *God, Sexuality, and the Self*, 102.
37. Coakley, *God, Sexuality, and the Self*, 102.
38. Coakley, *God, Sexuality, and the Self*, 104.
39. Coakley, *God, Sexuality, and the Self*, 104.
40. Coakley, *God, Sexuality, and the Self*, 105.

recognizable. I was being shown a way to honor deep commitment in covenant *and* the unresolved and resolving rages in my body.

Coakley paints what I call a *dance of orthodoxies* within which I could align, recognize, resonate as an enraged woman pushed to the periphery of so much Christian concern. "My own reading of this early patristic period," she begins, "neither reduces the history of the development of trinitarian doctrine to non-theological forces, nor assumes that the achievement of classical orthodoxy is the arrival at some stable place of spiritual safety. 'Orthodoxy' as mere propositional assent needs to be distinguished from 'orthodoxy' as a demanding, and ongoing, spiritual *project*, in which the language of the creeds is personally and progressively assimilated."[41] In classic Coakley fashion, she prays-thinks-feels-writes within what she's called God/de's *apophatic horizon*.[42] She names the integrity and even *orthodoxy* of being grounded in one's own visceral experience held in a prayer-based worshiping community able to witness and hold accountable in Love, all while being pushed to the periphery by a more ecclesial-grasping understanding of Orthodoxy as historic-propositional assent.

As Coakley sums it up, "My thesis is that this nexus of association (between trinitarian thought, prayer of a deep sort, and questions of 'erotic' meaning), caused sufficient political difficulty to press the prayer-based approach to the Trinity to the edges of the more public, conciliar discussion of the doctrine, even in the patristic period itself, and further marginalized it as far as modern histories of dogma were concerned."[43] For the first time in several decades, I could begin to imagine that the Wisdom unpacked in my own sacred bewilderment and blessedly assured visceral journey was still sacred within my own root wisdom streams. It was even *trinitarian* in a way that I finally had access, sensibility, hope. Though most of my life in Christian congregational life had attempted to require neglect or relinquishment of my woman-body's experience, here was an invitation into an ever-deepening openness to the whole self, a *theology in via*. Making sense of my own experiences, then, I call this the *dance of orthodoxies* that honors the elders of my own tradition *and* the bewilderment in my own intimate transformations, or more accurately, transfigurations, because the wounds *remain*. Coakley's *théologie totale*

---

41. Coakley, *God, Sexuality, and the Self*, 5.
42. Coakley, "What Does Chalcedon Solve and What Does It Not?"
43. Coakley, *God, Sexuality, and the Self*, 6.

created a space of invitation, even liberation, for understanding my own decades of awakening, abandonment, rage, and return to the body.

In sum, this renewed and renewing Trinitarianism breathes as an incorporative Trinity, inspired by Romans 8, willing to dance alongside the ecclesially orthodox Trinity of Father-Son-Spirit so in need of renewal today. God/de's desire is fundamental here, known as the divine spark in each of us, palpable in pleasure created, refined, and shaped into a Christ-like self-offering amidst God/de's delight and abundance intended for all. This Spirit-led approach to the trinitarian life of God/de gives my six-year-old self a vastly different invitation and landscape on which to understand and cherish her own embodied life. Desire is God/de's gift, a sign and symbol of God/de's movement within her, beyond her. When held well and cherished, its presence—no matter how difficult or delightful it may feel at any given moment—directs a human body toward life. Always toward life. Neglect and refusal of feeling shut down a human spirit, numbing us away from the Love that beckons, always. Our invitation is into *praying the Trinity*, a life of devotion and active waiting, deepened in worship and liturgy that is able to hold and witness our pain beyond traditional categories and into intergenerational healing.

Chapter Five

Forgiving the Divine: It Has Something to Do With Grief

THIS RENEWED AND RENEWING Trinitarianism may be the center around which the writing-unto-understanding finally landed, but the journey was anything but linear, perceivably faithful, or theologically assured. Welcome to the more demanding part of the journey, at least for my *feminist with a forgiveness problem*, making peace with my *conscious feminine theologian*, who, because of being a yet-silent *preacher's wife*, was able to steady some sort of trust while serving in ecclesial-academic environments hostile to H/her. Unable to avoid congregational settings, I was already getting weary of the rage. Its righteousness and my own deep hurt at its root had no place to go. I read a lot in this time, with little reprieve. Intellectually, I cherished mirrors that could honor my visceral experience, like *Rage Becomes Her*,[1] but my body was increasingly exhausted, even close to despair.

    The damage done to me as a woman, belatedly awakening to her giftedness in the F/feminine, *is* irrevocable, irredeemable. It has involved accepting that what I have lost can never be regained. As a feminist with my forgiveness problem, I am broken-hearted, in search of strategies to live bearably with the rage, as righteous as it is. I lost whole decades of my life, its wholeness, beauty. I lost entire decades of knowing utter delight at how wondrous my woman's body *is*. How responsive to love. How strong in work, defense, play, even necessary offense. How beautiful. How wise. Finally *consciously* returned to my own flesh, in the excruciating pain of

---

1. Chemaly, *Rage Becomes Her*, xi–xii.

those unforgivable Days in the Weeds, I was given the gift of myself as a woman, in a woman's body. *Womanheart* found me in relationships with awakening women, enlivening every cell. I was returned to what could be called *women's mysteries* just in the nick of time—the sacred power of my own bleeding, the contemplative mystical gift of Presence in the days right before my bleeding. I was landed again and again into deep wonder at how abundant and sacred All Life Is, *all of me* included—failures, flaws, light, shadow, gifts, graces all.

Yet the loss remains. For forty-five years, I did not know how deep the Love well went. I had thought—as does most of my ancestral lineage—that you had to perform and conform to be loved. You had to starve *yourself* if you wanted to belong. Today, I know that the F/feminine always arises in my body as *grief*. Pleasure felt deeply in my body always bring tears to my eyes. These signs and more will always arise in me as grief because the loss and wounding of my deepest self, for decades, is *irrevocable*. It can never be restored, nor can my bodysoul be easily reconciled to the role God's church has played in such devastating loss. Particularly as it continues and will continue to neglect the F/feminine well beyond my lifetime.

These signs and signals arise in my flesh now as *praise*, which I have finally learned is grief's "best friend." My ancestral lineages—and much larger segments of the population in our United States, I will argue—have little skill or understanding with grief as a *sacred art*. Martin Prechtel paints a vastly different, poetic picture that resonates deeply on this side of the story arc, though it was incomprehensible to me beforehand. "Grief is the best friend of Praise, because Praise is a grandiose griever! Without both Grief and Praise, life is only hate and mediocrity. . . . Because they are best friends, both Grief and Praise live together in the same building, but in opposing quarters: in the left and right chambers of Love's great thumping house called the Heart."[2] The tears, the return to my own body with its deep gifts in desire and pleasure, immerse me in the wonder that life even *is*. That I get to know Love so intimately, so deeply. That my beloved family is who it is. That I have been soul-hitched to my beloved for as long as we have, are. That I get to watch the Spirit work with my fearful, perplexed and perplexing colleagues and students as we all encounter a God/de more wondrous than our congregational communities could ever have embodied.

---

2. Prechtel, *Smell of Rain on Dust*, 5–6.

While the previous chapter is the *theo*-logical center of it all, this chapter is no less central for the challenges needing redress today. Enraged but weary back in 2017, I had absolutely no interest in *forgiveness*, of any kind. From anyone. For anyone. I'm a born-and-bred Presbyterian who has only understood forgiveness in an untenable, unreal but practiced-traditional way: a refusal of hurt, for sake of forced reconciliation; a theological window-dressing that neglects an irrevocable wound; persistent allowance of continued wounding "for sake of relationship" or "community." I am not alone in my confusion and skepticism. In his book, *Forgiveness: an Alternative Account*, Matthew Ichihashi Potts recounts the June 17, 2015, murders of the Mother Emanuel African Methodist Episcopal Church Bible study members by White supremacist Dylann Roof. He describes the offerings of forgiveness spoken to Roof at his arraignment by some (but not all) of the victims' surviving family members. Then Potts shares an interview of writer Ta-Nehisi Coates, who wondered aloud, "Is that real? . . . I question the realness of that." Potts concludes: "If forgiveness is real, then it's a real problem."[3] Amen, brother. I feel all of this skepticism, disbelief, resistance . . . in my own belly.

By this time, however, I also felt viscerally terrified in practices of silence, in solitude, in which I used to feel the most Presence. I was at a loss, with nowhere my logic or rage could take me. Many years into this *womanheart*, these *women's mysteries* in my life, it was apparently time to re-enter a more communal journey. Perhaps to heal? Bewilderment and acceptance. The 2017 Shalem Institute's nationally configured training program for spiritual directors felt safer than anything proximate or Presbyterian, and it offered a larger, contemplative container still identifiably Christian. The often unconscious communal assumptions around prayer made me anxious, since prayer had now become only unspoken, silent, embodied in a gaze as regularly as it would find me. The spoken prayers of "community" felt disingenuous, performative, even triumphalist and violent. On the intensives, the Shalem community gathered for times of communal silence. This felt just barely doable. As Spirit would have it, the familiar Sinai Jesus icon from my first real encounter with icon-prayer was in the communal space of our retreat center.

---

3. Potts, *Forgiveness*, 1–2.

Forgiveness Findings—Part I

My journal of that first day at the Shalem intensive began,

> *I don't know how to gaze into the eyes of the Sinai Jesus anymore, which I'm not sure saddens me that much. I keep sitting here, so I'm feeling something drawing me close, inviting, but it isn't sadness. I wonder . . . the difference between the gaze and a stare . . . ? I find what is most alive and sacred to me today in the gaze(s) into which I am welcomed. . . . From time to time, I feel the energy of the gaze in unexpected places—in the eyes of a student, yearning for more; in the eyes of a directee, for just a moment; and with an impish smile, in my dog's eyes too. Her whole being can invite the gaze, even when her canine instincts urge her to look away. My husband avoids what I mean by "the gaze," which I honor most days fairly well. His sacred is external to the intimacy of this internal gaze I so cherish. The eyes of Jesus in this Sinai Jesus icon feel to be closer to his external sacred than to my visceral, intimate sacred, I guess. So I stare into these iconic eyes, wondering why I am looking for so long. No One is there. I remember wondering what I could be seeking. Surely a release from fear . . . fear of those Days in the Weeds, fear of any extended silence imposed from beyond myself, fear of being left alone without eyes to see me into a life held by the F/feminine. My journal entry finished: I rest in the abundance that has been given. I no longer need Sinai Jesus, like I once did. So why does he beckon so? What do I want? What does he? What did I want or need from this Sinai Jesus? What did he need or desire?*

During the Great Silence of our Shalem retreat schedule, I took these questions with me on a walk toward the labyrinth there on the retreat-center grounds. I remember bumping into two men from the retreat on my way there. Today, I see how significant it was that they were *men*. One was a Shalem leader, who paused, smiling at me in our shared-sabbath-silence. Shortly afterward, another man met me. He and I had connected easily earlier in a table-fellowship conversation. We smiled at one another in the silence, hugged briefly before walking onward. I continued to hold my questions close to heart, feeling like I had been distracted, unaware it was all purposeful. *Solvitur ambulando*, I heard in my ear. *It is solved by walking*.[4] I began to walk into the labyrinth.

---

4. Often attributed to St. Augustine, it found me in McGowan, *Book of Love*, 191.

The first thing I heard, or felt, was a complicated rush of feelings, even resistance. "I don't want *anything* from the Sinai Jesus" arose, which I felt fiercely in my rage. Some tears were close behind. In all things masculine and church, I'd finally learned to not want anything, or at least anything specific. Why come to want something, only to discover that it is undependable or will leave you bereft in the end? Again and again, desires I have had, ways of being connected as I need, have had to wait or change in Brian's and my life in his church. It used to send me off the deep end into my abandonment wounding, but even by this summer 2017, I'd begun to learn to *not* to bite the hook (as Pema Chodron might say). I was blessed in my beloved's commitment to me, even as sometimes it felt compromised by his church. I could still feel the energies heightening, deepening, the closer I got to the center of the labyrinth. I heard a question from within, perhaps from the Sinai Jesus? *whether I would stay with him to the center . . . ?*

I walked closer to the center, remembering there was a prayer in the novel I was reading, a version of the Lord's Prayer to be recited in the six-petaled center of an 11-circuit labyrinth. The first petal of FAITH, "Our Father, Who art in heaven . . . " reads the opening. Then SURRENDER, "Your Kingdom come, Your will be done . . . " SERVICE, third petal, "on earth as it is in heaven." ABUNDANCE, "give us this day our daily bread . . . " The text from *The Book of Love*, the second volume of the Magdalen series I had been reading, nuanced the teaching: "There is nothing that you need or desire that will not be provided you when you live in the flow of God's grace, aligning your will with God's will."[5] The fifth petal stopped me in my tracks: FORGIVENESS. *Forgiveness?!* My gut twisted as the rage resurfaced.

Tears began and an unbidden question erupted into my awareness: *Does Jesus ever ask for forgiveness?* The prayerful instructions that two of the book's characters—Maureen and Matilda—receive, shining for me out of my Kindle read "Here you must list those who have harmed you, who have given ill witness against you, or who have otherwise caused you pain. And you must forgive them, while praying that they will one day be fully *anthropos* and realize their own connection to God and remember their own promise."[6] A complicated wave arose in my belly, my heart, my

---

5. McGowan, *Book of Love*, 220.

6. McGowan, *Book of Love*, 220. *Anthropos* in the novel (and in ancient texts oft-refused by orthodox Christianity) refers to being in right-relationship with God, grounded in the "commitment to create heaven on earth by acting in accordance with

mind. Utter bewilderment, confusion, fear. I knelt down in the fifth petal and wept. I sobbed, breathed, cried some more.

I have been wounded, been harmed, I heard myself whisper. *Those who professed to love me gave ill witness against me as a little girl. I have been caused pain, more than I could bear*—*in Brian's church, on those two terrorizing days in 2014, now whenever I enter a Christian sanctuary that feels like a salt bath on my woman's body with no skin.* Did I want Jesus to ask me to forgive him? Did I want him to finally take responsibility as God for those days of abandonment, rending, and terror in 2014? What *was* this desire erupting so fully within my body? My journal of that day, then:

> *To be clear, the sense of these questions isn't one of "wrong-doing" needing to be "made right"; a foibled, flawed woman like myself taking the place of God. No. The feeling I get from it is a deep sadness, infinitely shared, that the world is this way, that there is so much pain, that God could stop it if S/he chose power over Love. Which S/he does not do, time and again. How can Love choose as She does, again and again? . . . there's so much pain. To be infinitely aware of all that pain . . . Hellish. But as I received the question that was irrefusable and heretical, as I stayed in my unknowing and deep pain, movement happened. I felt the Sinai Jesus sidle up close to me in the fifth petal. Gently, H/he asked, "Will you forgive me?" I could feel my hardness of heart begin to moisten. I could feel myself being seen, being welcomed "on an other side" of this scary journey I had been on. I could feel his compassion, his companionship even, given his encounter with abandonment and death. I paused to text the question to a spirit-friend from California, to make it 'real' beyond my own head: "Do you think-feel-sense that Jesus ever asks for our forgiveness?" To be fully realized as human, H/he must have . . . but . . . [lots of tears, wide-eyed emoji].*

Receiving this question, in such a fashion, has to be one of the most startling and yet touching feelings-insights-images ever prayed into me. It came from somewhere unexpected, unknown, yet familiar. But it could not come from my theological mind, that I knew. So I sat with it, beginning to smile. If Jesus were truly human, as many of us profess him to have been in time, to be as Risen, he would have disappointed others, even hurt others who needed things he could not or

---

the Way of Love, by loving the Lord thy God above all else, and by loving your brothers and sisters on earth as yourself, for they are a part of yourself."

would not provide in the moment, because of the depth of his love, not power. Being divine, self-giving, he would ask for forgiveness in order to return to open-hearted relationship. Open-hearts only becoming open when moistened, when invited into supple receiving. Which the F/feminine had been shaping in me these recent years.

Pragmatically, from another angle: asking the question already transmits the desire to be restored, to be close, from 'his side' hidden deep within each of us. If asking the question would heal a wounded heart, H/he would ask the question to heal it. What arrived in my belly awareness befuddled all theological propriety but instigated *theo*-logical resonance too. *If the question itself would heal, H/he would ask it.* Regardless of the church organization and history that would utterly refuse *Jesus asking for forgiveness*. An ecclesial system that yet professes: within H/him, all transgressions become null. Or if we listen to Scripture: It would cost Him everything to ask it (divinity) yet he would therefore ask it (not regarding equality with God as something to be exploited) (Phil 2:6–11). The whole thing was so antithetical to what I had been taught. It's even offensive to the devout faithful, as it would have been to me as my graduate student self, defending the church at such unknown cost. Neither then nor now can I shake the deep felt-sense that I was asked to forgive, *so that I could be free*.

Here is where I became a feminist with a forgiveness problem. Rage unresolved for decades had made me a feminist, simply to survive. My covenantal commitment as a preacher's wife had shaped me into a conscious feminine theologian, continuing to serve in academic and ecclesial environments (un)consciously hostile to the F/feminine. Without any cognitive theological framework within which to hold this experience, however, it landed in my journals of the time before completely receding from awareness and memory.

I literally forgot about it until nearly four years later.

Forgiving Findings—Part 2

I have lost two grandchildren, the woman said, rather matter of factly. She then described her outrage—one was killed by a drunk driver, another by a rare form of brain cancer that lasted only six weeks. She named the grief that continues to come, though lesser now than immediately after each loss. The context? I was sitting in a Zoom circle series on *Forgiveness*, offered by two elder-teachers I had gotten to know.[7] I registered for the series mostly out of curiosity and a desire to be with them, but I had also entered into the series with a sense of pragmatism. I had been deeply hurt by the leaders of a women's community in which I'd offered my gifts for years. I figured I might learn some practical tips toward letting that injury go, even departing that community with a hoped-for grace. Two weeks into the series, however, it became apparent the reason I was there was a vastly different invitation than I had consciously chosen. *I have lost two grandchildren*, the woman said, rather matter of factly.

She described her situation, her grief, and then almost in passing, she spoke of her journey to *forgiving the divine*. I saw others on the Zoom screen respond with the quiet applause, the poetic "rubbing fingers in the air" gesture, as they recognized something significant in connection with their own experiences. Something imploded inside of me. I honestly don't remember anything anyone said after those words. All I could hear was noise. Unintelligible jumbling noise for what felt like an eternity. The words that invited me in further came from one of the leaders, a woman of African descent, her own words of divine accusation. Words I could *feel* in my own outrage.

You left me, she said (to No One in Particular)

. . . *I never left you. It just didn't look like what you thought it should.*

"Surrender," she said God said. "*No*," she replied.

"Surrender," she said God said. "*I don't trust you*," she countered.

"Surrender," God said.

"*You left me*," she accused.

. . . *I never left you. It just didn't look like what you thought it should.*[8]

Never before had I heard such bold words accusing the divine, *words that I could resonate with to my very core*. The words drove me into three days of stream-of-consciousness writing. I described anew my Days in the Weeds, the days when God had abandoned me. Unstoppable tears. Utter terror. The speech of a three-year-old the first day. No speech at all, the second day. Void. Abandonment.

---

7. Quanita Roberson, www.nzuzu.com. Tenneson Woolf, www.tennesonwoolf.com.

8. Quanita Roberson's Forgiveness series (see www.nzuzu.com).

In my rage and resistance, all I could feel back then and again was the very real possibility that God was nothing but human yearning crafted in myth and memory, kept alive by fearful human beings. God *is* that, after all, in human terms. I had wept in those interminable Days, as all that had been sacred and untouchable in my life was stripped away. This was my trauma, something landing on me, in my body, happening to my body, overwhelming all capacity to receive.[9] Not simply a rupture of some imagined continuity. To disregard the Days in the Weeds would continue the betrayal of myself, of my reality as a woman within established theological traditions that have disregarded women's experiences and voices for centuries. To hold onto the whole experience was exhausting and a choice for wariness over vulnerability, duty over joy, arm's length distance instead of intimacy-belonging. *Forgiving the divine* landed in my body as offense and hope, impossibility and potentiality. With utterly *no recollection* of my encounter with the Sinai Jesus in the labyrinth years before, something in me shifted open. My feminist lost her footing, if not her rage. My conscious feminine theologian was willing to sit with the unknowable by then, actively waiting in the silences becoming easier to sustain, in solitude and in circle. This phrase of *forgiving the divine* opened a space in my rage, a whiff of a sacred teaching I could mimic, or worse, theologically define, but which was still *not an option* for me.

My feminist-*gift* is *wrestling*—and forcing *others* to wrestle—with the righteousness of my pain, the purity and beauty I now know in my body, which offers me a peaceableness I never thought possible. Historic wisdom traditions have rarely had the best interests of women at heart, as women. In Scriptures, practice, and experience, sacred root traditions are horrifically one-sided, placing women and women's cadence primarily in the gaze of the masculine, the patriarch. The cadence of women's voices—the focal point of women's souls, bodies, spirits . . . what I call *womanheart*—is strikingly absent from historic Scriptures, practices, traditions of our historic root traditions. I don't think this is an overly bold claim, requiring much evidential work. Women are always faced with "proving a negative," which basically proves the point. Then came the unsought, undesired teaching from the circle series: "Your freedom is directly related to your capacity to forgive."[10] I am *steeped* in

---

9. Roberson, circle-teaching Fire & Water retreat.
10. Roberson, *Forgiveness* series, 2022.

theological discourses, none of which allowed this disruptive, unruly forgiveness to find me in my rage.

Then faced with an unexpected institutional offering of a sabbatical, a couple years after this encounter of the phrase *forgiving the divine* in circle, I decided to print out the over 800 pages of blog-writing I'd done over the last fifteen years. *Buried deep within all those words was the Sinai Jesus, waiting for me in my labyrinth walk in the Great Silence.* Finally grounded in my own body's wisdom, with a rebellious fence-pushing charism finally for my own good, I leaned into the accusation of the divine, inspired and enlivened by rage made holy in a Body of Humanity able to receive it, witness, hold unto healing, and trust. It wasn't the church, that was for sure, nor perhaps will it ever become the church. But I heard the question that has driven this entire project, though unspoken because *no one of faith would dare consider it*: **What freedom would be available to women (and to men, non-binary as well) on the other side of forgiving the Divine for centuries of patriarchy?** I remember laughing aloud when I first spoke the question into a circle. Then again when I would repeat it to rightfully enraged women and women-identified human beings, queering and nonbinary folks. This question enlivened most every human being I encountered, except for the most conservative, who understandably have no context for it. Or have only defensive refusal of it, in addition to my own experiences as a woman-identified human being.

Re-reading my blog-writings, I gasped when I read the entry of my Shalem labyrinth encounter. I felt the energies in the room, in my body, heighten with wonder and awe, tenderness mercy and love. These were my own words, *clearly my own words* from four years ago, even though I had completely forgotten such an out-of-the-box but deeply-healing experience. But *I had received it in my body*, so the entire unfolding back in 2017 returned to my memory in full. I could smell the wild bergamot, flowering on the grounds. The dampish smell of the landscaped pond, with a sun-dappled bridge across it. This question of *forgiving the divine* is a completely offensive and incomprehensible one to ask most people of faith. Clearly it was one that kept returning for me until I allowed it to have me, until I surrendered into its purposes for me in sacred bewilderment. I was now a feminist with a forgiveness problem and a conscious feminine theologian weary of being in congregational settings, feeling the weight of righteous rage.

It Has Something to Do With Grief

I remember where I was that morning in June 2015, when the news of the murders splashed across North American newspapers. Crawfordsville, Indiana, co-leading a mid-career colloquy with a woman of African descent who served as at least a conference-level leader in the African Methodist Episcopal Church. She and I had had an uneasy working relationship as women across the Black-White wound in our country's history, in higher theological education, on the leadership team. She disappeared from the leadership team for a day or two, tending to her ecclesial responsibilities with the blessings of all of us. Yet even today, I can still feel the inability of either of us to truly see the other through our own vastly divergent racial wounds, so easily triggered. For our purposes here, what did those AME church members know, utterly inaccessible to us theological scholars, beginning to be explored by Matthew Ichihashi Potts? What did they know that makes absolutely no sense in our current, rage-drenched politics? Or in our highly professionalized, litigation-dominated settings, for that matter? In my nearly thirty years of higher theological education—whether in student, administrator, or professor roles—I cannot remember *one* time in which forgiveness has arisen as wise-practice in a collegial-communal setting. Not once. It has no place in professionalized ministry, it would seem, unless as a point of research, like in Potts's case. So you can imagine my surprise when *forgiveness* began to pop up into my awareness.

Potts invites his readers into a reconsideration of forgiveness that is *real*. Instead of a theological framework within which all must fit, he begins with the Mother Emanuel AME church survivors' "angry and grief-stricken words while also attending to the forms of forgiveness they say they have offered." He observes that these forms "reject hate but not anger," "deny superficial healing and forgetting," and "refuse unearned reconciliation."[11] He wants to ask "what a Christian forgiveness that rooted itself in grief would look like"[12] The forgiveness he begins to chart as *real* allows for anger, rage and grief. It actually *preserves* mistrust, keeping a safe distance for victims who may need it. Forgiveness in his alternative account acknowledges hurt rather than promising healing. It reckons

---

11. Potts, *Forgiveness*, 2.
12. Potts, *Forgiveness*, 3.

uniquely with the permanence of the wound, rather than hastily dressing that wound with a thin reconciliation.[13]

Ultimately, Potts proposes a theological defense of forgiveness rooted in *grieving*, evolved beyond classical and contemporary models that are economic or virtue-restorative. As such, forgiveness becomes a "refusal of retaliatory violence," a "forswearing of vengeance and rejection of retribution." It involves "accepting that what has been lost cannot be regained." It is "more broken-hearted than whole-hearted," "a strategy for surviving an irrevocable wrong." "Forgiveness is not reconciliation. . . . It may provide a first step to reconciliation, or it may simply occasion a lasting nonretaliatory estrangement."[14] It is a way "we learn to struggle with and through and in a loss we cannot redeem."[15]

Here is a contribution to my wrestlings and rage that I could begin to recognize, if not fully enter into as a feminist with a forgiveness problem. I could hear whispers of my own words, offered in lament within settings I could trust. The damage done is irrevocable . . . What I have lost can never be regained. . . . I am broken-hearted . . . For forty-five years, I did not know how deep the Love well went . . . If we listen to Potts's work, we can begin to make some sense of this fierceness for women, rage, but more importantly, *how to release the rage* for . . . something . . . ? It has something to do with grief. It has something to do with praise.

In these encounters—labyrinth and circle series—I was invited into an "other side" past rage and shame. A peace of mind and body found me, not depending upon the conditions of peace. Not depending upon whether any one in my faith communities got it or not, honored my experience or not, was curious about what I know to be Truth's superb surprise. Capacity for presence has been renewed for me in previously intolerable settings of neglect and hostility to who I am as a woman. I find myself more curious than reactive now in the extremities of emotion available to us as human beings. A gentle courage revisits me again and again, delving more deeply into the life that has been given me, regardless of how others perceive it.

The cauldron of rage within which I have known my sacred work remains. It simmers and occasionally spits out fire when the world pours its disregard of the F/feminine into my own small life. Most days, however, I find myself outside of the cauldron somehow, grateful for it, all.

13. Potts, *Forgiveness*, 5.
14. Potts, *Forgiveness*, 8.
15. Potts, *Forgiveness*, 10.

It has something to do with *forgiving the divine*. It has something to do with *forgiveness finding me* when I was not remotely interested in offering it to anyone, or receiving it from Anyone. Finally landing in wisdom community intent upon belonging, especially across our divisions today, I learned it has something to do with the wisdom of grieving that is praising, praise that is also grief. And within the same renewed and renewing Trinitarianism with which we began, it has something to do with God/de's *ontology of desire*, the concentration of desire—intensified and refined in this whole journey, shaped and being shaped into a cruciform offering/receiving. T. S. Eliot came barging back into my awareness: "With the drawing of this Love and the voice of this Calling / We shall not cease from exploration / And the end of all our exploring / Will be to arrive where we started / And know the place for the first time."[16] I now understand our entire lives are drenched with grief—and praise—when we are living into its fullness. I still have a lot to learn, however, about *how to grieve* within my own ancestral lineages of faith and family.

Grief Unveiled, Unveiling . . .

For years now, circle-way community regularly invited me to *grieve*, to discern *what sadnesses I was unwilling to feel*. Which is all fine and good, except I didn't know how to grieve or even what grieving looked like, felt like. Talk about beginner's mind. I have pockets of experiences when I have lost someone beloved to me: choral director and seminary organist, David Weadon; mentor and PhD advisor James Loder; my heart-dog Marley in 2017. But I presumed I'd not been initiated yet into grief. I thought grief was an invitation that would come to me eventually, but had not yet.

Unbidden if disconcerting, circle-companions would ask me gentling questions whenever my anger flared up into the center. *What sadness is there in your body? What have you been unwilling or unable to feel . . . yet?* So much so that I began to weave it into my classroom teaching. When the energies of the room would arise from a deep woundedness I could sense in the room—whether around race, gender, or progressivism from ex-Evangelicalism—I would gentle the room a bit with a pause, with silence, then tender the question: *What sadness is in your cells? What sadness have you been unable or unwilling to feel . . . yet?* The

---

16. Eliot, "Little Gidding."

entire learning environment would shift open. Curiosity and surprise would arise. Sometimes answers were spoken, but oftentimes, the energy shift was enough.

This meant my own learning journey shifted in unexpected directions, not ordained necessarily by power-over or authority-of-Scripture habits of mind/body, or in alignment with tradition or even belonging within Christian community. My human dignity mattered. My body was now the purveyor of wisdom in relationship with colleagues, students, circle-companions. Decades I was shaped in the assumption that anger was a sin. That forgiveness is a "seventy-times-seven" act of will as commanded by Jesus in Scripture. When I finally began to allow the sadnesses to be felt in my body, to come into *visceral awareness*, to allow my body to release them in whatever manner was offered me, *freedom entered into my cells too*. I wasn't consciously considering forgiveness at all.

But there began to be a lightness to my step, a calmness in my spirit, a peaceableness in my body *no matter what situation I found myself in*. I began to be able to enter into Christian sanctuary spaces again without feeling the raw pain and stinging salt-bath I'd known for years. I began to observe the behaviors and choices of my worshiping communities with more patience, without enraged malice. Their refusals of language that would honor women as women, for instance, no longer was the uphill battle that made any sense to me, that had defined liberal or progressive feminists for ages. Freedom had already come to me (largely) without that, after all. The triumphalistic theologies of Evangelical or Pentecostal preachers no longer (as easily) triggered my feminine abandonment or sensibilities of being unseen and unheard. I began to understand that my learning journey was such an essentially human one, regardless of how we may identify ourselves in the rages of the day. I began to belong to myself, in the Body of Humanity.

Unbeknownst and even unbidden, I was *grieving*. I was being shown *how to grieve* while living in an immediate family, civic, and ecclesial ecology utterly unskilled and unwise in *grief*. Life and forgiveness found me here. I had had no inkling how grief-drenched my entire life has been, if no less effusively drenched with *praise* too. When we lean into wonder, into bewilderment, a body-door can open. I began to re-appraise my sensibilities around *grief*. I could begin to see my unresolved griefs as what I had known only as a cauldron of rage. While they are not the same things, I've learned and continue to learn again and again: anger is unresolved grief; rage is unresolved *collective* grief.[17] They are intricately related, connected to our capacity to grieve, to surrender, to allow and receive.

Martin Prechtel's work and Francis Weller's *five gates of grief* provided me with the sense-making I needed to be able to see how completely drenched in grief my entire scholarly, ecclesial, vocational life has been. How also drenched in joys, lived but misunderstood as "creative renewal," which it *is*, but also something *more*. Julia Cameron had led me for decades into *creative renewal*—imaginative, artistic ways to resolve early childhood wounds, sensations of deep loss, sadnesses I would discover as I engaged her work, then so many others' written works as well.[18] Each was actually a pathway to grief being resolved and relearned consciously as praise, though I had absolutely no inkling this was the wisdom underneath it all. Awakening to the groundedness and freedom that comes in resolving grief, now within a renewed and renewing Trinitarianism offered to my body in God/de's ontology of desire, I am finally able to see more of the whole picture. More ways to see the complementary pieces I had needed in order to become articulate about the Force or Flow that has never let me go, Who breathes so deeply within me, Whom in my own forgiving-findings becomes Present again and again.

Martin Prechtel, Francis Weller, and Others

Prechtel was the first one to challenge all of my preconceived notions about grief, which is also praise, given I had been shaped for decades in ancestral, civic, and religious misunderstandings so prevalent today. "Grief is the sound of being alive," he observes. It "is an obligation to the life one has been awarded, an obligation to life to make more life."[19] I was first struck by the word "sound," because what I know as grief in my family *has no sound*. We speak rationally and within ancestral or elder sensibilities of reason. No one is to speak too abundantly about one's own creations or losses, for inherited fears of being shamed, disregarded as selfish.[20] Prechtel continues, "Necessary grief when shunned or unat-

---

17. Roberson, personal conversation.

18. Cameron, *Artist's Way*. See also Elsheimer, *Creative Call* and Millin, *Women, Writing, and Soul-Making*.

19. Prechtel, *Smell of Rain on Dust*, 5,3.

20. My generation of "the cousins" is getting better at this, demonstrated by the last family reunion. One invited each of us to share something of which we were proud, whether from work or family or daily life. But it had to be a *good enough brag*. Those too-self-demurring were challenged by the whole as *needing more brag*.

tended can easily hide for years, even generations, in the skeletal structure of the family collective psyche. Like light, matter, sound, and energy, grief will eventually manifest even among those in the future who did not consciously experience the loss."[21]

I began to wonder about the griefs of my grandparents, whether paternal or maternal in relation. I know my paternal grandmother yearned deeply to be a social worker when she graduated from college (a stunning act just as it was, for a woman of that era, age, in the 1920s). Her father could only imagine her as a school-teacher. Ruth being Ruth, she struck up a deal with him—whichever letter of offer arrived first. She wept bitterly when it was the invitation to teach. But what losses did she feel in her body? In her being? In *A Companionable Way*, I tell the story of my nearly-thousand-mile round-trip drive one July weekend to place a pomegranate at the gravestone of my great-grandmother, Elizabeth M. Musser Hess. The obvious reason my family could receive for my presence there was the memorial service of my father's cousin Wilmer, but I knew even before I left I was there for another purpose: to leave a pomegranate on her tombstone. I had been reading Sue Monk Kidd's *Traveling with Pomegranates*, a mother-daughter travelogue, concurrent to my conscious feminine leadership training. When the service began, I slipped out the side entrance to find Elizabeth M's tombstone. It was not as I had imagined at all—we were a simple farm people at that time, so she didn't have her own gravestone. Her name was listed under her husband's name, Abram Z, which erupted in me as rage. And tears. Unstoppable tears which for the first time, *did not feel like my own*. Yes, I was participating in this release, which my body needed as its own. Today, I wonder whether I was also brought there to weep on behalf of so many who no longer can, who lived through things I cannot imagine *without a sound*. Without any opportunity to be seen or heard in their pain, imposed shames, wounded ancestral lineage with the body. Who knows? My body knew what to do, until it could do so no longer. I returned to the memorial service, utterly changed inside, if inarticulate about it.

One cannot grieve that which one does not love. One does not know love—fully, deeply, searingly—unless one is willing to grieve. "Grief is a worker on life's big highways," suggests Prechtel, with "Praise [as] Grief's eternal freight train, forever hauling the vision of life's bigger picture from stars whose light hasn't got here yet, which Grief uses to refill the potholes of our losses."[22] Each relies upon a common currency

---

21. Prechtel, *Smell of Rain on Dust*, 4.
22. Prechtel, *Smell of Rain on Dust*, 6.

of Beauty. Each gives sound and form to "all parts of the world and universe, each living according to its own nature, each entire in itself, each a willing participle in the great prayer of praise singing the world back to life."[23] The task Prechtel ultimately identifies in their work together, their dance, is *singing the world back to life*.

In his poetry and in the prose that embodies each chapter of his book, Prechtel paints a portrait of grief intuitively obvious to me today but which remained conceptually incomprehensible for a long, long time. Grief is not disappointment, for instance, though when something or someone we love dies or disappears, we grieve. It is natural. As natural as "peeing, eating, singing, dreaming, running, or looking under rocks for bugs to feed your frog." Deferring or refusing grief is what has made our world so sick. He encourages us here: "To truly and freely grieve as an entire people can revive an entire culture just as much as it can bring back to life an individual." Grief takes many forms, across lineages and across cultures, but surprisingly, it is not sorrow. Some phases of grief are *sorrow-filled*, he argues, but "real grieving refuses to remain in sorrow." It is active, purposely done, movement. Grief is not depression either. "Depression comes from *not being able to grieve*, which converts our losses into violence." Most importantly, "grief thinks nothing of impossibility, only of what makes life more deliciously alive."[24] No one in my ancestral or faith lineages understands this intricate dance, this intimate one-ing of grief and praise singing the world back to life.

Francis Weller's *five gates of grief* then opened a much more expansive, if no less poetic way to understand how grief-drenched my life—our lives—have been, are today. The popularly assumed sense of the word *grief* tends to focus on the first gate alone: "the sorrow we experience with the loss of someone or something we love."[25] Here Weller equates sorrow with grief, but as you delve more deeply into his work, you see a deeper resonance with Prechtel's claim that they are not synonymous. Weller's gates include other ways to enter into grief consciously, seeing its ever-presence in human life, though it is the *second gate* that is most significant here, for my own story arc.

The other gates *do* give a sense of Weller's scope, however, beyond *sorrow* yet incorporative of it. The fifth gate acknowledges *ancestral grief*,

---

23. Prechtel, *Smell of Rain on Dust*, 6.
24. Prechtel, *Smell of Rain on Dust*, 3–6.
25. Weller, *Wild Edge of Sorrow*, 23.

what we carry in our bodies from losses experienced by our ancestors.[26] The fourth gate points to *what we expected and did not receive*. Grief arises naturally at that intersection.[27] The third gate overwhelms us, of course—*the sorrows of the world*—opening only when we become more cognizant and capable to enter into the sufferings of others. When we become globally aware, the grief can become extreme, particularly outraged, even violent in our overwhelm.[28] It is Weller's second gate that Michael Lerner observes is the most original contribution, for so many of us. "The first gate is known to us all," Lerner writes in the Foreword. "The second gate surprises us: *the places that have not known love*."[29] This was the gate into grief that broke open my own awarenesses about grief as an ever-present but hidden companion throughout my entire life. Our lives. Particularly Christianized lives steeped in historic tradition.

Weller describes this avenue into grief as any and all "places within us that have been wrapped in shame and banished to the farthest shores of our lives. We often hate these parts of ourselves, hold them in contempt, and refuse to allow them the light of day."[30] They are untouched by love, and "profoundly tender places precisely because they have lived outside of kindness, compassion, warmth, or welcome."[31] Brené Brown's decades of research into connection, wholeheartedness, vulnerability and shame gift us with some depth too. Brown defines shame as "the fear of disconnection." It's "the intensely painful feeling or experience of believing that we are flawed and therefore unworthy of love and belonging." She then challenges our predictable defenses with impish humor: "The things I can tell you about [shame]: It's universal. We all have it. The only people that don't experience shame have no capacity for human empathy or connection. No one wants to talk about it. And the less you talk about it the more you have it."[32] With that, in Weller's work, I saw how powerfully my ancestral lineage work is *second-gate-work*.

My family and faith lineages are doused in shame, apparent when anyone steps out of expectation, out of intellectual-philosophical-demurring norms, out of socialized congregational behavior. I know the look

26. Weller, *Wild Edge of Sorrow*, 63–69.
27. Weller, *Wild Edge of Sorrow*, 54–63.
28. Weller, *Wild Edge of Sorrow*, 46–53.
29. Lerner in Weller, *Wild Edge of Sorrow*, xiii.
30. Weller, *Wild Edge of Sorrow*, 31.
31. Weller, *Wild Edge of Sorrow*, 31.
32. Brown, "Power of Vulnerability."

of disdain and disbelief to use that will insure no shame comes *my* way. Let it land on someone else. We know the power-plays to become special in our communities and less vulnerable to being seen poorly, being unworthy. We know how to sit in our pews faithfully, making sure no one else knows about the things we hate or don't want others to know. Alana Levandoski and James Finley's teaching-song from *Sanctuary* played in my body's ear: "Do not perpetuate violence against the parts of yourself that need to be loved the most."[33] I have perpetuated my faith's, my family's, and my own violence against the parts of myself I feared the most. My body was wracked with shame from my earliest memories, crystallized in my awakening to desire when I was six years old. Desire was never spoken about openly, which meant my desire threatened my most intimate belonging. It was to be shunned from all conversation, discourse, at least until marriage, though after decades of shunning, so much damage was already done to hold the mysteries of desire well. My entire body experience had to go underground, embroiled in shame for decades. As Brown says, "The less you talk about it the more you have it." This entire book is *second-gate-work*.

Then Weller gentled me, my fears. "These neglected pieces of soul live in utter despair," he laments. "What we perceive as defective about ourselves, we also experience as loss. Whenever any portion of who we are is denied, we live in a condition of loss. The proper response to any loss is grief, but *we cannot grieve for something that we feel is outside the circle of worth*."[34] Walking through this second gate of grief has opened my heart, my mind, all because *my body* could withstand it all. Because I was awakened so early. Because my body was anointed into protection, a seal irradicable. Because I was abandoned so thoroughly, with rage driving the freight train at first. Rage was the only thing that had enough fire to get me where I needed to be—a labyrinth and then a community of deep witness exploring *forgiveness*.

Forgiving the Divine

Today, from this other side, I don't try to flatten or make theological sense of *forgiving the divine* in historic doctrinal terms or the highly polarized and fear-drenched politics that drive us into disembodied certainty,

---

33. Levandoski and Finley, "Do Not Perpetuate Violence."
34. Weller, *Wild Edge of Sorrow*, 31.

imposed from the past. None of this need *make sense to my mind* for me to receive its fruits and giftedness of belonging in my embodied spirit, en-spirited body. From my woman's body, I simply say that forgiveness is not as or what my tradition has espoused for centuries. Nor are we Christians the best ones on the planet to teach its hidden gifts. Forgiveness is not about reconciliation, though one can become more peaceably reconciled on the other side of rage. It is not a debt owed to God for how God has forgiven us. Nor do I find it to redeem suffering, or even worse, reimburse suffering in any classical Trinitarian logic. Economic and virtue-restorative understandings of this term have fostered more wounding in an already wounding world, using ancient scriptural texts to reify our thinking in that way. Forgiveness also has no necessary relation to positive, affective change.[35] It doesn't necessarily restore anything. Forgiveness doesn't even free us from the wounds of our past.

I remain thankful for voices that helped me find my way into this committed bewilderment, of course. The *fourfold path* so clearly practiced and then taught by Desmond and Mpho Tutu, for example: telling the story, naming the hurt, granting forgiveness, renewing or releasing the relationship.[36] Mary Hayes Grieco's book, whose title offended me in my rage: *unconditional forgiveness*. "Forgiveness is a private process that we do for our own sakes," she explains, "there is no experience of hurt, loss, betrayal, or disappointment that is beyond our power to heal and resolve."[37] She was the first one I encountered who systematically addressed the "big one" of *forgiving God*. "I believe that if your concept of God has failed you—if you are closing down instead of opening up when things are hard—it's time to 'fire' that particular version of God. Forgive it and send it packing. Then ask the Universe to show you a new concept that brings you forward—one that keeps you open and learning."[38] Grieco even provides a step-by-step practice for *forgiving God*.[39] Here was someone with whom I could be challenged to keep learning, even as I couldn't in my own integrity "just send Jesus packing." Jesus has been much more than a concept, given the visceral memories in my own body. But I have also now experienced the visceral truth of her work too. Then, Mark Umbreit spoke directly into my own resistance and rage, unlocking something I needed

35. Potts, *Forgiveness*, 7.
36. Tutu and Tutu, *Book of Forgiving*, 49.
37. Grieco, *Unconditional Forgiveness*, 1.
38. Grieco, *Unconditional Forgiveness*, 130.
39. Grieco, *Unconditional Forgiveness*, 135–36.

to hear: "And here lies the paradox of forgiveness, the mystery to which we stand in awe. The less said directly about forgiveness... the more likely many people choose to go there, entirely of their own volition."[40] A sensate image for what I was experiencing began to form.

If anything, this forgiveness that has found me is more like a *salvific peripheral vision* than anything directly articulate, visible, demonstrable. You know how you can see things peripherally that when you try to look at them directly, they vanish? Best I can "define" forgiveness-findings for now is like that. Today I can see that forgiveness, however else it may come to be defined, has freed me again and again to see and sense God/de indirectly, again and again, amidst excruciating pain and irrevocable loss. I have been shown in such indirect-seeings some futures more free and hopeful than anything I could have imagined in the direct-sight aims I or we impose upon our world(s). It is my hope that these words can contribute a compelling here-and-now way to reconsider forgiveness anew, at least for enraged, wounded human beings persistently refused and denied by people of faith, by visible institutional expressions of the church.

This expression of forgiveness, guided by Matthew Potts, allows for anger, rage and grief. It acknowledges hurt rather than promising healing or reconciliation. It allows space and time to "preserve mistrust" and "keeping a safe distance" for the victims of injury. Most importantly, it reckons uniquely with the permanence of the wound rather than dressing it too hastily for the easing of others (most often, the wound-ers). As such, I still consider myself a feminist, a woman steeped in the conscious feminine, even if I am willing to relinquish the word *feminism* with its roots in the wounds of power-over structures and history. In this healing journey of forgiveness finding me, I am no longer anti-anything, per se. "Healed persons are not anti-anything, they are *for something*,"[41] came the teaching. I have now lived into it long enough to know this truth in my own flesh and bones. Stunningly simple: I am for the utter dignity of all human beings[42]—all earthly beings, actually—and for a renewed and renewing way of healing ourselves—always only one heart at a time—by covenanting into practices of community in the Body of Humanity that celebrates the individual voice but not at the expense of our earth,[43] of our most proximate beloveds.

40. Umbreit et al., *Energy of Forgiveness*, xiv.
41. Roberson, personal conversation.
42. Riley, *This Here Flesh*, 3–15.
43. Brosmer, *Women Writing for (a) Change*, 7.

Personal Healing into Collective or Social Forgiveness

My fierceness for the well-being of women (and women-identified human beings) has only strengthened in my awakening, in my rage resolving. I've also not *left* religious traditionalism(s) behind, though many of my most conservative brothers (and sisters) will surely believe I have. Because I do not accord much sacred authority in the ways we have in the past, which has become intolerably stale in a viscerally present relationship with God/de. My feminist continues to cherish her forgiveness problem, it would seem, though now it is less a problem and more a mystery. Not unlike *forgiving the divine*. Our current theological formulations have no space nor any willingness to even begin to consider this phrase, yet it held the key for everything that is offered here.

Re-shaping forgiveness as *salvific peripheral vision*, as *something that finds us when we're ready to heal* gives my body oxygen amidst the polarized, wounding disputes all around me. I am reminded again and again, in surrender if with impish smiles: not everyone is interested, willing, or ready to take responsibility for their own healing journey into a more expansive sense of faith, hope and love than their current body could withstand. This journey has required every conceptual, emotional, spiritual and embodied tool—gifts, really—given to me as a deep-feeling woman, in a remarkably beloved and wounded family lineages with elders who yet could find a way to stay in relationship with me amidst the years that terrified them. Now into the years that simply bewilder them. See how we're learning? All I can do is testify that there is a freedom on the other side of rage and forgiveness both. It is available to each and every one of us enraged embodied-souls, mired in ancestral-wounded lineages, yearning for new maps of love and better ways of gathering as human beings able to listen deeply and make healthier decisions *together*. Not without pain. Not without injury. But now—at least in my own life and my proximate spaces—with deepening intention and skill to grieve the losses that are irreconcilable, even irredeemable. My body, rooted in the ontology of God/de's desire, knows there is freedom here on this other side of all sides.

Any practical implementation could seem impossible, or at least implausible. I get that. But a first implementation of it all arose near the ending of this writing, unexpectedly, as the president of my seminary got emotionally-spiritually hammered by bishops in one of the UMC Conferences, who clearly have unresolved grief, even wildly projected rage directed at him, at all of us, because we love and serve with *those who left* the denomination. In our small faculty community that day, we asked then listened then wrote and edited our best estimate for how to live into this *forgiveness findings* wisdom so unexpected for any of us, not least of all *me*. The first statement draft was mine, with all the poetry I desired. The final statement, strengthened for its purposes by being cut in half, was approved unanimously by the seminary faculty—clearly an act of God/de, as this group rarely does anything unanimously. It is uploaded to the seminary website for "protecting the learning environment for all."[44] The first day we even considered drafting anything, the words nearly wrote themselves.

The practices to which we've committed together focus on long-standing, even cross-traditional wisdom aimed at disrupting our world's familiar *forces of unforgiveness* with forbearance, a willingness to listen, a willingness to catch ourselves in wounded narratives, and shared learning toward the encouragement and support of institutional integrity without political retaliation. William Bole, Drew Christiansen, SJ, and Robert T. Hennemeyer define *forces of unforgiveness* as cycles of revenge, distorted memories, victimhood, and institutional breakdown.[45] Cycles of revenge are self-explanatory in all areas of violent conflict around the world. Their volume highlights Northern Ireland, Yugoslavia, Bosnia, but one could immediately remember Israel-Palestinian Territories, Rwanda and more. Distorted memories are those that continue to fuel the cycle of revenge, often by fostering a collective story of victimization that becomes what is called a *mytho-history*, "a distorted memory retrieved and recycled for use in a current confrontation."[46] Recycled memories like this "typically 'forget' aspects of their own history that do not conform to images of vicitimization and might actually fit the profile of an aggressor."[47] What to do with enemies then, with whom we must unavoidably live in proximity?

Donald Shriver's work wrestles with this question writ-large in global and ecclesial politics, leaning toward the possibilities of social or collective forgiveness in our world today. He too acknowledges the double-edged sword of memory, its necessity yet unavoidable danger too. "Pain can sear the human memory in two crippling ways," he writes, "with forgetfulness

---

44. United Theological Seminary, "To Protect the Learning Environment For All."
45. Bole et al., *Forgiveness in International Politics*, 11–29.
46. Bole et al., *Forgiveness in International Politics*, 15.
47. Bole et al., *Forgiveness in International Politics*, 16.

of the past or imprisonment in it. The mind that insulates the traumatic past from conscious memory plants a live bomb in the depths of the psyche... But the mind that fixes on pain risks getting trapped in it. Too horrible to remember, too horrible to forget: down either path lies little health for the human sufferers of great evil."[48] The context for his words was the Shoah, the Holocaust within twentieth-century history, but two decades ago within these United States, Shriver proleptically laments the forces of unforgiveness so apparent today. Cycles of revenge. Memories distorted by intergenerational wounds and mytho-histories of inherited pain, stories of victimization and the apparent decline of institutions. He asks wearily, as do I, "Will the planet earth ever host a species who, by a great majority, will gladly say, "We are all humans?"[49]

This work of allowing forgiveness to find me, to find us, continues to unfold with excruciating difficulty and "pockets of possibility"[50] that yet give me hope. The practices to disrupt the forces of unforgiveness are recognizable in most wisdom traditions, but for me, they are visible within some of Jesus's most neglected, radical teachings. Practicing forbearance in mercy. Learning to listen ever more deeply amidst rage-sadness-pain, getting curious of others' stories while drenched in our own "side." Placing ourselves in multiple communities—forming and unforming as the Body of Humanity—so to have our stories mirrored, in hopes of catching ourselves in any distorted memories, stories of victimization. Finally, learning to reconnect with institutions—even in their decline and perceived de-evolutions—so to honor our elders and support reconnected lineages for future generations. Here lives this paradox of forgiveness finding me in purely proximate practice, no longer resisted but surrendered into a larger Flow and Force in nonattached impassioned hope for collective renewal into new life. Bemused am I that it has been my inability to avoid over twenty years of resistance to *being a preacher's wife* that brings this all home.

---

48. Shriver, *Ethic for Enemies*, 119, cited in Bole et al., *Forgiveness in International Politics*, 17–18.
49. Shriver, *Ethic for Enemies*, 5.
50. Palmer, "Thirteen Ways of Looking at Community," vii.

Chapter Six

The Teaching No One Wants: Surrender

BECOMING A PREACHER'S WIFE over twenty years ago offers an impossible teaching I did not want to learn, but which has probably saved my life: *surrender*. None of us actually *wants* to learn it. I say it's impossible because it lives and breathes underneath ego, language, and social norms in a power-over history we've so deeply ingested. Especially people of faith know to say we're surrendering all to God when we are actually grasping the most. Surrender awaits us, hidden underneath things we prefer like agency, will, even our own desire. Not unlike the Void, surrender vanishes as soon as one speaks it aloud. Nothingness cannot be discussed or described in words, in cognitive substance. Neither can surrender. Even worse, for a conscious feminine theologian, for a feminist with a forgiveness problem, *surrender* looks like the antimatter of awakening.[1] Yet it remains part of the unspoken force that unlocked the freedom I now know, that I had to be shown over years, accompanied by the Body of Humanity, accompanied by wisdom elders consciously outside my frameworks of expertise.

    I had intended this chapter to be a gentle-truth-in-love offering for congregations today, naming the ways in which we've co-created congregational Christianity as costly for all involved—pastor-preacher, beloved, disempowered congregational members. Some of that may happen, in Spirit's tether. But even as late as all that, I had not fully surrendered because there was some energy in me to *teach them a lesson*. That would be the voice of my pain, my sadness, resolving but not resolved. More germane to the flow of the story here, even more amusing, is the

---

1. See Coakley, *Powers and Submissions*.

deeper purposes here: a prolonged demonstration of a *refusal* of surrender, which is really the only sure human way to see or hear it. As that became clear to me, I couldn't help the belly laughter here too. In a role unsought, unchosen, imposed, and undesired by me, I get to grieve and praise the depth of covenantal love I now know, and the main characteristics of surrender by which Spirit has room to breathe in our bodies despite our wills, strategic sensibilities, and resistances.

I can now see things I hadn't noticed before, for instance. Being a preacher's wife is how I first encountered a forgiveness finding me, even when I was not looking for it.[2] Unchosen, the role has taught me the power of choice, always in diverse discernment. Imposed, it has shaped in me an empathy for the (un)conscious impositions of others. Undesired, it has taught me about raw intimacy and the depth of covenant across differences of many kinds. Silent for decades, my preacher's wife voice has finally come forth in the power of story, always seeking the larger Story within which another voice can be welcomed, challenged, even sometimes bounded *so to grow* toward deeper spiritual resilience and grounded, embodied faith. Honoring the deep inner work it has taken to say it aloud, I can today bow to the exquisite purpose of this role in my life, chosen for me if not by me. *Because* I am learning more about its roots in surrender, I am receiving my own small place in the divine order of things, which mysteriously grants a largeness within my own body that has become so very blessed.[3]

Surrender-Refused Can Be Seen in Resistances

Most pastoral-rabbinic-spouses don't have the melodramatic wrestlings I have had with it over the years, though I *do* come by my struggles honestly. They have served sacred purpose, in other words. Gender roles in the pursuit of ordained ministry were already a minefield of academic and ecclesial challenges in my own seminary formation. Back then, arguably still true today, congregations rarely sought women candidates to fill their own pulpits. When they did, congregants would impose old stereotypes of "preacher's wives" upon them, with presumptions of subordination and inferiority. Congregations are simply not practiced at welcoming a woman's particular gifts for ordained ministry, even as

---

2. As recounted in Hess, *Companionable Way*, "Grounded in Exile."
3. Kidd, *Book of Longings*, 13.

women need to stand in their own power regardless of congregational desires. All this is further complicated by women-candidates' socialized need to *learn to lead like a man*. Most often, a straight white man with a wife and kids.[4] I joked in chapter 3 that I was "my father's son for over forty years." Not surprisingly, then, I swore throughout all my graduate school years that I would *never* become a preacher's wife. And to my credit, I *did* get engaged to an attorney.

So why the melodrama and the struggles? Over the decades, I've had to learn a vastly different way of being alongside my husband's role and world, quite foreign to who I am as a conscious feminine leader *or* a feminist. Honoring his vocation meant holding my tongue when I felt the need to speak. His pastoral calling had vastly different norms and expectations than my academic one. Often he and I would get caught in the cross-hairs of our academic and ecclesial settings, having to resolve institutional or congregational tensions somehow between the two of us first. Since being a preacher's wife is a role I never chose for myself, *never* would have chosen for myself, there has regularly been a deeply felt-sense of *in*authenticity. Of being made small by a congregational body unable or unwilling to receive anything more than socialized expectation. Its systemic influences were out of my reach, with no apparent relationship to my desires at all. This often left me with intimate scars and no communal recourse, which neither my beloved nor I would have wished on me, on us. Still, this is the voice in my economic trinity that can ultimately speak most gently about the choiceless choices we make in covenantal love, with a spouse and a congregation. She can speak to the rawness of intimacy within the complicated dynamics of congregational presumption and life. In the end, my hope is that you can catch a glimpse of *surrender's wisdom* amidst my resistances and refusals. Not unlike Brené Brown describes her struggle with vulnerability, my journey with surrender has been a twenty-"year long street-fight." It's been "a slug-fest." Surrender "pushed, I pushed back. I lost the fight, but probably won my life back."[5]

---

4. For my contexts of Presbyterian Church USA.
5. Brown, "Power of Vulnerability."

Surrender Is Unchosen Yet Assuring

No one *consciously chooses* surrender, no matter how faithfully they may aspire to it or even claim to. I particularly dislike the romanticization of *surrender* in contemporary Christian music. For my part, if it's not a streetfight, it's not actually something you're alive enough inside to care about. Therefore, it's quite significant here that I did not consciously choose my role as preacher's wife. My first love from college days contacted me via email shortly after my Comprehensive Exams in grad school, to ask about joining the Presbyterian Church close to his home in St. Paul, Minnesota. One thing led to another, and a renewed romance sparked into a holy Fire between us. Several months later, Brian arrived so to spend Thanksgiving weekend with me. I wanted to show him some of my sacred spaces, including the walking paths at the Institute for Advanced Studies and the historic Quaker meetinghouse that had become a spiritual home for me ("rebuilt in 1679"). On the path, my first-and-renewed-love, my attorney friend from the Twin Cities, proposed a life together, marriage. I said an enthusiastic *yes*. We then sat on the meeting house steps, calling our parents on his new firm's cell phone. I got engaged to an attorney on Thanksgiving Day, happier than I ever knew I could be.

The next morning, we went for a walk on the canal paths behind my seminary apartment. We were aflush with an old-new love, with assured commitment, needing to plan how this was all going to work with him in Minnesota and me in New Jersey. The obvious choice was for me to move to Minnesota where he had a good paying job and I could finish my dissertation without a job. Except we got to talking about how he had applied to seminary right out of college, never going because there was no community around him to confirm any call. He daringly floated for the first time, "I could come to seminary while you finish your dissertation."

I remember being viscerally startled, stunned even. I stopped us on the path and looked at him in my surprise. I saw a light in his eyes, his face softening, almost to a glow. I am an intuitive and an educator, so those parts of me, fully devoted to him as my life-partner now, went running with the idea neither of us had ever spoken to one another. *He could come to seminary,* moving our lives into one *here*. It was so obviously the right path. He was so happy to consider diving into theological studies. I wasn't thrilled with staying on the East Coast, which I named aloud to him, but it *was* familiar to me by now, after seven years. I could see the logic of it all. We probably enjoyed a bottle of wine to toast the entire plan.

Until 3 a.m. when I woke up, *angry*. Only then did I realize I had gotten engaged to an attorney but *now I was marrying a seminary student*. I felt trapped. Furious. Afraid in a way I had not been fearful before. I was unable to disregard that it still felt the right pathway for him and for me, but now . . . there was an outside chance I was going to become *a preacher's wife*. I woke him up in my quiet fury, insisting we go to the 24-hour Dunkin Donuts.

Over twenty years later, clearly I did not leave him for becoming a seminary student. What woman in love would do that? I didn't like it for *me*, but I loved how it enlivened and fed him. I loved beginning our marriage together as two graduate students with the remains of his legal career finances and my own administrative work to support us. Besides, we had time and space to delve into theological studies and life passions. He wasn't sold on congregational ministry yet, so perhaps it was all just my own fear, I reasoned. Then I was stunned, deeply touched, when Brian willingly advocated for my professional path first, his own secondarily. "Academic jobs are harder to come by than other jobs," he rationalized. We had not focused on any particular calling for either of us, at this point, so again, who knew what would happen?

Feeling into it, knowing what I know today, I'm struck by the characteristics of surrender writ large into our lives in this moment of covenantal origin. For me, it came as utter delight in seeing the awakening of desire and purpose in someone I love, only later, becoming fear then fury in how it might affect me. I've learned to look for—sense into—awakening of desire and then accompanying fear or fury. Surrender made me feel trapped, powerless, because it required the relinquishment of my own power, alone, so I thought. The situation may confirm the path forward as the discerned, sacred one, but the fear and sense of suffocation don't go away with that discernment. Reason can also undergird surrender, as my beloved embodied in his own surrender to my (then undesired, unexpected) academic calling. It also doesn't remove the sense of uncertainty in the least. I've often wondered what kind of professor my beloved Brian could have been in this life. A stunning one, I suspect, as he can make history come so alive you can *smell the people*. His fear of a two-academic-calling and his own desire to *teach within a congregation* eventually led him to his own surrender, in my view. When I wonder aloud about *what could have been*, he is quick to change the subject. Surrender is an intimate thing, with tinges of fear and a need to belong, to be about shared purpose. It can be entered into in faith, and then discerned anew as life changes.

Surrender becomes sacred when it leads into feeling a part of something larger, whether it's shared purpose or something more mysteriously sacred. Brian and I were blessed with this bookended-assurance of our unchosen choices. The Saturday after we had gotten engaged in 1999, Brian and I visited some seminary friends who were living in Pennsylvania, serving as a clergy-couple at a church there. They now had two small children and a busy pastoral life, co-pastoring. It was a lot of new people for Brian, for both of us. To regain our intimate balance, he and I took some time for ourselves, driving to a local park they recommended, not far from their home.

It was nestled between three hills or small mountains, a sunken lake with a variety of spots to park, to walk to the water's edge. We parked and walked out to the water, soaking in the dusk twilight. A mist had come in, making the whole valley closed in by low clouds. We noticed a pair of swans in our little inlet of the lake, bringing us to quiet speech about our soul totem. Swans mated for life. "Ugly ducklings" made beautiful by discovering they were swans. I had found a Celtic ring of swans when in Scotland, shortly before we'd gotten engaged: a feminine rendition of the mythological Norns, with one swan looking backward, one swan with head bowed to the present, the third swan looking ahead. Past, present, future.

Then we saw another pair of swans, then another. An entire flock of maybe 40–50 swans took off from the far side of the lake, flying around the lake, passing over us again and again. They circled and circled, unwilling to fly into the clouds that enclosed us all.

Brian and I were stunned, both of us moved to tears.

"Did you see that?" he asked me.

"Yes, I saw it too," I whispered.

We had never seen so many swans in one place, ever or since.

We embraced. We kissed for a long time before we returned to all the people who would come into our shared life together. Complicated and complicating of our covenantal belonging.

Recently, just as I was beginning to come to voice as the preacher's wife that I am, I was looking for a pair of pearl earrings. I wanted to accessorize the fancy-formal dress I would wear as Brian's "plus-one" at the wedding he would officiate, the reception we would attend that night. I startled at the gold ring of the Norns, resting on the jewelry-bag fabric. I had not worn it for well over a decade. I smiled, remembering the overwhelming number of swans, the sign or seal, the veil that had blessedly covered us both all these years. A Celtic rendering with swans of an ancient feminine mythology, companioning a preacher's calling.

How appropriate, I thought, putting on the ring. Because now I know, in a settled freedom in my own belly: when we live purposefully and consciously into our own best lives, we will find that we get what we need. We can surrender into the unsought, learn a deeper intimacy in the undesirable, honor the personhood of those who (un)consciously impose upon us. All of us really are participating in patterns socialized into us, offering only what we know, so often without malice or ill intention at all. All of us have been shaped so to refuse our own pain, to project it outward onto whomever we can get to hold it. That cannot continue to be our most humane *way*. It never has been. As a preacher's wife with a conscious feminine theologian and feminist at her back, I can offer some invitation to those who will listen into deeper spiritual maturity,[6] as uncomfortable as it may be sometimes.

Surrender Is Undesired yet Intimate

Undesired, my role as a congregational spouse has taught me all I did not want to learn about raw intimacy in covenantal commitment, marriage being only one kind of covenant in play, I belatedly learned. It is a beautiful thing to fall in love, to find that love reciprocated in lifelong commitment. I am fortunate to still know that beautiful thing today, with the same man. But as David Schnarch says, *intimacy is not for the faint of heart.*[7] We imagine we'd like to see the love letter from a lifelong partner, offering the breadth and depth of intimacy for which human

---

6. For definition of *spiritual maturity*, I rely on Maggie Ross: "Spiritual maturity is not an option: it is our coming to be, our confluence with God, self, and community in ungrasping, eucharistic engagement. . . . We move from dependence to independence to interdependence. . . . We no longer mistake individuality for authenticity. . . . We are able to live in ambiguity without leaning on props or propositions. We have deepening love for Scripture and symbol and liturgy, but realize that they are feeing us only so that we may go into the desert and wait, watching in the dark. . . . We recognize that there is suffering that will come to us that must not be avoided but embraced and lived through, that there is suffering that we must hand ourselves over to in order to continue to mature." *Pillars of Flame*, 188–91.

7. Schnarch, *Passionate Marriage*, 100.

beings *were made*. Raw honesty in such a letter would rarely be see-able today *as love*. Our most intimate partners know us like no other, ways we want to be seen, but more importantly, ways we do *not* want to be seen or even know ourselves. While we are much more drawn—seduced by—the flashy notions of romantic love, hot sex, affirmations from our partner and confirmations in who we are, as we are, grounded love is deeper than all that. Raw intimacy is the stuff of crucibles, the stuff of excruciating spiritual maturation or refused growth; pain held in deep ambiguity while growth is refused until finally . . . usually after much suffering by both . . . it is no longer refused. Schnarch's work highlights this deepening of intimacy naming the power of self-differentiation *concurrent with* emotional commitment to the relationship as the holy fire of true intimacy. Letting yourself be seen in your growing edges or unpalatable aspects you've not figured out yet. Staying with your partner even as s/he/they do something you'd wished they'd not done. Loving them fully as they become someone you did not know they would become when you committed to life with them. Another one of Schnarch's quips is that no one is ready for marriage. *Marriage* makes you ready for marriage.[8] True intimacy is also expressly *theological* in my view because its shape resembles the shape of God/de's love for each of us: being deeply seen and heard, known warts-flaws-foibles and all, and *loved anyway*. Pure grace. Unearned but so deeply desired, to be loved *just as we are*. We impose our own societal-familial norms on one another, then call those *God*, or God's church. Necessary structurally, but eternally differentiated, known as such when becoming strong enough to mature into the realities we did not choose but can now welcome as grace-filled, purposeful.

But what is this intimacy supposed to mean when your marriage covenant is *not the only covenant in play*? Religious leaders enter into contractual arrangements with their congregations, interpreted scripturally and theologically as *covenant*. Every pastoral-rabbinic spouse will recognize what needs to be asked or named next. When push comes to shove in a shared life, *which covenant takes priority*? Each of us is a human being, living in time, particularly a time with strong senses of causation and linear order of importance. Which covenant is *more* sacred? How do these covenantal commitments coexist in the light-and-shadow of human relational dynamics, stretched into relationships with over ten, twenty, fifty, a hundred, or a thousand people?

---

8. Schnarch, *Passionate Marriage*, 2.

These questions arose again and again over these twenty years. I have had various lenses through which I could try to navigate Brian's congregational calling amidst my visceral awareness of abandonment by my family, church, and God. I even wrote (an unpublished) "Open Letter from Wife to Mistress Church" upon his tenth anniversary at one church. I was doing the best I could, but it was utterly drenched in little but rage and woundedness. When he had to choose his church over our agreed-upon-time-together, I would get enraged, feeling abandoned. Which served its sacred purpose, at times, as his fear of my rage would counterbalance his natural assumption of duty-to-many-others before duty to *one*. A natural inclination, of course, which he denied verbally, always expressing his primary commitment to me. Which I did not believe, because it would arise so often, this conflict of plans we made and the actual plans that were possible alongside a congregational need. I no longer find this framing of church as mistress redemptive, though it was necessary for me to name at the time. It *did* demonstrate that the ambiguity in this multiplicity of covenants has been incredibly costly to me over the years. To Brian as well, if in different fashion, alongside his utter love of what he gets to do as an installed pastor of a congregation.

For those unfamiliar with the communal dynamic, allow me a basic description, from my experience. The life of a congregational spouse is peppered with what might be called *microaggressions*, the unconscious slights and impositions of presumption arising out of the congregant's desires and assumptions more than the spouse's own personhood, identity, or desires.[9] You are constantly unseen and unheard as primarily yourself. You become a functional vessel for the pastor or rabbi. An unavoidable stand-in or strawman (woman, in this case). People make you privy to whispered medical diagnoses or gossip-mongering "to tell the pastor or rabbi." Friendship overtures come that are simply (un)conscious means to get close to the pastor or rabbi, often a father-figure upon which projections of safety and security land. There can also be a presumption of free leadership and hospitality tasks to support the congregation, regardless of propriety, giftedness or desire of the spouse. The famous stereotype for small Christian communities with a preacher's wife (not husband, for some reason) is leading the bell choir, which someone in Brian's first church *did* suggest to him that I should do. After

---

9. Sue, *Microagressions in Everyday Life*. See also Merrit and Fenimore, *Wounded Pastors*.

sharing his hesitation to even tell me—"You'll only get angry," he said—we both laughed aloud. I probably did feel anger.

These are the mundane, daily slights that you learn to stomach. Or you leave your marriage. Many marriages under the strain of congregational dynamics *do* break under such burden. These are the ways in which a calling into congregational leadership imposes its priority in your own life and choices. Actions will always be decided looking through the screen of congregational perception and congregational reaction. Whether you want to or not, you begin to make unconscious and conscious choices to not speak, to avoid possible reactivities, or to simply *not be there*. Which is the strategy I chose earliest on in Brian's ministry at a smaller-city church. These smallish slights cannot hold a candle to the daunting challenges that are no less unlikely.

For myself, I got manhandled at the after-worship coffee hour by the head deacon of his first church, with few to little personal or communal resources by which to redress the inappropriate behavior. We then lived with the splinter in our marriage because it was unresolvable as pastor-husband and clergywoman-wife. Who gets priority when the economics of the job requires the regular imposition of congregational priorities over marital or family ones? It took us over four years to figure out how to resolve that one. Blessedly, the entire narrative was one of the first instances of *forgiveness finding me*, which I detail in my previous book as the invitation to "Grounding in Exile," in *A Companionable Way*. I no longer paper over the excruciating pain and cost upon us both from that collision of old-boy religion with my woman's body. These things happen all the time in socialized, largely (un)conscious civic-religion norms favoring those with positional power. Spouses have little to no voice in any ecclesial system to redress them without feasibly dire consequences to the leader and his/her/their congregational relationships.

Even with all my standings and titles, however, I learned to rarely exercise any of those in the vocational life of my husband. Undesired, this role was not mine, I reasoned, though I did want to honor his own calling in every way that I could, with integrity in my own awakenings. This meant our lives had to have an autonomy and differentiation we *grew into* because of his congregational calling. If you're not conscious and intentional about choosing *your own life*, independent of all of them, you can begin to live your life as secondary to the pastoral calling, his/her work, the needs of the congregation over your own. Which I have fallen into, from time to time, even with my own professional identities and responsibilities. In the role undesired, you develop an excruciating sensitivity to the impositions of others into your most intimate life. It was an easy additive to my well-developed rage and fierceness for women at the time, even though it had given me a taste of forgiveness-findings.

Ironically, both freedom to live into your own life and empathy are born here in surrender to an undesired role, again usually without intention or will. Given who I am, I honestly don't think I would have faced up to the ways I needed to grow in my feminine self, *but for* the challenges I could not avoid *because* of my love for, my life with, my beloved. For one, I grew up as the second daughter of two in a loving faithful family in small-town Ohio. There were lots of gifts in this for me, but it did shape me in being habitually *unable* to *say what I wanted* or *needed*, for *myself*. People who know me today usually express surprise at this. I can be quite outspoken. Rarely if it were *only for me*, however. I wanted to be in Blue Birds, but my older sister's choices were the ones easiest for my family to accommodate. I wanted to join 4H and learn how to care for horses. My family valued academics and music, so I learned piano and became good in school. I learned early on to mimic the desires and needs of those who would keep me safe, which would offer me the attention and the side effects of parental approval for success. But there were so many things I wanted to do that were different, that were regularly inaccessible or simply not supported. Again, I observe this of my beloved family without malice at all. They couldn't hear me, true, but I also couldn't name what I really wanted, even when I was asked. Long-ingested shame silences even awareness of desire.

Blessedly, if painfully, being a preacher's wife forced me to *choose my own life* again and again. Often it would take getting so angry that I simply didn't f***king care how Brian or the congregation might feel about it. But step by step, I began to choose my own life, especially through the creative renewal tasks and hobbies in which I could feel the oxygen of curiosity, spontaneity, playfulness and fun. This led to fun hobbies, then blog writing, then, finally, a circle of women writers with whom I could write stories I'd never told anyone before. A bridge was being built to an entire life *outside of congregational life*, just for *me*. Surrounded by these circles of women, I had a counterbalancing force to the human collective that ran my husband's life, our shared life together. For many of these years, I simply relinquished our physical-emotional home to his life, *his* collective, because it was easier. It wasn't until the COVID lockdown that I was forced to re-integrate all of my life into our own home—all of my

F/feminine, all of my circles, all of my spirit-friendships—regardless of how difficult or easy it would be for him.

It was the undesired role that invited his own surrender then, which ultimately strengthened our covenant together, on this side of things. I did not enter into the community-formation work with Women Writing for any reason associated with my marriage or my job. If anything, it was my attempt to provide an exit ramp from my job, and at a couple points, perhaps our marriage. So while in many ways I had "left" the congregational structure behind in my own wisdom-walking way, it was precisely that structure/analogy that could communicate deeper learning for my pastoral-husband. Finally, in an organizational trope he as an Enneagram Six could feel and understand: *I had my own congregation that was persistently coming first in my life.* He became a "pastor's spouse" to the WWfaC community work I was doing. And he began to understand, in his body and in his spirit, even if in his mind he thought he had always been choosing me first. Faced with the realities of "my" congregation of women's circles, he then began to make different choices in his own vocational life. Because I had begun to choose my own life, I became more able to name what I needed and how, which gave him ways to meet me there. He and I began to work more collaboratively together on a *shared life*. I was not just tolerating or avoiding his vocational life, nor was he begrudgingly tolerating or avoiding mine.

Which is where empathy grew, cultivating it as we were, unaware. The mutual surrender embodied in Brian's and my stumbling into separate yet linked vocations could be argued as quite costly. It has cost both of us a lot. Slowly, and with some occasional help from the larger Body of Humanity, we began to empathize with one another's costs, with one another's injuries not deserved, unbidden, yet seemingly unavoidable in how congregational Christianity is co-created today. Was it the resistance that was costly? Or the surrendering? Yes. Our entrance into an academic and a congregational calling taught us both the power of choice in choicelessness, trust in devotion to One Whom I can now name God/de, he would say God, lived out with each other. Raw intimacy is rarely what we say we want, but I have found it to be the most powerful in the healing and intergenerational work Spirit has seemed to be about with me, with us. It's the stuff of crucibles, to be sure, but also new life. Brian and I like to joke together that we've been married three times now, each to the other, necessary when one of us has grown or changed so much that it required a "new" marriage between us.

Surrender is Silent Until It Isn't

Until recently, the phrase *preacher's wife* gave me a place to put all of this abandonment pain endured over the years. The unsought, unchosen, undesired role of "helpmate" within an institution that I have experienced as abandoning women for millennia sort of summarized everything I detested about congregational Christianity. But seeing it as *a role* formalized it somehow. I could keep all of this at arm's length, almost like it's not personal *to me*, or even *at me*, so it's not *mine*. A part of me that was not of my choosing, therefore not of my authentic life or self. Then I began to see that it was this very *unavoidable* dynamic and role that required me to choose my own life, even come to voice as the woman I am, in covenant with the one I love. I began to see how twenty years of unchosen service embodied devotion, as I had learned it. These twenty years could seriously be construed as active waiting, being attentive for whatever God/de might offer, which had funded faith from seminary onward in me. In the heat of the awakening and abandonment years, one of us would ask the other, *Why do you stay?!?* usually through quietly gritted teeth. Neither of us had a logical response. Only an action. Devotion. Active waiting. Staying. Even the most shadowy-dynamic we humans create can be used for transformative purpose, if devotion holds and the active waiting of prayer breathes in your body long enough.

Being a preacher's wife unfortunately makes you an easy mark for congregants' dysfunctional attachments and refusals of their own spiritual growth. I cannot count the numbers of times well-meaning human beings have projected things they wished were not true about their *own* lives onto my life instead, my deepening capacity to make choices for myself. Such persons fault *you* for things you never did or said. If you're not careful, you can become a lightning rod of a whole slew of (un)conscious baggage that congregational religion harbors, organized as it is today. Long-term members especially feel no consequence, as they know the pastoral spouses won't speak transparently, at least not without the aforementioned economic and relational threat to the pastor and his/her congregational relationships. All of these things—small and large—shape a religious-leader's life without any care or concern for *anything* the spouse may need or desire. The contract, named in covenantal terms, is with the leader, not the spouse. The spouse rarely has any independent voice in the leader's ecclesial systems, and no direct agency at all. Leaders today are not positioned amidst the financial risks so to help their congregations learn of their own shadows, given the voluntarist arrangements of faith communities. The desires and needs of a pastoral spouse are hardly ever considered, systemically.

What made the difference for me in my own coming to Voice as the preacher's wife I am is because I had a clergywoman's presbytery resources and the standing of a full professor in a theological seminary. A situation in my beloved's work life arose in which I eventually realized *the only strand of the story missing* from a leadership discernment was *my own*, as a *preacher's wife*. No one was more surprised than I when she came to voice, empowered by myself as clergywoman at her back. The conscious feminine theologian fierce for a *church-woman's* truth also roared to life to protect the integrity of the ecclesial community, his congregation whom I have come to love from my more removed or complicated role. Gently, with as much covenantal care as could be mustered, I as *preacher's wife* began to speak—to protect, to honor the discernment of the community (however it might unfold, independent of me or others), to speak truthfully to a difficult situation and potential threat to the congregational life as a whole. Because I *do* have resources to speak to what I have experienced that are less easily ignored in systems built upon certification and expertise. I do have resources that cannot be denied in my *marriage*, who Brian and I were sealed in faith to be and who we have become together in these two decades. All things considered, my beloved and I have navigated all of this so very well. Only once have I moved this newfound Voice into a conflict between what I knew I needed, i.e., what would be healthy and necessary for me in our marriage, and what I could bring to bear *from my professional roles as clergywoman and professor*. It was not a pretty week in our home, but I was finally *heard* with the seriousness that the situation required. We both know now that our covenantal commitment to one another comes first. The threat has borne out as I knew and said. And it's been a complicated journey here.

For the Love of Congregational Life: Learn to Shadowdance?

If I were to speak plainly in this sacred-work-role into which I have now surrendered, at least for now in this purpose, I would invite goodhearted, faithful people gathering weekly or more in congregational practices to consider a spiritual practice I've called *shadowdancing*.[10]

---

10. Hess, "Shadowdancing," 77.

No, it's not the Andy Gibbs's rendition of it, from the 1970s, though it could be introduced to a congregation with a seventies dance party. It *is* a process of awakening in which fear—to be held and heard within a small community able to witness, trust, hold and not fix—is both gift and pathway to spiritual resilience and congregational transfiguration. *Shadow* simply refers to our greatest hidden potentials/passions and our greatest fears/sacred wounds. It is both light and dark, in other words, but unknown and unclaimed. Responsibilities or responsiveness refused. Spiritual maturity within faith community only comes with the capacity for speaking the truth, receiving the truth, assured of love *anyway*. No congregational system I know today can do that, perhaps shouldn't even try. Nonetheless . . .

Shadowdancing invites a vulnerability to our deeply hidden potentials which, when left unconscious, we project outward onto others. Sometimes this transference appears as adoration of the pastor or idealization of the mentor. That is projecting one's own strengths onto another you'd hope would do your work for you, even save you from your own fears or loneliness. This can pad a pastor's ego but is largely unhealthy. Eventually, the pedestal crumbles and we all become human again, with hurt feelings and energies of blame. Sometimes the transference comes in the form of blame and shame—projecting things true inside of someone but which they fear the most, are most wounded by. These projections can implode a ministry today, given the polarizing climate and our incapacities to connect with one another as fragile human beings, perfect in our imperfections.

But we *can* learn to reverse this outward-imposition process and withdraw our attentions back to the sensations of fear and anger in our own bodies. It's incredible how much energy returns for a beautiful life when we catch ourselves in projection, pull it in to learn from it *inside of ourselves*, then feel the *a-ha!* of insight that frees us from fear, connects us to the earth and more. All the energies used to refuse and project and hide come back to us as generativity, inspiration, creative possibilities with others. I have learned to watch for a couple red flags in the shadow and projection dynamic in congregational life. Whenever suffering is utterly disregarded, even used as a punchline, shadow and projection are in play. Politics today is the projection of viscerally felt but largely unconscious suffering onto the other, in utter refusal of both the pain to be metabolized or the opportunity to listen to suffering that is not one's own. Either/or thinking. Polarizations. Info-gorge of expertise to make sense of senseless violence. Whenever hatred is espoused as impersonal or warranted, shadow and projection are also in play. Herman Hesse quipped this nearly a hundred years ago: "If you hate a person, you hate something in him that is part of yourself. What isn't part of ourselves doesn't disturb us."[11] If you don't feel connected with something, or someone, then there is little feeling or awareness of it.

Which is not to say that suffering or hatred should not be or will not be amongst us. Life *is* suffering and hatred is a natural aversion experienced slightly or intensely in all human beings, at some time or other, whether admitted or not. It's a visceral responsiveness in fear, not the moral failing we accuse in ourselves or others. *Shadowdancing* is simply bringing into conscious spiritual practice the energies and fodder for spiritual maturity that will always be with us. Projection is "a perceptual process that tests and evaluates the object in terms of its acceptability to self. . . . It is the insertion of self into the object with the immediate and mostly unconscious purpose of assessing the object either as nourishing or toxic." This is the most expansive sense of the word. All human beings project in order to come to know what they have not known before.[12] Projection is also an aggressive refusal of that within us we do not want to know or feel. In this sense, it has been characterized as an aggressive act of defense in which a person inserts hated parts of him/her/themself into the other in order to harm or control that object and refuse whatever is within for sake of perceived safety. The object is then perceived as the "persecutor," absolving the ego not only of responsibility for this hated part, but also deflecting any need to integrate, perceive deeply, grow in any new ways. Sound familiar today? Ultimately, projection is "ubiquitous and inevitable," says James Hollis. "It employs multiple strategies" in its dynamic of inner shifting energies within the connections desire in relationship, in the push and pull of *eros*.[13]

Each of us can explore the pathway of *withdrawing our projections*, not unlike the pathway of awakening to being in the body you are. Through yearnings met and unmet, a person first conceptualizes experience as "out there"; inner experience feels like it is coming from beyond the self somehow. Any other is therefore an outward focus of inner experience and communion. The second stage of projection involves a gradual awakening to increasing discrepancies between inner

---

11. Hesse, *Demian*, cited in Mizen, "On the Capacity to Suffer One's Self," 314.
12. Malancharuvil, "Projection, Introjection, and Projective Identification," 375–76.
13. Hollis, *Eden Project*, 35

experience and the realities presenting themselves to be perceived, "the widening gulf between who the Other is supposed to be and our concrete experience."[14] Questions arise, growing into doubts. Consternation arises too, as one attempts to hold onto the reality of who one desires. Inevitably, however, one begins to question the reality of the other. The projection is beginning to get lost, unattributable anymore in the same way. This can be a most painful and grief-stricken moment or duration of moments, because nothing seems to be as it so surely was before. Violence can often erupt here, if the fear is great enough.

The third stage requires a willingness to see anew, to really ask "Who *is* this one? Apart from my fear?" The most promising practice here is one of curiosity. How can one learn to become curious amidst the felt-sense of loss, the uncertainty in what had been so certain before? The fourth stage of Hollis's schema for withdrawing projections leads one "to recognize that what one perceived was actually not real, that one was not experiencing the Other out there, but the Other in here."[15] Hollis calls this moment an act of ethical courage. Here the one projecting himself onto another can magnanimously learn to free them from the needs and desires arising from within himself. The person can face forward in all frailty and passion, becoming precisely who he is and allowing the other to be just as they are. The fifth and final stage of the projective process then requires "the search for the origin of that projected energy within oneself."[16] What was the meaning of the projection? Which part of the self was projected and why? The journey to wholeness requires the integration of these projections, withdrawn, received, assessed, welcomed and understood more fully *within*. The other is then free to be him or herself, in all flawed, fabulous humanity.

The visceral signals are what can alert a person into the dynamics of shadow and projection. It may show up simply as discrepancies from what you thought you knew. Cognitive dissonance. Surprise. Aversion and disbelief. There are other ways to get savvy to our projections, however. Intergenerational healing work encourages us to *know our own triggers*.[17] Each of us has predictable situations in which our past sensitivities, complexes, or projections are likely to be activated. Intimacy brings much

---

14. Hollis, *Eden Project*, 51.
15. Hollis, *Eden Project*, 52.
16. Hollis, *Eden Project*, 52.
17. Hemphill, *What It Takes to Heal*, 155. See also Davidson, "Beyond Trigger Warnings," 251–56.

of this to bear—all facets of earliest years, nourishment or neglect, and socialized ego dynamics (repression, denial, etc.) prevalent in y/our own family of origin. Self-reflective practices can instigate awareness of projections playing out in collective ways. The body will give its clues as well: "a churning stomach, a quickening heart, sweaty palms, etc. are somatic states that can alert us to the likelihood of projection."[18] Finally, any situation in which a tremendous amount of energy erupts or arises, energy that is disproportionate for the activities at hand, suggests projection may be at play. Or, in intergenerational healing streams of reference, a trauma is presenting itself to be healed. Which can only happen within a community skilled and willing to witness without judgment, hold without fixing, trusting each of us to do this work of becoming more conscious of our own shadow—gifts and challenges both.

Shadow and *projection* name the dynamic two-dimensional movement human beings have done toward deeper understanding—or deepening woundedness—for ages. *Shadowdancing* is the threefold key holding this two-dimensional dynamic in a third-force container strong enough to hold it, which I call the Body of Humanity. For years now, I've named the only container strong enough to do this healing work a circle. The longer I have traveled in the circle-way, however, the more diverse lineages of circle-holding I have encountered. The more diverse lineages, then the larger this sense of a Body of Humanity can become. Congregations will always have a part to play in the journeys into spiritual maturity, resilience and deepening belonging. No less true: no part of my own economic trinity knows a congregation skilled and willing to witness, hold, trust and ultimately heal as I have experienced in these last years. My preacher's wife knows to look now for "pockets of possibility" made possible because of the role she's in, regardless whether it was sought, chosen, imposed, or desired.

It's one of the bemusing ironies today that it was my coming to voice *as a preacher's wife* that ultimately spurred this entire book to completion. This wisdom-stream of *being a preacher's wife*—unsought, unchosen, undesired, imposed—can finally be spoken truthfully in love, a sign and seal of God/de's nurture-with-rigor *of me* toward becoming the woman I am today. You can't always get what you want ... And I knew it, even as I didn't want to know it, way back in 1999. Brian and I both knew it enough to remember it through the growing times, because of the Flow Who would

---

18. Hollis, *Eden Project*, 53.

never let us go, Who was even breathing deeply within us, gentling us as O/one with the most extraordinary ordinary seal upon us.

What I as a preacher's wife, feminist and conscious feminine theologian, can say today is that I am overwhelmingly grateful for *all* I have experienced, in this and many other narratives. I'm even honoring the pain, as without it, I would never have been goaded outward into the much more expansive sense of *faith* that breathes in my body, lives in my uncertainties, guides me to unforeseen abundance and freedoms I know today. Without this pain and rage, I would not know the web of deeply intimate spirit-friends who bless my life *every day,* from their disparate and geographically diverse locations. This pattern of surrender, perceivable or sense-able only in my resistances here, is important for us all to begin to wrestle with, to learn, to practice, to hold for one another. It's the unseen side of the Gestalt. It's the salvific peripheral vision where forgiveness can breathe. It has both everything and nothing to do with power as we consider it today within institutional dynamics. For my part, it came through a covenantal commitment—partner devoted to partner, no matter what—a feminist willing to rage while carrying the problem of forgiveness, and a conscious feminine theologian with decades of formation and devotion to the best in her own root tradition able to point to potential implications for congregational life and religious leadership.

Because surrender changes *everything* I thought I knew about *leadership.*

Chapter Seven

The Body of Humanity, Scripture, and Faith... Oh My

ONE AIM IN THESE pages has been utter honesty with myself as a woman now conscious of being in a woman's body in a world often dangerous for women, made more so by historic wisdom traditions I am yet unwilling to disregard or deny. My rendition of Elizabeth Gilbert's affirmation of writing to make sense of her own journey was not so transparent, however, nor her words in full. Yes, she wrote a travel memoir—*Eat Pray Love* (Pilgrims, 2006)—to make sense of her life at that moment. Her own words, however, were ones *untrue* for me, so I edited them. Her words in full read: "*I once wrote a book in order to save myself.*"[1] Writing this book was the next step for an impassioned, creative non-fiction writer in her integrative, healing work of *orthodoxy*, what Sarah Coakley defines as "a project, the longed-for horizon of personal transformation in response to divine truth."[2] *Living on the Other Side* has been my own sense-making of an excruciating-into-peaceable life of awakening, abandonment, anointing, if eventually, now, assurance. I may even come to say some day that writing it was salvific for me in my capacity to be fully present in God/de's desire for this world, for my life within it. The glaring untruth in Gilbert's words required my elision of her words, however: I could never have *saved myself*. Each of us comes into this earth out of ancestral lineages, out of community, in which we are ever

---

1. Gilbert, *Big Magic*, 98. Emphasis mine.
2. Coakley, *God, Sexuality and the Self*, 90.

embedded and responsible. My salvation comes not from myself, from any one of us, not even from one Man.

It was the Body of Humanity enlivened with a renewed and renewing Trinitarianism who labored hard to birth this conscious F/feminine within me, to ultimately return me to my root tradition in faith as the most whole in belonging I have ever been. A collaborative-emergent community saved me in its willingness to form and unform, again and again, in an ancient yet new configuration of circle and shared energetics of hope. A generative, collaborative wisdom of spirit-friend companionship and circle-way gathering was able to come alongside the traditional-institutional expressions of human-collectives today in order to offer gifts and spaces our institutions are particularly unable and unskilled to offer: a motherline within which to be nourished, a whole-hearted welcome of me as I was/am, a safe harbor from my worlds' (un)conscious refusals to see or hear deeply amidst untended intergenerational wounds, a way to become more fully human in the deep listening, seeing, and hearing I desperately needed in order for me come home to myself,[3] more healed and whole as the woman I am. This emergent community amidst spirit-friend companionship was able to witness without judgment but with accountability, to hold open spaces for me to awaken to God/de's desire within me, so to be gifted, intensified, refined—nurturing me with compassion and rigor at the same time.

It's taken *years*, and I still miss it more than I embody it, but *surrender unto bewilderment* has been the rub of *forgiveness finding me*, of a peaceableness not depending upon the conditions of peace,[4] of a return to wholeness in a root tradition that has abandoned women as women for centuries. Surrender. Trusting the divine order of things amidst the urgency of conscious and unconscious pain.[5] A deep wisdom of a living, subtle-body *faith* is hidden here, most often out of sight and mind in formally trained religious leaders serving yet so faithfully today. My thirty years of formation in higher theological education have also shaped my mind and even my spirit into otherizing and externalizing prevalent assumptions and workings of leadership. I recognize savvy skills developed *are* necessary to participate and even succeed in the institutions we've inherited—wisdom of serpents, innocence of doves. Despite my

---

3. Woodman, *Coming Home to Myself*, 15–20.
4. Levandoski and Finley, *Sanctuary*.
5. Quanita Roberson, personal conversation.

woundedness, I have been shaped to value institutional thinking,⁶ so much so that I yearn to weave the wisdom of institutional thinking to now be *shaped by the ethos and emergence of circle wisdom for the Body of Humanity*. What does the *respect-in-depth* of institutional thinking bring in *support* of emergent communities alongside our institutions, such that each finds just enough stability over time for the benefit of future generations? How does all I have offered here alter my understanding of faith, of community, even of Scripture held to be sacred? I offer what I have been given amidst such conundrum, beginning with the Body of Humanity, its breaking-open of my scriptural habits of mind, ultimately, an invitation to *faith* conceived within them both, palpable in my body.

Body of Humanity—Community

"Whether we know it or not, like it or not, honor it or not, we are embedded in community,"⁷ begins Parker Palmer in a now-classic online piece from 1998. It found me shortly after my Days in the Weeds, shaping my perceptions of deeply healing, gathering community that was yet *not* congregational, nor even necessarily *Christian*. I was finding myself in gatherings of women, then gatherings of human beings unaffiliated with any historic root tradition of any kind, exploring practices of intentional community. Each of us amidst all of us seemed to be seeking connection, belonging in places safe to become vulnerable, deeply seen and heard, held and encouraged. In contrast to the congregational forms of gatherings I had been shaped in my entire life, it was these non-church, non-congregational gatherings that became most nourishing for me, beginning to heal my wounded body-heart, soothing my enraged spirit. I remember pondering with a spirit-friend, "What am I supposed to learn when I experience 'church' where 'church' is not welcome nor visibly present?"

We arise out of relationship—what Palmer calls "a complex ecology of relatedness"—and without it, "we wither and die."⁸ Community is therefore not *achievable* by leadership today, in the sense with which we are most familiar. It is a *gift to be received*, even *relaxed into*. Hopefully *surrender* comes to mind by now. Community also differs from intimacy,

---

6. Heclo, *On Thinking Institutionally*, 4–5. Thanks, Uncle.
7. Palmer, "Thirteen Ways of Looking at Community."
8. Palmer, "Thirteen Ways of Looking at Community."

simply because it broadly covers everyone from relations with "strangers (e.g. the poor around the world to whom each of us is accountable)" to those "with whom we share local resources so must learn to get along with (immediate neighbors)" to those we "relate to for getting a job done (coworkers),"[9] etc. Community is both more what we yearn for, and less than our cravings demand. We are created to thrive in community. Community—this broadly conceived—is what (painfully or at least uncomfortably) grows us up into adult human beings—initiated adults[10]—so to offer our gifts to the whole and to receive what the community can offer. No more. No less. You can imagine how naturally a conscious feminine wisdom rests here—receptivity, nourishment, capacity to hold new life amongst the old, nurture with rigor at the same time.

Presumptions of expertise within leadership distract and hinder community today, however. "When we try to 'make community happen,' driven by desire, design, and determination—places within us where the ego often lurks," Palmer observes, "we will exhaust ourselves and alienate each other, snapping the connections we yearn for."[11] Contrary to presumptions imposed upon religious leaders, community is in fact an *emergent phenomenon*, one to be cultivated, certainly not presumed or imposed as responsibility on the few. Even more challenging, this kind of community requires more leadership, not less. It requires a leadership not exercised through power—as in bureaucratic and power-over actions—but in genuine love and an authentic exercise of authority, more than power. "Authority is granted to people who are perceived as authentic, as authoring their own words and actions rather than proceeding according to some organizational script. . . . it consists in creating, holding, and guarding a trustworthy space in which human resourcefulness may be evoked." Not assigned. Not expected nor commanded. *Evoked.* A conscious feminine-conscious masculine space, in other words, able to hold space and protect it while human beings *grow up* into deeper capacity, greater resourcefulness, strengthened faith to perceive interconnection. The archetypal masculine is in balance for this work, but only when women claim their own voice and power. Only

---

9. Palmer, "Thirteen Ways of Looking at Community."

10. My paraphrase in learning from Quanita Roberson: An initiated adult is one emerging from community and returning to community, able to claim responsibility for his/her/their actions, gifts, lives in the work of healing, in deep gratitude—grief and praise—interconnected with ancestral and future lineages. www.nzuzu.com.

11. Palmer, "Thirteen Ways of Looking at Community."

then are men freed to love without power.[12] This requires a capacity in leaders today to be patient, to evoke a community's awareness of its own resourcefulness, much of which said-collective will resist and refuse, projecting it back onto "leadership."

Ultimately, our inherited notions of institution-drenched "community" require that leaders *suffer* while their communities refuse to surrender into the divine order of things in which they've been incredibly gifted with a wondrous capacity to love, to wonder, and co-create. In Palmer's words,

> Suffering is what happens when you see the possibilities in others while they deny those same possibilities in themselves. Suffering is what happens when you hold in trust a space for community to emerge but others lack the trust to enter the space and receive the gift. Suffering is what happens while you wait out their resistance, believing that people have more resources than they themselves believe they have. But leaders do not want to suffer. So we create and maintain institutional arrangements that protect leaders from suffering by assuming the worst of followers and encouraging leaders to dominate them by means of power.[13]

Sometimes even using sacred Scripture to do so. These are simply the words of one man, invested in education that transforms, but they speak to the need for these kinds of communities alongside the ones we are traditioned to focus on. Leaders cannot sustain such suffering unless they have a safe-enough space in which to have their suffering seen, heard, honored. "A community can hold multiple purposes," observed a couple elder-friends with one another recently. "You cannot build a community... Every time you try to build it, it fails. You can create the conditions that support an emergent phenomenon, but you can't build one."[14] Just as we cannot *make plants grow*, none of us can be tasked with making or creating community.

Each of us *can* learn to be receptive, however, in moments of *surrender* and the *inner work* required to participate in life around us, within us, all while staying as connected to our communities (of faith or none) as bearable, feasible. We can learn to cultivate capacities for connectedness, to create conditions within which community *might* emerge, on the periphery, in "pockets of possibility" amidst tribalistic and individualistic

12. Quanita Roberson, personal conversation.
13. Palmer, "Thirteen Ways of Looking at Community."
14. Roberson, "Individuals, Teams, Tribes and Communities."

energies. We can honor the light that tribalism brings in its fierce commitment to the sacred, to what has been, even as we learn to temper its shadow, its refusals of the individual. We can honor the gifts that individuals bring into the community, even as the community needs to temper the individual's tendency to separate and divide for sake of ideological purity or an incapacity to sustain the rage, the woundedness sustained *in litigated "community."* In the words that taught me: "Tribes serve important purpose, even as they have both shadow and light. Yes, tribes can be unforgiving, but they also keep traditions, rituals, and ancient knowledge in place. Individuals can forget to consider the tribe, but individuals gift the world with unique genius and purpose we all need."[15] The intersection for entering into this energetic Flow of things is a practiced willingness to move inward, to trust the internal transformation of your own heart *is enough*. Is what is *invited*.

Each of us is tasked with growing up, which means here *developing a capacity for connectedness* in a world predicated on divide and conquer, fear and buy, conform and belong. As Palmer in his Quaker wisdom observes, "Community begins not externally but in the recesses of the human heart. Long before community can be manifest in outward relationships, it must be present in the individual as 'a capacity for connectedness'—a capacity to resist the forces of disconnection with which our culture and our psyches are riddled."[16] Everything here in *Living on the Other Side* aims to awaken and invite deeper and deeper capacities for connectedness. Only in the groundedness known deep in your own flesh and bones can you begin to resist the forces of disconnection all around us—polarization, shame, rage, certainty and more. The sad thing is that when we are flourishing, we disregard any need we may have of community. Only when we are mired in failure, loss and suffering do we remember we cannot thrive, perhaps even survive these days, without some relatedness, some capacity for connectedness, some community willing to emerge amidst it all.

Blessedly—or cursed as we have co-created our world to be—more and more of us are becoming overwhelmed with suffering, loss, and failure. It is getting harder and harder to maintain our illusions of separation. A pandemic, centered upon our inability to grieve, which often shows up in our physical lungs. Fear-mongering politicians doing precisely what

---

15. Roberson, "Individuals, Teams, Tribes and Communities."
16. Palmer, "Thirteen Ways of Looking at Community."

we've shaped them to do—refuse to govern, refuse to listen, refuse to compromise. Wisdom traditions battening down the hatches to grasp onto the sacred that we've known before, distrustful and unwilling to risk into the Sacred we could become *together*, with a sustainable relationship to our planet, a willingness to practice trust and forbearance amidst increasing violence and tribalism. By what practices do we face our own inner separations—narcissism, egotism, jealousy, competition and more—and how can communities (whether congregational or not) hold space for the inner work required? By what means do we penetrate "the illusion of separateness" and "touch the reality of interdependence" so overwhelming but increasingly obvious post-COVID today? How may we disrupt "the forces of disconnection" within ourselves, so to cultivate deeper capacity for connectedness with those most proximate to us?

I remain challenged and curious to *think institutionally* here, given I have a fierce commitment to the continuity of lineages that have made me who I am, gifted me with both an intense capacity for deep feeling, relationality, and precisely the intergenerational wounding to push me into the light of sacred work. Human collectives *need collectively-decided-agreements able to weather decades of time*, if not *institutions*, to hold responsibly the gifts of our ancestors for the sustained life of human wisdom in generations to come. Hugh Heclo's book is now a classic in this wrestling and cauldron of paradoxes within which our shared life is boiling today.

Heclo observes our modern impasse in the dance between institutions that are changing—if not declining—and our declining capacity to trust, becoming largely *distrust*. "We are compelled to live in a thick tangle of institutions while believing that they do not have our best interests at heart."[17] Speaking as a woman in her enraged and yet healing review of history within wisdom traditions of faith, I say, *damn straight*. I can provide evidence that institutions as we have co-created them have *rarely* considered the best interests of women *as women*. Half of the human species. Distrust is therefore a viable even legitimate consequence. To smile with him in his impish prose: "Today's institutions have gained our distrust the old-fashioned way. They have earned it."[18]

Yet Heclo also observes the underbelly or the shadow side of our liberal democratic presumptions—our *live and let live* doctrine, our

---

17. Heclo, *On Thinking Institutionally*, 12.
18. Heclo, *On Thinking Institutionally*, 15.

reliance upon institutions only for the protection of "other people." We have co-created a shared life that is a recipe "not for freedom, but for continuous confusion, anxiety, and dread." Traditionalists lament the loss of the Transcendent here, blaming secularism for our plight. More progressive voices blame Traditionalists for not relinquishing that which has wounded them most. Regardless of how we identify, collectively we do not find ourselves in the "free, liberated condition that seemed promised," but instead are left "perplexed, burdened, and looking for some fixed points of reference."[19] And yet . . . And yet . . . Amidst all the tumult and polarizing chaos of today, we still "depend in some senses on a basic institutionalized trust that makes meaningful human interactions possible. It depends upon our tacit acceptance of common social knowledge and expectations, as well as our willingness to do the accommodative work that keeps our conversation meaningful."[20] We go to the grocery store and on good days, have meaningful encounter with the cashier and bagger. We go to church and on good days, have meaningful encounter with one another in a familiar socialized form. We go to the baseball game, and on good days, josh and connect with those sitting nearby. Our impasse, according to Heclo, is that we roll the distrust that institutions have earned around on our tongues, savoring our righteousness, while we then feel betrayed when *others* refuse what we consider common social knowledge and expectations. Fewer and fewer of us are willing to do the accommodative work that keeps our social contracts meaningful, alive. Somewhere between *live and let live* and *we belong to one another, we are one another* lives and breathes the healing way forward.

Therefore, ironically and with my uncle's great bemusement, I land here with a plea for more collaborative explorations in *thinking institutionally*, informed and shaped by the cadences, voices, and wisdoms of those most often marginalized or unheard. It's not an unusual or innovative plea, given so many voices before me have sketched visions and invitations. Letty Russell comes to mind: "I have always found it difficult to walk away from the church," she wrote, "but I have also found it difficult to walk with it."[21] Decades ago, she argued for *church in the round* challenging solely hierarchical institutions and leadership with those shaped by the architecture and ethos of *circle*. Round table connections,

---

19. Heclo, *On Thinking Institutionally*, 39.
20. Heclo, *On Thinking Institutionally*, 41.
21. Russell, *Church in the Round*, 11.

"overturning the Masters' Tables"²² with kitchen table solidarity, communities of hospitality, welcome table partnerships. She urged a "spirituality of connection" nodding to Sister Choice, Sister Outsider, and Sister Circle—all invitations into relationship within one's own F/feminine, exploring the margins, opening the circle to all.

Feeling very much in her lineage, I wonder how we begin to develop practices that honor what Heclo calls *respect-in-depth*, a respect that engages our sense of obligation to community both living and dead, reconnecting wounded severed ancestral lineages into intentional communities. It requires embodying a messy essence of (emergent) community able to witness, hold, heal and trust. It requires sustaining connection and commitment to institutions that have wounded us, that are perceived as failing, as those in proverbial decline. It requires a mixture of cognition and emotional attachment that yields habits of action congruent with valuing the utter dignity of all sentient beings by deepening listening, witnessing, holding space for, healing, and trust. It means acknowledging and somehow *countering* both the performance-based distrust—which institutions have earned—and culture-based distrust—the *live and let live* which has fragmented us—with seasoned, wisely chosen actions of trust in an increasingly distrustful world. All of which will never appear as flashy or successful in our professionalized environments. This *institutional thinking* is undramatic, unassuming, and certainly unfashionable, when considered externally.²³ Considered internally, within the framework of inner work or the internal transformation of the human heart,²⁴ this way of thinking and acting actually paves a bewildering pathway toward fulfillment, satisfaction, integrity and what I call an expressive delight able to companion the suffering of self and others.

Given that there really is no consensus definition of the word *institution*, we are first challenged to confront our own assumptions of what *we* mean by it. For most deeply wounded by religious traditions, institution refers to "organized religion." It's also popular to consider the term referring to abstracted social collectives like government, civil services, sports, school, etc. Yes and no, for our purposes. Heclo provides a chart of over twenty social-science definitions of *institution*, able to summarize only by saying, "at the end of the day, we might want to capitulate and say that

22. Russell alludes here to Audre Lorde's classic writing, "The Master's Tools Will Never Dismantle the Master's House."
23. Heclo, *On Thinking Institutionally*, 82.
24. May, "From Cruelty to Compassion," 1–3.

'institution' is a basic, elemental concept that cannot be defined (except through synonyms . . . which means no definition at all)."[25] He defines it himself as "the irreducible word pair I–We."[26] At most, he encourages us to develop sensitivities for a more comprehensive way of life proximate yet open-hearted. An appreciative viewpoint in collective matters, not projecting fear onto "them" nor receiving others' projections on "ourselves." A *habitus* that builds upon appreciation without becoming cynical in distrust or Pollyanna-ish in unfounded optimism. Willingness to live into communal values and purposes undergirding the utter dignity of all sentient beings means living committed to these ends more than solely—soul-ly—organizational or bureaucratic norms.

Institutional thinking means being mindful in that way, accepting that there can be anguishing choices to be made in matters of personal duty and organizational loyalty. It also means practicing both receiving and innovation, mindful of the long lineage of ancestral wisdom within which one lives and breathes. These lineages have given "a world charged with meaning and calls to commitment. What is on offer is an invitation to engagement that goes well beyond self-engagement."[27] It does require the willingness to surrender to what has been received, however. What is being received. Ultimately, *institutional thinking* involves being mindful about time reaching back further than one can imagine and reaching forward further than one could hope. It is being attentive to precedent as a form of solidarity, recognizing that our craving for liberation imprisons unless we have done the inner work to know our own woundedness. It means living "an implicated life, always both inheriting and bequeathing."[28] Today, institutions are what Heclo calls "weathered presences." What "weathered presences" can we commit to in daily or weekly action, so to become more intentional about reweaving our communal fabric(s)?

For me, these questions became the frustrating covenantal reality of unavoidable interconnection with all those in my own root tradition who continued to—and probably always would—refuse to hear my sadness, my experience, my voice *as a woman*. While I envy those who live into what seems an utter ideological separation from those with whom they vehemently disagree, I also know that illusions of separateness lie

25. Heclo, *On Thinking Institutionally*, 51.
26. Heclo, *On Thinking Institutionally*, 51.
27. Heclo, *On Thinking Institutionally*, 98.
28. Heclo, *On Thinking Institutionally*, 109.

there too. As I was viscerally returned to my own body, gifted with desire, palpable in pleasure, a peaceableness of the present made possible things and even presence I had considered impossible. A forgiveness found me, easing the rage and putting in its place curiosity, empathy, wonder at the Life we get to live today. Which leaves me with only deeply embodied, grounded and covenantal practices of what Donald Shriver has called *social forgiveness*: practicing forbearance, learning to listen more deeply, honoring rage-sadness-pain while getting curious of others' stories, catching myself in my own stories of victimhood, and learning new ways to encourage and support institutional integrity without political retaliation. Practiced in collaboration and hope in the present moment, encountering one heart at a time.

This is how I continue to show up in ecclesial and academic environments (un)consciously hostile to the F/feminine, even to me personally, with presence, newly grounded in my woman's body. I lament regularly, wishing it were different, even as I continue to live into the wisdom of the silent treatment in irreconcilable settings. I remain present, available, but no longer offer my voice to any of the corporate practices that silence, refuse or denigrate the F/feminine. In every congregational worship service, I sit or stand, present to all around me while remaining silent in honor of all silenced in these practices of tribe. Sometimes, I permit myself the unhelpful release of circling everything that is masculine in a printed order of worship, but my gift to the whole is to take it with me instead of leaving it on the pew.

The Body of Humanity in which I continue to participate alongside these more institutional environments makes these covenantal practices possible, even bearable. My husband and I laugh as he attempts—and regularly fails—to count the number of circles and open-space communities in which I participate so to nourish my woman's body for the complicated covenantal work I continue (for now) to offer. Without regular nourishment, encouragement, and yes, accountability to my highest values of egalitarian community, emergent leadership, and truly collaborative co-creation of communal containers practicing ancient-new circle-ways of being more humane—more human—together, I could never sustain the dissonance in traditionalist settings. Which leads nicely into the arena of largest dissonance and irreconcilable loss for me as a woman rooted in Protestant Christian traditions: Scripture as Sacred.

Scripture

How does a conscious feminine theologian re-encounter sacred Scripture, here on the other side of rage, abandonment, and a forgiveness that has found her? What is at least a tentative approach that can be constructive, healing, yet also not become complicit in the silencing of women's voices by ancient texts—and centuries of masculine-ized interpretive strategies? Is there a way to hold Scripture as sacred, rooted in a forgiveness of its woundings in our shared or co-created power-over history? How does Scripture invite us to the luminous perception of the interconnection of all things? The short answer for me today: I have not found the way, nor do I expect to find any reconciliation within my own lifetime. I can continue to participate with integrity in Christian congregational practice, honoring how the community holds these ancient texts to be sacred and the Word of God. For myself, Scripture only speaks truthfully for me when it is *decentered* yet *authoritative in witness to the Resurrection*. This is a completely enchanted conviction, if not in the fashion that will comfort the ecclesially regulated orthodox.

I want to begin smiling with one of my earliest visceral memories on a summer Sunday morning in the First Presbyterian Church in my hometown. I was sitting next to my mother, cranky to be there, probably overly warm, as we didn't have air-conditioning in the church yet. The organ began for the singing of a hymn but my stubbornness prevailed. I refused to stand, arms crossed, frowning. My mother responded brilliantly, probably mostly from her frustration with a recalcitrant daughter, but also with an authentic faith. "*I* don't mind if you sit, but I'm not sure how *God* will feel about it." I can still remember the visceral charge, the surprise, the wonder filling every part of me. *We weren't the only ones in the room?* My world became enchanted in that moment, I'd say today. There was a Presence beyond what we could see or hear, somehow interested in us, however small. A mother, frustrated with her willful younger daughter, planted a seed of something deeply grounding for me, for the rest of my life. God was a *Person* in the *room*.

Rarely did I know that visceral resonance in *Scripture*. The Bible was Sunday school, then memorizations and tests of achievement. My folks made it as bearable as they could, creating verses so to memorize, with which we could play Go Fish. Rather clever, actually. Except Scripture was the yardstick against which I was judged while saying "You should not judge." It was the playground on which the boys had power and the girls were subservient and property. It was rule book for well-shamed women and men, willing to submit their very lives to things—including having children or completely dissociating from their bodies—assuming this was the faithful path to meaning. A meaning that so often seemed to fail to bring light to their eyes or lightheartedness into their step. Scripture eventually became the battlefield within which one's intellect could challenge and conquer another, simply by knowing more, citing the right sources, and bringing the conceptual cannon to whatever knife fight the men in the room had decided. After nearly thirty years of ecclesial formation in the Protestant assumptions and practice of the *authority of Scripture*, I made my best peace with it, demonstrating my expertise in exegesis and preaching—mostly pulpit supply in our local presbytery. Like any faithful Christian, I have texts that have spoken deeply to me along life's pathways. But Protestant authority of Scripture is so much the water we all swim in to ever consider we might have dirtied the water so fully that fewer and fewer of us can breathe.

Then I sat in a circle of women writers, in love with the power of words and the power of community to encourage the development of individual voices. Week by week, we would light a candle, passing it around in silence to invoke a holiness of space, time. One of us would read a poem as event, as provocation. We'd pass a talking piece around the circle, inviting *each voice* to respond to the Event, the poem, or an aphorism from the top of the agenda, etc. Then we would write together in the silence for a while before gathering in smaller groups to share our words. Often, we'd come back together as a *listening, witnessing community*, to receive whatever words any woman wanted or needed to have heard. The community would then offer what we call *readback lines*, those words or phrases that touched a heart, connected a writer with her listener. "The words that had found good ears," we would say, citing another poet. An acoustics of intimacy would develop in this performance of the Word—communal, egalitarian, befriending of things easy to hear . . . and things not so easy to hear. A synergy of the group would develop over the course of the semester's circles, becoming an energetic whole unto itself. More than the sum of us somehow. We would talk about "catching courage" from one another and deepening consciousness of our own gifts, the gifts of others. When conflict would arise—as it inevitably does with human beings in any collective—there were "the practices" able to help deeper listening, opening to unexpected graces within and even sometimes beyond the conflict.

Speaking as a lifelong Presbyterian, this way of gathering was so eminently theological, so *Presbyterian*, I could hardly stand it. Every voice matters. Each voice is welcome. A community gathers to invoke a sacred Center. Prayer and practice unfold, together. The word is proclaimed and shared, deeply received and graciously offered. This Word is the Event in which the Sacred takes shape, again and again. Except in this circle, it is the *women* whose cadence, voices, and words mattered. Eventually this became "women-identified human beings" as well as some men who were hungry for what this Center had to offer, to receive. It was not just one person's interpretation of the word, but a communal, collaborative offering of the word, received together. It grew a faith in each of us as a luminous perception of deep interconnection. It spurred a courage to live more fully into our own gifts, encouraging the gifts of others. It regularly affirmed and confirmed the power of the word when celebrating the individual voice in the practices of community.

Today, I feel like I was granted—utterly gifted with—how *word* used to be *event* in human collectives of old.[29] Before literacy. Before our habits of mind were distanced from our bodies and focused upon some page with scratches and scrawls. Before the writing of the few became the power-over the many.[30] Before women were relegated to the home and men with their fears and voices were prioritized into the court and eventually even the printing press. Free for millennia to demonize the feminine in writ that would be passed down, generation to generation. Free to pour their fears of loss and insecurity into power-over habits of mind to control, imprison and wound, written into sacred texts now deemed Holy Writ. Texts which imprison and enslave them into power-over habits of mind, just as much or more so than they have women. Here is where my own intergenerational woundedness broke open into fearlessness. Here is where I began to resonate with just the possibility, however minute, that we might confront *gently* the Protestant obsession with the authority of Scripture as power-over by the few at expense of the many. Here we might consider returning ancient texts to their original home as a *derived authority* held in honor but not bondage. *Decentered* ancient texts might better

---

29. Ong, *Orality and Literacy*, 37–49. The duality of orality and literacy no longer holds, of course, but the framework opened deepening scholarship into diverse communicative strategies at the heart of circle/open-space gatherings in some contrast with more traditional congregational habits.

30. Shlain, *Alphabet Versus the Goddess*, 1–3. See also his *Sex, Time, and Power*.

craft Spirit-companionship in our journey of faith without enslaving us in dualistic, divisive, power-over habits of mind.

Several times in recent years, I've encountered the lashing out of a fearful white man, seemingly terrified of losing his sacred center when encountering something I said or did. None would or could *physically* injure me in these settings, though I don't discount the possibility of fear driving men or the women who love them to do so. I read the news. But each time, the gift for me was becoming aware of my body-response. I was absolutely overcome with a visceral response, what trauma-informed healing resources identify as a trauma-reaction. The body's precognitive, preconscious, visceral response unregulated but proven sufficient over the years to protect and preserve the body. It is an overwhelming impulse in my body to flee, to get away, perhaps to freeze in hopes some threat will pass. My stomach clenches. I sweat. My heart rate spikes and the energetic field around me turns from a vague anxiety into a visceral *fear*. Blessedly, I was reared in environments where physical violence was not common, but the fear of being shamed, shunned, ultimately *not belonging* or being *left out in the cold*[31] was pervasive. More often than not, Scripture was used to create this conformity, to silence any experience I may have had that did not fit into the expectations of my elders. I can now honor how my body goes into visceral fear when men and masculinized women wield their understandings of Scripture against anything I may offer, refusing whatever my experience as a woman has been.[32] Living for nearly thirty years in higher theological education means my body has responded this way, subconsciously, *for decades*. So I know Scripture as what is wielded today in denominational disputes and schismatic refusals of one another's human dignity. None of which leads me—or us, I will argue—to a deeper faith in God, certainly not Godde, so therefore, not God/de.

For myself, I no longer approach my own tradition's Scriptures—both Hebrew and Christian Testaments, with the Apocrypha thrown in

---

31. Rita Sinorita Fierro, personal conversation. See Fierro, *Digging Up the Seeds of White Supremacy*.

32. Jungian Jean Shinoda Bolen also speaks to this intergenerational trauma in women's souls and cells: "Somewhere in our souls, we remember the burning time, when women were persecuted and burned alive as witches. This went on for three hundred years of the Inquisition. . . . This collective memory has an effect much as any personal repressed trauma does; it makes women anxious when we discover our own sacred experiences and find words for them. We need courage to bring forth what we know." *Crossing to Avalon*, 80.

for greater diversity of Wisdom—with what I would call *authoritative habits of mind* expected today. This does not mean these writings have *no authority*, but I no longer primarily look to Scripture to hear God/de's voice. Godde and H/her divinely sparked F/feminine expressions are omitted, abused, raped, pillaged, dismembered and more within ancient texts. I do not say this lightly, as I have lived for nearly sixty years in a model of authoritative witness, first as laywoman and then as clergywoman and then theological scholar. I find our largely hermeneutical-textual worship of Scripture to be—at the very least—lacking, divisive, increasingly fragmented, and even violent within human community. At worst, Protestant Christianity's utter grasping focus on Scripture to the exclusion of any other revelation is idolatrous, refusing revelation from within creation, community, even the massive depths of our own tradition's voices, let alone Wisdom from other traditions. The work of the Spirit, recognized in the fruit of Spirit, beckons me beyond where my community seems to be today.

Yet the power and influence of this compilation of texts cannot be denied nor simply severed, disregarded. Such an act would dishonor my elders and my communities of faith. I know that speaking so clearly here will worry—even deeply concern—brothers and sisters in Christ I continue to hold dear, particularly those of African descent. I receive gladly the scriptural wisdom of friends within black church traditions, in awe that they have somehow been able to take what was used as utter *poison* for them—history of chattel slavery and more—making it yet into a *balm*.[33] I listen and receive, hopeful for some reconciliation like that for myself. Waiting, actively, still. Similarly, I felt an expansiveness within me, receiving the well-plastered aphorism of Thomas Berry: "We need to put the Bible on the shelf for twenty years until we learn to read the scripture of life."[34] I resonate deeply with so many of us who have been wounded by the use of Scripture as an only or single focal point for determining wisdom in the world today. Yes, yes, I know it is human beings' *use* of these texts, not the texts themselves, but, to quote Eddie Izzard, the text *helps*.[35] Which presents me with irreconcilable paradoxes, particularly in my woman-identified body.

33. Callahan, *The Talking Book*, cited in Evans, *Inspired*, 38.

34. Berry, remarks at "Seeking the Meaning of Peace," cited in Brunner and Swoboda, "Creation Care and the Bible," 414.

35. Izzard, *Dress to Kill*: "The National Rifle Association says that, 'Guns don't kill people, uh, people do.' But I think, I think the gun helps. You know? I think it helps . . . If you just stood there and yelled BANG, I don't think you'd kill too many people."

Spreading out from its Hebraic origins into the siblings of early Christianity and rabbinic Judaism, empowered and distributed by means of empire, the Bible as "both text and physical entity has been and continues to function as an icon: an image that mediates between the material and spiritual world and thus is a locus of religious power."[36] Encounters with scraps of Scripture, gazed into as icon, received as visceral invitation to liberation feels in alignment, feasible. Lee Martin McDonald's thorough review of authoritative habits of mind across centuries of transmission and translation of texts also points a direction that is obvious, yet so resisted today in fear. "Wherein lies authority? If we carefully interpret the earliest Christian communities correctly, the earliest canon of faith for the church was Jesus. All Scriptures are, of course, a derived authority . . . Jesus and the gospel he proclaimed are at the heart of the Christian message, and we would do well not to place a written text with numerous variables in his place."[37] Perhaps the Authority of Scripture—*as we have come to conceive of it*—has simply run its course? What might it mean for Christian communities to encounter these ancient texts more as *icon*, inviting us into encounter with the living God/de, than *word*, over which we control, wield, and argue?

I am extraordinarily grateful to have encountered and been shaped in the sacredness of these texts, so to have language and context for this Jesus Christ, Messiah, Anointed One, with testimony to his bodily resurrection in the power of the Spirit. I *do* honor our Hebrew-Christian Scripture as *authoritative witness*. This is the testimony within which I know who and Whose I am, have always been, even as I have also viscerally experienced *divine abandonment* as a woman, in a woman's body. Jesus is the One whose sacred signature my body has recognized for a long time, has gotten me into this entire story arc and to this other side. His energetic signature, confirmed and affirmed alongside scriptural witness, shows me the One Who has met me along the way, Who has sidled up next to me in the labyrinth so to hear me. He is the One Who knows the woundedness of abandonment, could be present for the work of healing. I have learned surrender to these texts as authoritative witness to the Resurrection, to which I impishly refer in my classes as a "dead man walking." Authoritative witness is to the Resurrection, even as the historic church, mired in power-over habits of mind, idolizes the *man*, to the detriment of all. The

---

36. Parmenter, "Bible as Icon," 298.
37. McDonald, "Wherein Lies Authority?," 237.

Good News is the *Resurrection*, in other words. Jesus is Lord is a partial truth in our ecclesial-fearmongering age that seems to demonstrate more a human shadow of domination than a kenotic, Christ-centered expression of divinity. I can say Jesus is Lord and mean it, even as I know in my body I am to grow out of that long-conditioned power-over habit of mind and body. Scripture provided me with the ancient testimony, the elder-honored continuity within lineages of human beings woven into and proclaiming salvific truth. Scripture and tradition have led me here, in other words, while Spirit continues to show the irreparably damning evidence *in Scripture* and *Scripture held as idol* for the damage done to women and the F/feminine, irreconcilable with the gospel, irreconcilable with faith as it has breathed in my woman's body.

Decentering Scripture in this way challenges the utter focus of congregational life on the preacher and preaching, which, if consciously redressed could enliven more of us into a living, active faith, freeing more of us to see our interconnection with all things. I hold as irreconcilable the life-giving encounter of the Word I've experienced in women's circles that differs so completely from how we conceive of encounter with God's word in Scripture in worship today. One voice offering his/her/their interpretation of Scripture alone while *everyone else passively listens.* To my bodysoul, gathering around the words of women offers much more nourishment for women, with strikingly fresh ways to perceive the complete omission of women's voices whenever Christians gather around the word to study together, focused upon the ancient text alone. I don't pretend the social architecture of congregational life will ever change, nor that it needs to. But I do smile when clergy bemoan the lack of congregational engagement in a more active life of faith. We lament the "services for compensation" concierge ministry we have systemically co-created by means of a one-voice-centered worship service, or scholar-oriented Bible studies, listening in this way week after week.

When congregational members *do* deepen their own discipleship or spiritualities in a deeper dive into our historic tradition, wisdoms that find them along the way, many wind up outgrowing their congregational family entirely. Communities draw the line and those who venture beyond those fences are simply no longer welcome. Some into ordained leadership, which instills a functional separation, often creating spiritual isolation; some into another congregational setting where deeper-faith questions are more welcome. Some of us simply move completely outside of congregational structures altogether, so to breathe in this larger, more expansive—if lonelier—sense of Spirit-led encounter and faith as luminous perception in a wilding and bewildering world. Here where the Body of Humanity awaits.

All of which I hold in the bewilderment I've encouraged as method to be *sacred*, allowing this to evolve in my own understanding, encounters in the years to come. Three days after the manuscript finally landed in its final form here, I was sitting in my husband's congregation for Sunday worship. I try to attend once a month, balancing that commitment with what my own enspirited-body needs, rarely provided in today's congregational practices. I startled to hear an Invitation, so clearly recognizable in my body's utter resistance to it: *Read the whole thing, then, from cover to cover.* The resistance, fear, and fury I recognize so well now as an invitation to surrender erupted in my body. *You have to be freakin' kidding me*, is the less profane version of my silent response, sitting there in the pew. Smiling, getting savvy to my own rhythms amidst bewilderment and rage, I stopped by the church library to pick up a variety of translations for this next invitation then, reading the Bible from cover to cover as the conscious feminine theologian I am today.

What I noticed most fully as I began the read-through was how genuinely sad and deeply grieved I am as I read it, perhaps will always be. I am genuinely sad for all I (we) have lost, grounded in sacred stories used in ways we can no longer undo, unsee, unfeel. The two millennia of Eve's condemnation and imputed shame robbed my own little girl's body of its sacred beauty, its invitation and mystery in the natural rhythms of maturation into the power of bleeding, the mysteries women alone know when connected to the sacred in their bleeding times. The one line of Miriam's Song and the nearly entire *chapter* of the Song of Moses demonstrates the common pattern of pushing little girls behind the boys again and again, hindering them from trusting their own voices, their own wisdom that the world needs so very desperately. The Levitical model of obedience and penalties for disobedience has literally plagued our world with power and powerlessness, condemnation and judgment befalling those without standing or voice. Numbers' revelation of the priestly *curse of bitter water* upon a woman whose husband is simply *jealous*—she need not have done *anything* at all—touches the visceral fear that every woman knows in her own body, once she awakens to being in a long line of women cursed, raped, burned at the stake, and more. Finally, nothing can prepare a woman for reading Judges 19, with the Levite who, to avoid his own rape, sends his concubine to be raped all night long. When she attempts to return to what had been her home, the Levite takes her out to dismember her very body, sending the pieces throughout all the territory of Israel. I grieve how numb we've gotten to such stories, given their prevalence in news and even worse, unspoken testimonies by women or women-identified beings too threatened to know their bodies—they—matter.

None of that discounts the texts of raw beauty, prophetic urgency for being human together in ways that protect the orphan and the widow. I breathed a little easier making it to Ruth, reveling finally in an ancient rendition of something I could feel, have experienced myself: the fiercely loyal companionship of two women, Naomi and Ruth. Even cloaked in the polygamous, chattelizing-of-women norms of the time, a seed of something woman-centric breathes, if just for four chapters. The poetical books or the Writings (Hebrew), what my tradition now deems "wisdom literature"—Job, Proverbs, Ecclesiastes, and the Psalms, as well as Sirach and the Wisdom of Solomon from the Apocrypha—welcome a much easier passage for a poet such as myself, surrounded by women writers observing the ordinary and extraordinary of their own lives. I'll never see Job the same, now companioned by Alicia Ostriker and Cheryl Bridges Johns who reframed reconsiderations for me: decentering benevolent patriarchy, learning to ask how Job's wife might have felt about God's murder of her children so to be replaced with ten *new* children. Like children can be replaced? Really? The Psalms bring humanity back to itself, in all glory and shadow. The Song of Songs points to what ancient men feared most. We catch glimpses of radical teachings and visions of a reign of God/de in Isaiah, Jeremiah, prophetic texts into the Beatitudes and more: a different ethos of love and life coming into Israelite observance and norms. We get to see just how very body-centric Jesus and his healings ministry *was*, as he is recorded as *bodily-healing* way more than he is recorded *teaching*, as we would consider it.[38] The parables, regardless of gospel-rendition, create space for new insight, for challenge of perceived norms often violent or neglectful of women.

None of which resolves the grief and sadness in me, in my body, for all women and women-identified bodies have lost over centuries of historic wisdom traditions. It's unspeakably difficult, clearly, to approach these ancient texts without drowning in my own cauldron of rage. I must become a human body of sorrows, it would seem, well-acquainted with grief. Which is where I land—praise that has become grief, grief that

---

38. Moltmann-Wendel, *I Am My Body*, 56ff.

someday may become praise once again. I smiled when some new work coming out of a movement called Wild Church began to show a way to continue to sit with my sadness, to tend my body's grieving whenever and however it arises. Kara Markell argues for engaging the Big Book of Revelation—the natural world—toward the *rewilding of religious leadership*. The Little Book (in comparison), the Bible, need not be neglected or ignored, but just like Job, it *does* need to be de-centered. She argues, "In the natural world and in superorganisms like forests, one finds life's genius and the revelatory presence of the sacred power of life. Mutual relationship with the more than human world in a posture of humility and openness, opens the way to receiving ancient wisdom."[39] How might this Big Book of Revelation come to contextualize and contextualize our Little Book of Revelation, i.e., the Bible, all ancient texts considered sacred and revelatory, so to encourage us toward participating in and leading the Body of Humanity as a *living organism*? *Rewilding* in this way brings my body a sense of hope. It resonates deeply with years of sacred bewilderment, honoring the rebalancing of F/feminine and M/masculine by means of a much larger Revelation *all around us*, and *so deeply within us too*. In this wilderness, then, I know S/she awaits me. Finally, I get to say, *here I am* (1 Sam 3).

Faith

Given these musings on community and Scripture, it won't be a surprise that I now understand *faith* in much more expansive, non-sectarian way without underpinnings in a modernistic conception of God or as I say, God/de. Think relational quantum physics, less Newtonian science. What I want to offer does not necessarily *contradict* my tradition's scriptural understandings, but it would never be considered traditionalist. I can see this non-sectarian definition throughout Scripture, in other words, but I also know it may be my new hammer, which makes everything look like a nail. Once you see what you've been given, you can't help but see it *everywhere*.

The entire story arc of this journey demonstrates faith to be an expansive, curious, even infuriating nourishment of Life, sensed first in a body and then lived with confirmation and guidance amidst intuition, companionable discernment, and serendipities some of us call signs or

---

39. Markell, "Rewilding Religious Leadership."

Providence. It is the *be not afraid* in times of great discomfort or fear. Love in the face of distrust. Graciousness in the face of enmity. Cynthia Bourgeault received the encouragement from her imaginally covenanted partner, Rafe, as "Trust in the invincibility of your own heart."[40] Trusting into an unknown with a sense of being deeply related to it, within it. Even in the painful things we co-create and inflict upon one another. Decades later, Bourgeault now points to *faith* as *a luminous perception of the invisible golden thread.*[41] Those words resonate with my own experience here. Faith is that in which we have found ourselves most whole and connected, surrendered into the divine order of things, abundantly loved and grace-filled, in grief that is praise. Faith is perceiving *in the heart* the interconnection and purpose of all things, even or perhaps most especially while our conceptions are being transfigured.

Throughout this story arc, I both knew and did not know what I was choosing, saying *yes* to, following this thread. Sometimes it was a nudge I felt consciously, with a conscious *yes* given. Other times, it was a leading in my body, while I was completely unaware but somehow willing to brave-risk-enter into the setting without knowing why or for what purpose. It's significant to me that both of these are *saying yes*, as our world is configured as *free*, so for Love, not Power or coercion. I also recognize that this more expansive sense of faith grew most in the *unchosen* or *unknown* yes's. Those that bewildered me grew a deeper trust and confidence *within* me. A strengthened capacity to even see my own utter abandonment as purposeful now, if I honor how viscerally the wound remains.

So I've come to see *faith* as this *luminous perception of the interconnection of all things*. It doesn't loosen my sense of intimate personal relationship to this Force or Flow who would not let me go, Who breathes so deeply within me. But faith does not rest in Him, or Her, or Them alone, regardless of my body's experience or sensation. It is a deeply embodied, engaged phenomenon, part of God/de's creation as much as part of me. I'm living in faith when I am most present, most perceptive, to the highest frequencies of Life we humans get to know: mercy, compassion, lovingkindness, hope. It is a luminous perception and knowing of the Heart in me, seen and unseen at the same time.

---

40. Bourgeault, *Love Stronger Than Death*, 70–75.
41. Bourgeault, *Eye of the Heart*, 16..

This sense of faith had to come first for human beings before any ancient texts were ever written, compiled, or canonized. Faith is prior therefore even to Scripture. It does not depend upon any ancient writings, though it can be nuanced and made articulate by them. On the contrary to how most conceive of it in my root tradition today, faith is a primarily relational term, not a received literary or conceptual one, connected to the "biblical sense of God of the church." It is not equated *with* the Bible, but to be pointed to, even broken open, *by* ancient texts considered sacred for millennia. I will guess that most seasoned in a living faith would actually agree with me, though be discomforted by my decentering of Scripture. Faith in this reoriented sense returns us to a time when it was lived and breathed in primarily oral communities, well before human beings ever had access to written language that would abstract our minds.[42] I'm simply arguing for a return to what is primary before empire and biblical studies, the golden handcuffs of expertise, got a hold of everything. Highly literate people, in contrast to historically primarily oral or today's secondarily oral cultures, fragment and abstract into words on a page, away from the body, away from our sensorium. Faith that lives and breathes however is a primarily oral—today secondarily oral—sensate capacity to perceive connection in the Heart, a luminous thread of interconnection.

Living faith connects you with anyone and everyone who senses the Sacred, regardless of tradition, theistic or not. Beliefs, in contrast, separate and divide, requiring the fancy analytical footwork of dialectical synthesis that never quite integrates into one. Or further, a movement from either/or thinking into the non-dual awareness of both/and, which gets you closer to living-faith, integrative presence. My life and work here is a testimony to this distinction, though it's not because there's anything particularly special about my gifts. Living faith always draws other human beings living in faith to one another. It is the thread that interconnects and the human heart's capacity to perceive it, follow it. *When the student is ready, the teacher appears*, say the Buddhists. *Trust the divine order of things*, says Quanita Roberson. *Leap and the net will appear*, invited Julia Cameron decades ago.[43] Different aphorisms I have found to be true of this sense of *faith* risked and breathing, again and again, in a subtle, living theology *in via*. While my most recent

---

42. Ong, *Orality and Literacy*. See also his *Presence of the Word*.
43. Cameron, *Artist's Way*, 2.

language for the means of living into the world this way is a *method of sacred bewilderment*, it was delightful to be reminded that Spirit was planting these seeds all along the way. I used to call this *a contemplative empiricism in an artisanal way*, trusting in the divine order of things enough to *seek the question* in which grounded collaborations, deeply rooted amidst wisdom traditions, might emerge.

Seeking the Question into an Emergent Leadership "Method"

Early in my scholarly vocation, I crafted some jargony language for *theology in performative mode*, arising from a sustained encounter with music as "container" for spiritual insight. Performative mode aimed to point to all the things beyond interpretation and theory/practice discourses that prevailed in my day. I argued theology in performative mode must be primarily "relationally-formed through a methodological commitment to compassionate companionship(s), lived within practiced rhythms of life-giving covenantal relationship." "Explicitly embodied." "Indwelt operations of contemplative inquiry with heightened attention to sensation toward awakening in new insight." I argued this way of being becomes explicitly multidimensional in "an *erotic* rationality" and "an extension of tasks beyond interpretation toward the fullness of human living through *contemplative wondering, impassioned gentle conviction, intimacies of difference, and joyful celebration that yet knows sorrow.*"[44] Then I spent the next fifteen years doing just that: living primarily into covenantal companionships with those deeply rooted in wisdom traditions and those with no explicit traditional commitment of any kind. To be honest, I forgot the themes and language that had felt so necessary to name in scholarly form. *Sacred bewilderment* as method of *seeking the question* and *surrender* into the divine order of things offers more contemporary language resonant with my woman's body today, but I belly laughed to realize that, in some ways, I've been writing this same book for nearly thirty years. *Seeking the question* is where it started, but then a three-imperative invitation into surrender enfleshes how to breathe more deeply into the inner work and emergent leadership collaborations suggested—and hoped for—here.

"How can I develop a relationship with my teacher when he only visits for a teaching once a year?" This question was asked by an earnest

---

44. Hess, *Learning in a Musical Key*, 167–207.

Buddhist practitioner as we were discussing Rig'dzin Dorje's book, *Dangerous Friend: the Teacher-Student Relationship in Vajrayana Buddhism*[45] at Gar Drolma, where the sangha meets close to where I live in Dayton, Ohio. I had landed in this sangha book club while companioning a spirit-friend from my husband's church. She felt drawn to Buddhist wisdom, which made sense to me because her husband self-identified as Buddhist. I had been manhandled by the head deacon of my husband's church, so was seeking a way to become "grounded in exile" from what had presumably been "our" congregational home.[46] Gar Drolma held this healing space for me for years, though I wrestled with what my own role could be in a Buddhist sangha, given I could only be an affiliate practitioner at best, a tourist at worst. I knew my Presbyterian and UMC seminary communities would be more shocked than supportive that *this* is where I had been led.

The *Dangerous Friend* book discussion opened up issues of relationship and practice in profound ways. I felt for my practice-friend who only got to see her teacher once a year, particularly as the teacher-student relationship in Tibetan Buddhism is so fundamental to practice. She was faced with cultivating intimacy with a man who had been in a Chinese prison for over twenty years, freed and therefore planting Buddhist sanghas all over the United States. He visited Dayton, Ohio, maybe once a year for a weekend's teachings. How does a Buddhist practitioner cultivate deepening intimacy with her teacher, her lama, under those circumstances? My heart ached for the impossibility of it all. My heart startled more at a felt-congruence or resonance with this vastly "other," even non-theistic wisdom tradition of Kagyu-Nyingma Tibetan Buddhism.

As she asked her question, I was stunned to hear it in my own *Christian* spirit-body-mind. How are *we* who profess Jesus as Lord to develop a deepening intimate relationship with *our* teacher, a carpenter from Nazareth with 2000 years of Christian and imperialized history? How are we to develop a relationship with this Risen Lord when bodily visitation is so rare, if ever? This brief incident crystallized several elements within my own path of teaching and scholarship, moving into the theologies of religious pluralism, a companionable way, and conscious feminine leadership in institutions quite disinterested in H/her as S/she is. But in that moment, I became aware of a calm abiding, a felt-sense of a new way to

---

45. Dorje, *Dangerous Friend*.
46. Hess, *Companionable Way*, 20–23.

be in this Buddhist sangha with integrity to my own tradition. I could share in this question, *from my own root tradition*.

Ultimately, I was being taught the importance of *sitting with practitioners* of various faith/non-theistic traditions, actively waiting for the question that impassions the practice of each yet remains distinct to the traditions or norms present. Focusing my practice as "befriended outsider," I moved into *learning to pray* with other *practitioners of prayer*, persistently assessing how to do so *as a Christian*. My sense of *prayer* then expanded to include observance, meditation, breathwork, and more—any *practice* in solitude or community that required open space and curiosity, willingness to risk in heart and in community.[47] I wanted to learn how others confront the particularity of religious traditions or their own woundedness by such traditions, while living into the necessary but rooted openness to other wisdom from which all of us may learn, *need to learn*. Ways in which all of us may become wiser to our own root traditional wisdom *and* the Wisdom beyond our gates, however S/she might arrive. Congregationally or traditionally-historically socialized Christians do not welcome this approach easily, I might add. Particularly in a refused-grief-drenched world in which so much of what we have known as Sacred is changing before our very eyes. I empathize yet am no longer bound by such fear (on a good day).

As I inhabit my story ever more deeply in a restorative-wisdom fashion—re-storying it year by year as I live it—a method of sorts came into speech in multiple contexts of circle quite resonant with what I used to call a contemplative empiricism in an artisanal way. The primacy of prayer, devotion, active waiting that seeks the question in the Body of Humanity has guided my living honestly and as transparently as I know how into deeper and deeper mysteries that none of us will ever fully understand. It has fostered in me a loving and being loved ever more deeply the longer I practiced in this way, with proximate beloveds, inspired by spirit-friends from all over. It's fairly simple, yet

---

47. The implicit non-negotiable for me here, significant to name, is a willingness to be proximate together in some practice of prayer, observance, meditation. *Something* that opens contemplative spaces for unknowns to emerge. Inclusivity in popular presumption suggests "all," but inclusivists are rarely as inclusive as they imagine. I am certainly not. Everyone has an incapacity or inability to be-with: this is mine. I have little capacity or interest in the truly secularized, or truly fundamentalist—those who in my experience of them refuse *any* sense of the unknown beyond their own conceptualizations, those whose need for certainty is so great that there is no practiced curiosity that could lead to surrender.

excruciatingly difficult to embody today, particularly in communities of faith. *Show up. Unlearn why you're here. Offer your gifts and receive what you need.* Three imperatives that require practice, failure, and commitment to keep practicing if our leadership is to become emergent and responsive to a sustainable universe around us.

First of all, show up. Fully. Get all of your body, all of your stories—particularly those most feared or shamed—present with you, in your body, in the room, with whomever you're with. This is much harder than you think, especially amidst technological and polarizing distractions. Most of us are highly practiced at only partial presence, anywhere we are, while being completely unaware we are only partially present. Those in trauma-informed care speak of this kind of presence as one's awareness of one's own reactivities or "triggers."[48] It means being as conscious of one's own ancestral and faith lineages' gifts and wounds as possible, honoring that our bodies are reacting way before we know how to healthily respond.[49] It means *shadowdancing* and getting savvy to your own capacity for projections and *withdrawing them* so as to do the least harm. It means staying at the inner work required, held in communities able to witness into healing, so to self-regulate and be grounded, present, amidst other human beings who may or may not have tended to their own personal or intergenerational wounds yet.[50] Showing up like this is excruciatingly vulnerable, even if you don't speak a word of any of your stories. Stories do not need to be spoken aloud to *be present with you in the room*. We often experience inappropriate story-sharing as *over-sharing*, usually for some unhealthy attempt to belong, be loved, become special. That's not what I'm talking about here, nor what is healthy for the over-sharer or the community. I'm talking about becoming present to your own deepest fears, which you've probably been traditioned to think of as darkness or sin. I'm inviting a curiosity to *be with them differently*, in communities able to love without judgment, witness without accusation or condemnation. Probably not congregations, and probably not small groups or book groups. Consciousness raising-circles (they used to be called). Writing circles. Conscious-feminine communities which then allow you to *show up, fully present, grounded in your own body.*

---

48. See Nsoroma, *Wisdom Walk to Self-Mastery*, 38. See also Hemphill, *What It Takes to Heal* and Brown, *Dare to Lead*.

49. Menakem, *My Grandmother's Hands*, 5.

50. Ginwright, *Four Pivots*, 16–17.

The second imperative is to *unlearn why you are there*.[51] Most of us enter into human settings with an anticipation or expectation of *why* we're there. Leaders today survive and thrive by anticipating, becoming as strategic as possible. School is the largest shaper of this, with its socializing methodologies. Educational theory talks about it too. *Explicit* curriculum we consciously choose. The *implicit* curriculum is the unconscious or subconscious learning simply by being in that space. Null curriculum, when even considered, points to everything that is missing or not even being considered at all. Unlearning why you are where you are is an implicit-to-null focused task. Reconsidering why we gather where we gather, for what known—and unknown—purposes. Think church. Town meetings in government. A sports event, etc. This second step of fully inhabiting our bodies and spaces in bewilderment that can become sacred is to relinquish as many assumptions or presumptions as possible. To un-know *why* you are where you are so you might learn all the unknowns inside of yourself or inside others. Get curious about anything that could happen in the moment, altering all expectation. A friend of mine says it this way, "I wonder what could happen next?" Living with that unlearning expectation *habitually* opens up spaces for surprise, abundance, co-emergence that are largely impossible when we leaders are focused on our own strategizing anticipations.

Finally, the third imperative aims to encourage living into a culture of true generosity, grounded in presence and connection. *Offer your gifts and receive what you need.* I originally thought the last task in my learning was simply to offer my best. I had T-shirts made with my "method," offering the first two imperatives, followed by *offer your best*. I stand by that. All we can offer is the best we can offer, with great freedom in being finite. You cannot take someone where you have not traveled yourself. At least not healthily or well. The Body of Humanity teaching for me here was that one is not truly generous if one *cannot receive well*. Chameli Gad Ardagh calls most of what we consider generosity today a *near enemy of generosity*.[52] We offer what we have *in the hopes of receiving what we want*, whether that is security, belonging, being helpful, being special. Most religious leaders in the church today offer their gifts because of their vocation, yes. What they have been called to do. But they also offer them *because they are paid to do so*. Professional employment lives within

---

51. Slaughter, *Unlearning Church*, 1–2.
52. Ardagh, *Living Goddess*.

the ethos and practice of *professional ethics*, naming the contractual facets of paid employment. As a result, most pastoral leaders I know, including those I love most, are less and less skilled at being able to *receive what they need* or to practice into a culture of true generosity.[53] Increasingly absent is any communal center of gathering for *koinonia*, with a truly generous communal ethos of becoming-living-faith-together. More of us therefore need to begin doing the inner and communal work that *enlivens*—instigates and expresses our desires and passions—while living into a commitment to a communal center, an *ethos of open space*, discovery, co-emergence. Each of us is to practice generosity for the sake of the whole, *which also means learning to ask for what you need*. Mostly, we experience a penalty for this within established institutions, which I believe is instigated more by envy than anything else. We *can* be for deeper connection and collectivity without being enslaved to what has been, as we have always done it. But leaders will suffer to lead so.

The longer I have traveled within—and been healed by—a more expansive Body of Humanity beyond congregation or tribal-identity community, the more I have experienced an abundant way of being and embodying a lively bewildering path into companionship, laughter, lament, and more. *Show up. Unlearn why you're here. Offer your gifts and receive what you need.* These phrases have become my mantra or instructions received along such a sacred rupturing-healing way. Another colleague recently gave a slightly different but resonant version with scriptural nuance, good for Scripture-centered people of faith: *Don't be afraid. Listen to everyone you can. Look for a sign.*[54] My hope has been to share the harvest of some of these traditional fruits of Spirit in this excruciating-abundant journey. If it blesses congregations to invite "pockets of possibility" for new ways of committing to deeper spiritual maturity through inner work and exploring circle-way ethos together in collaborations yet unseen, unknown, all the better.

---

53. Merritt and Fenimore, *Wounded Pastors*.
54. Kent Millard, personal conversation.

Epilogue

Ancestral Wounds Healing—
Absence Becomes Presence

I SIT MOST MORNINGS with a cup of buckeye-blend coffee, stunned there is this freedom beyond forgiveness, a belonging accessible to me within visceral awareness of the Body of Humanity, feeling shyly grateful in the renewed Trinitarianism that made it possible through an awakening to desire, palpable in pleasure. It's easy in our world to focus on the fear, the tumult of polarizations tearing our communal fabrics to shreds, doomsday scrolling hours on end attempting to go unconscious about this Great Turning, as some call it, or climate catastrophe as others call it, or the near-implosions of representative democracy we seem to be seeing, or the decline of the church amidst the rise of fundamentalisms all over the world. Writing this (much larger) volume (than I ever intended), I sit most mornings no less accompanied by an Assurance that makes little sense in such a world. Which is not to say I don't get anxious or that I'm not afraid. I am, both of those things, regularly. Yet God/de has shown me again and again, in ways I cannot deny, that our world is more mysterious and more hopeful than any of my fear(s). To go scriptural about it, the gates of Hell will not prevail against the Life that has died and risen, the Life that somehow is intimately personal yet energetically shared in visible and invisible interconnectedness. Seeing it requires an attentiveness to chiasmic patterning, trusting long enough to see a spatial causality suggesting a Presence beyond our expectation, no less Present. The return to the body, delving into the subtle energies with much higher frequencies—mercy, grief-praise, forgiveness, compassion, lovingkindness—points to worlds within which we may practice, what Bourgeault points to as the imaginal realm within which we *do* have sacred purpose. The Great Exchange, she calls it. Writing honestly, without care for profession or vocation, I smile sheepishly at the revelatory happenings demonstrating this Assurance, in both ancestral woundedness and divine abandonment. They give me faith and courage to live here on the other side of rage, even in a world of rages.

Ancestral Wounds *Can* Heal and Be Held with a Smile

One year after my labyrinth encounter amidst the Shalem retreat, one year after any notion of *forgiving the divine* had long left my memory, I was immersed in a Great Silence at a retreat center held by the Sisters of Mercy. The Shalem program had required it, so there I was, a bit panicky about being disconnected from spirit-friends and women's circles but also curious and breathing amongst the Elders, the stately trees well over two hundred years old scattered all over the property. I was sitting in the dining room, the silence made companionable for the sisters and me by a CD player, crooning rather Muzak-y old hymn tunes. I was lost in thought but something caught my attention. A tail-end of a piece that somehow felt familiar but unplaceable. Lots of folks were still eating so I couldn't easily approach the CD player to hit "repeat." This forced me to pay attention to the album as a whole, which I then realized was a collection of "hymn-tune mash-ups," like the form that became popular while the movie *Pitch Perfect* and the TV show *Glee!* held sway. Finally, the last sister left the dining room. I pulled the CD out of the player, stunned with what I found.

The first time I had ever heard what is popularly known as Lakmé's "Flower Duet," I was in my graduate student years, watching an art film with my acapella group. The "Flower Duet" is a two-voice aria for soprano and mezzo-soprano in Léo Delibes's opera *Lakmé*. In operatic form, it is sung by the characters Lakmé, daughter of a Brahmin priest, and her servant Mallika, as they go to gather flowers by a river. It has a lilting question in its tone, a poignant dulcet quality. Two women's voices intertwined, soaring into the ranges above, cascading back into the orchestral harmonies. Listening to it today, I *still* catch my breath with tears at its visceral beauty. In the 1987 Canadian award-winning art-film, *I've Heard the Mermaids Singing*, it was a lyrical accompaniment chronicling a love triangle of sorts between three women—an artist, a studio-owner, and an affable soul trying to find herself through her own photography in a complicated, modern world.

That entire year, as I named in chapter 2, anger had become conscious in my body while laboring as the intern of a battered woman's shelter, supervised by a dear woman-bodysoul partnered for life with another woman. Both were more self-disclosive with me than was wise for that era, particularly where I was, yet they introduced me to sacred energies available between women that had largely been foreign to me. They invited me into their closeted Christian community gatherings, stewarded with other LGTBQIA folks (mostly LG, perhaps B then). I got to experience the integrity of a love beyond expectation, at some threat to everyone there in their ecclesial circles. The sacred timbre of the group was undeniable, palpable, so accepting of me, fierce for my well-being. Then in watching a movie with friends, this song of two women's voices, interwoven and dancing together, moved me to my very core.

I felt the sacred center of my supervisor and her partner, allured by their devotion to one another. I also felt the longstanding shame of my body for feeling this desire so palpably myself, for considering something like devotion for women *sacred*. Of course, I told no one. But from that point onwards, for the decades to come when I learned of this gift of devotion, palpable as desire viscerally in my own body, the "Flower Duet" became an audible icon for me. I would pause, honoring what my body felt, then what my body could release in feeling. It became the vehicle whereby Godde reattuned my own body to honor desire as utter gift, no matter what. It was the release of my shame and the whispering of something beautiful, holy, sacred in my own flesh. The "Flower Duet" became a song of liberation, an icon of sacred transformation, if also a song of deep sadness for all my youngest self had never known was beautiful in her. My body remembers and now can cherish the innumerable ways that women in circle have viscerally, physically, spiritually healed my woman's body, clearing the energetic lines so to be able to attune, self-regulate, ultimately respond to Life, to Love, to all that God/de intends as Gift between human beings in bounded, covenantal intimacies with one another.

It was also the tune that caught my attention in the retreat center dining room, providentially paired in a hymn-tune mashup with my family's table blessing, *Grosser Gott*, or "Holy God We Praise Your Name." When I looked at the CD playlist and saw those two tunes together as one title, my body viscerally *lit up*, resonant with awe, wonder, a little fear and joy from root to crown chakra, from the soles of my feet to the tips of my fingers. In an album my classist, stuffy musical self would have considered too schlocky for praise—*Divine Light: Music to Inspire* created and instrumentally crafted by Peggy Duquesnel and Steve Hall—I heard the full musical icon of my entire story arc here. "Holy God We Praise Your Name" and "the Flower Duet" were dancing in beauty, one-ness, harmony and witness, just as they *were meant to be*. I was struck by how I almost *missed it*. What if my body had missed this clear *sacred whisper* meant so obviously for me, that night, in this faith-filled yet excruciatingly painful journey? To this day, I don't know whether it was the "Flower Duet" tune or the *Grosser Gott* tune that finally got through to me. I like to think it was the duet, with its questioning lilt and dulcet tone, able to reach me without any fear at all. When intimacy speaks union, it doesn't really matter.

Absence Can Become Presence When Ancestral Wounds Heal in a Return to the Body

I still can and do say wholeheartedly that the God of the church did indeed abandon me as a woman, made known to me in the power of the Spirit in my woman's body in those Days in the Weeds. *Divine abandonment* of women and women-identified human beings is real within congregational forms of Christianity today, with no traditional ecclesial body (I can imagine) able to convince me otherwise. Come to think of it, there may be *one* ecumenical Christian community within which my woman's body has not been regularly abandoned. Not surprisingly, she would be called *Holy Wisdom Monastery*, where some of this was written as their praying the hours, their communal liturgies, returned to me in my woman's body. But divine abandonment was made complete in my family's ancestral woundedness, in faith communities' regularly socialized incapacities to honor much beyond solar Christianity or Christian faith held in certainty or power-over scriptural authority. It was confirmed in the pilgrimage to the Holy Land, *for Christ's sake*, said intentionally, without blasphemy.

It was the summer of 2017, before the labyrinth walk, when I was leading a conscious feminine leadership academy at a retreat center, stewarded by the Sisters of the Transfiguration. A stately, grandmotherly gingko tree holds her visceral greening energies over the gathering spaces, so much so that the circle-sisters that week named her Grandmother Gingko, even creating a communal ritual of leaving small gifts of gratitude and intention in her branches, at her roots throughout the week we were there.

I got nothin', I said to myself about day five of the week. I am a symbolic-item junky, always carrying things in my pockets and setting up little altars whenever I travel anywhere for long. It matters deeply for me to feel the connection in the intention, in the sharing of the symbol. I'm too often in inherited rituals with sacred energies that seem to imprison more than liberate, create a culture of "getting it right" more than feeling part of an emergent community making time sacred together. So I waited. And waited. Five days in, I still felt *nothing*. I felt a little disconnected from all the energies gathering at the community altar, which brought sadness. Curious how each fierce woman was finding her way there while I seemed to be kept at bay somehow.

Morning circle opened on day six with two women pouring their sorrow into the opening check-in. Anniversary of the unexpected loss of a child. Violence on the land nearby us, by landscapers with no felt-connection to creation as alive. I had chosen a steel-edged butterfly totem that morning, sending it around for women's voices, stories. We paused together, everyone having spoken. Getting on with the agenda did not feel ready or right. The energy was inviting something else. I scanned my brain for what I knew about butterflies. A song alighted upon my shoulder, just in time. I invited the circle to sing . . . for the young lives that had been too short, for the sorrow of the mothers and families left behind, for the rising grief in the circle that departure was coming soon . . . *Fly, fly little butterfly fly, to the calling of your spirit, fly free and purposefully, and know you are held in Love.* It's a sweet little chant, learned at a Red Tent circle.

Its sweetness means a soft voice, opening tone, and so we began . . . I invited humming, anticipating a couple rounds before moving into the agenda. But as the circle entered in, my body knew we were in it again, this fierce flow that can*not* but bring release, toward healing. Voices joined in as the words were learned, the stone went around again. Time out of time opened once again. This sweet song, sung fiercely, was the medicine of the morning. The stone returned to me as we sang at the tops of our lungs, standing, swaying our bodies, letting the sorrow be released. The circle began to ease again, and we drew to a quiet, returning to our seats. When each was ready to move on, she raised her hand in our "A-Ho" sign. We moved into the morning agenda. And I knew what I could offer, was *supposed* to offer in deep belly gratitude, at the roots of Grandmother Gingko: the little butterfly token that had been given to me by a friend, iridescent colors on one side of its little metal frame, engraved words on the back: *Be Yourself.* It had been held and blessed by all of us in the circle.

Later that afternoon, when I had the psychological space to enter in, I took the little butterfly from my window sill altar. Holding it gently in my palm, I neared Grandmother Gingko's dripline, bowing to her marvelous presence, energy. I walked around to the other side, to gaze with her all the way around. I gasped.

A plastic mannequin who a couple circle-sisters named the Rescued Lady was leaning nonchalantly against Grandmother Gingko, nearly smiling (if she'd had a head). Startling white, with a black-lined inside, she was all body, no legs, no head. All body, to *be* there, not think too much about it, not move away from her own presence. A Rescued Lady, leaning nonchalantly against Grandmother Gingko, *both* smiling, if *either of them* had had a head.

The Holy Land pilgrimage, the icon of divine abandonment, all came back to me. The Temple Mount, cobblestone streets of Jerusalem, the tiny trash truck, the turning the corner, the smashed lady on the street, left behind in her fragmentation ... all the memories and belly-feelings of that terrible, wondrous day in the Old City came rushing back into me. Tears of recognition, of amazement, even of joy streamed down my face as I sat in wonder on the grass underneath Grandmother Gingko's arms.

I *was* this woman, fragmented and left behind on the streets of Jerusalem, *found again*, because the trash truck didn't get to me in time. I am this woman, Rescued and nonchalant (outside), called forth into unimaginable but deeply felt work by fierce circles of women over a decade. I was companioned in sacred flow of companionship, pushed along with my rage to the holy site "where the women waited." I released a symbol of that rage and brokenness into the shrine of Mary Magdalene, pushed by Eastern European pilgrims wanting to get close to pray. This Rescued Lady has black within her, a union of black and white. Aware of my own whiteness, I could wish that the white were not forefront even here, but I bow to the messages we receive, when we receive them. I am as I am, just as I am.

Conclusion

The words bubble up out of me, for those who want to receive them then: we are this woman, each of us and all of us. Our power-over, yearning-to-be-*post*-patriarchal world shatters the black woman, the Dark Lady, those of unfamiliar bodies, those unlike our own we hold in fear. We leave our bodies behind on the streets of (yet blessed) wisdom traditions, more and more mired in hatred, shame, and violence. We see the shattering of women and girls daily, hourly, minute by minute, left behind in alley ways and in laws disregarding our own voices. But we are also the ones who have waited, who are waiting still, for more and more of us to join together in a more hopeful, fearless way. In a landed-leadership way, all body, all present, all presence.

I still have more questions than answers after thirty years of theological education. My body is still overwhelmed with grief some days, buoyant in praise on others, or more often, by the hope of others who seem to breathe hope into my own body when I most need it. None of this takes away the tumult of the Great Turning we seem to be in, nor does any of it written here redress the seemingly unending rage in our world today. Only you can do that, in your own body. Only we can do that, exploring new configurations of I–We with an in-depth respect for what has come before. Even as all has wounded us so.

Yet I breathe more fully when I hear a human being speak what I have found to be deeply true, with the same Spirit breath within them as testified here. Eve Ensler proclaiming the interconnectedness of all things, for instance, not unlike a Baptist preacher: "For me, it is all of this, all of this, *all* of this, in my body, in these words, in the world."[1] I am grateful to know faith now as a luminous perception of the golden thread connecting all things. I am blessed with the return to my own body that granted me such freedom in a forgiveness that found me. I am blessed and committed to the Body of Humanity able to witness, hold, trust, and participate with me in healing unto great joy made palpable in sorrows shared. I know nothing for certain anymore, except that assurance grows unwavering in a bewilderment become sacred, belonging to and with one another amidst our beautiful, wilding Earth. So may we all breathe more fully . . .

> *Though the fig tree does not blossom, and no fruit is on the vines; though the produce of the olive fails and the fields yield no food; though the flock is cut off from the fold and there is no herd in the stalls; I will exult in the God/de of my salvation. God is my strength; S/she makes my feet like the feet of a deer, and makes me tread upon the heights.* (Hab 3:17–19)

---

1. Ensler, "Suddenly, My Body."

Appendix

Resources for Open-Space Communities of Practice

Art of Hosting (harvesting conversations that matter)

A highly effective way of harnessing the collective wisdom and self-organizing capacity of groups of any size. Based on the assumption that people give their energy and lend their resources to what matters most to them—in work as in life—the Art of Hosting blends a suite of powerful conversational processes to invite people to step in and take charge of the challenges facing them.

Methods:

- The Circle Way
- World Café
- Open Space Technology
- Appreciative Inquiry

https://artofhosting.org/

Regional Contacts: https://artofhosting.org/connect/contact/

Awakening Women

We are a women-run organization. Together, we explore a business model based on ease, freedom and honoring of the cyclic nature of creativity.

We aim to live true to our values of integrity, trust, generosity and honest, open communication. Our team members work remotely from many places in the world. And yes, we have a zero-stress policy. Lead teacher, Chameli (pronounced sha-meh-lee) Gad Ardagh is a yogini, mystic, and a Goddess Wisdom Keeper. Her love of decoding and experimenting with ancient wisdom teachings through her own practice in yogini circles all over the world has crystallized maps of spiritual awakening and leadership that are accessible, practical, and honoring of women today. Rooted in earth honoring, devotional women's spirituality and goddess-centered tantric yoga, she is especially appreciated for her love of mythology and storytelling as a key to spiritual awakening and embodiment.

https://awakeningwomen.com/

The Center for Courage and Renewal—Circles of Trust

2435 East North St. Suite 1108—111
Greenville, SC 29615
+1 206.466.2055
hello@couragerenewal.org

Mission: to nurture deep integrity and relational trust, building the foundation for a more loving, equitable, and healthy world. The Courage & Renewal approach is distinguished by principles and practices intended to create supportive communities of reflection and belonging that help people move towards personal and societal wholeness.

Circles of Trust
Foundations of the Courage & Renewal Approach
Courage & Renewal Practicum

The Circle Way

A lightly formalized, lightly facilitated social structure that allows people to use circle process in a wide range of settings

- to mainstream circle as a shift in how organizations and communities' function and work together.

- to grow a diverse inter-generational community of circle practitioners promote racial, gender, disability, ethnic, economic, and environmental justice.
- to incubate and accelerate the growth of circle practices.

https://www.thecircleway.net/people-1
https://www.thecircleway.net/
https://www.facebook.com/groups/thecirclewaypractitioners/

Fire & Water: Leadership & Rite of Passage

A leadership program that calls forward unique gifts and genius in leaders of all ages. It calls forward abilities and instincts to work with clarity and kindness, humility and confidence, transparency, and awareness that we all seek meaning in our complex environments. *Coming of age in this age, because this age is calling for wisdom, because time passing is inevitable, but growth is a choice.*

Quanita Roberson
www.nzuzu.com

Flow Game: a way of finding clarity alone & together
Toke Paludan Moeller: https://www.interchange-tomo.com/flow-game-1
Mary Alice Arthur: https://www.getsoaring.com/the-flow-game
https://playflowgame.net/

Group Facilitation, Consulting, and Circle Way

Tenneson Woolf: www.tennesonwoolf.com
Christina Baldwin & Ann Linnea, elders in PeerSpirit and Circle Way
https://peerspirit.com/
https://christinabaldwin.com/
https://annlinnea.com/

Restorative Practices—Restorative Justice Circle Trainings

International Institute for Restorative Practices: https://www.iirp.edu/
The Restorative Center: https://www.therestorativecenter.org/

Mediators Beyond Borders International: https://mediatorsbeyondborders.org/

CircleUpEducation: https://www.circleuped.org/

Way of the Rose

The Way of the Rose is an open-hearted, inclusive community of beings dedicated to the forgotten Earth wisdom of the rosary ... and to the Lady, by any name you like to call Her. We are not affiliated with the Catholic Church or any other religious institution. Nor do we seek to build a new one. We have no dues or fees, no buildings to maintain or capital campaigns. We pass the hat from time to time for our modest needs. There are no priests or levels of mastery. Instead of lineages of power, we value circles of friendship. We support one another in praying for our heart's desire. Every rosary circle honors the Five Petals of the Wild rose: free, inclusive, praying the rosary, pray for our heart's desire, leaderlessness.

https://wayoftherose.org/
https://www.facebook.com/groups/wayoftherose
https://www.facebook.com/groups/256562762046210

Wilderness & Circle Way

School of Lost Borders: https://schooloflostborders.org/

Cascadia Quest: https://cascadiaquest.org/

Rites of Passage—Wilderness Quest: https://wildernessquest.org/

Animas Valley Institute: https://www.animas.org/

New Moon Rites of Passage: https://www.newmoonritesofpassage.com/

Women Writing for (a) Change

(with affiliates in Bloomington, Indiana, and Jacksonville, Florida)

Vision: a world that nurtures creative expression and silences no one

Mission: Create a community that embodies equity and encourages people to craft more conscious lives through writing

Values: Community. Joy. Respect. Connection. Hospitality

6906 Plainfield Road
Cincinnati, OH 45236
513-272-1171
info@womenwriting.org

World Café

Using seven design principles and a simple method, the World Café is a powerful social technology for engaging people in conversations that matter, offering an effective antidote to the fast-paced fragmentation and lack of connection in today's world. Based on the understanding that conversation is the core process that drives personal, business, and organizational life, the World Café is more than a method, a process, or technique—it's a way of thinking and being together sourced in a philosophy of conversational leadership. https://theworldcafe.com/

Bibliography

Althaus-Reid, Marcella. *Indecent Theology: Theological Perversions in Sex, Gender and Politics*. London: Routledge, 2000.
Ardagh, Chameli Gad. *Come Closer: Spiritual Awakening for the Feminine Heart*. Grass Valley, CA: Lighting Source, 2006.
———. *Living Goddess*. https://awakeningwomen.com/living-goddess-podcast-2/.
Barnhart, Bruno. *The Good Wine: Reading John from the Center*. Mahwah, NJ: Paulist, 1993.
Berezan, Jennifer. "This Is to Mother You." Track 8 on *Home*. Albany, CA: Edge of Wonder Records, 2013.
Berry, Thomas. "Remarks." Seeking the Meaning of Peace conference, San Jose, Costa Rica, June 27, 1989.
Berman, Morris. *Coming to Our Senses: Body and Spirit in the Hidden History of the West*. Brattleboro, VT: Echo Point, 2015.
Boehme, Jacob. *The Clavis: Or Key And Dialogues On The Supersensual Life*. Whitefish, MT: Kessinger, 2010.
Bole, William, et al. *Forgiveness in International Politics*. Washington, DC: United States Conference of Catholic Bishops, 2004.
Bolen, Jean Shinoda. "Athena, Artemis, Aphrodite, and Initiation into the Conscious Feminine." In *To Be a Woman*, edited by Connie Zweig, 217–21. New York: Jeremy P. Tarcher/Putnam, 1990.
———. *Crossing to Avalon: a Woman's Midlife Quest for the Sacred Feminine*. New York: HarperCollins, 1994.
Brosmer, Mary Pierce. *Women Writing for (a) Change: a Guide for Creative Transformation*. Notre Dame: Sorin, 2009.
brown, adrienne marie. *Pleasure Activism: the Politics of Feeling Good*. Emergent Strategy series. Chico: AK, 2019.
Brown, Brené. *Dare to Lead: Brave Work, Tough Conversations, Whole Hearts*. New York: Random, 2018.
———. "The Power of Vulnerability." Filmed October 6, 2010 at TedXHouston, Houston, TX. https://www.ted.com/talks/brene_brown_the_power_of_vulnerability?subtitle=en.
Brown, William P. "Job and Comforting Chaos." In *Seeking Wisdom's Depths and Torah's Heights: Essays in Honor of Samuel E. Balentine*, edited by Barry R. Huff and Patricia Vesely, 249–68. Cambridge: Smyth and Helwys, 2020.

Bourgeault, Cynthia. *Eye of the Heart: A Spiritual Journey into the Imaginal Realm.* Boston: Shambhala, 2020.

———. *The Holy Trinity and the Law of Three: Discovering the Radical Truth at the Heart of Christianity.* Boston: Shambhala, 2013.

———. *Love Is Stronger Than Death: the Mystical Union of Two Souls.* New York: Bell Tower, 1997.

———. *Wisdom Way of Knowing: Reclaiming an Ancient Tradition to Reclaim the Heart.* San Francisco: Jossey-Bass, 2003.

Brunner, Daniel L., and A. J. Swoboda. "Creation Care and the Bible: an Evangelical Perspective." In *The Oxford Handbook of the Bible and Ecology*, 413–24. Oxford: Oxford University Press, 2022.

Callahan, Allan Dwight. *The Talking Book: African Americans and the Bible.* New Haven, CT: Yale University Press, 2008.

Cameron, Julia. *The Artist's Way: A Spiritual Path to Higher Creativity.* 30th Anniversary Edition. New York: TarcherPerigee, 2016.

———. *Seeking Wisdom: a Spiritual Path to Creative Connection.* New York: St. Martin's Essentials, 2021.

Chemaly, Soraya. *Rage Becomes Her: the Power of Women's Anger.* New York: Atria, 2018.

Chittister, Joan. *The Breath of the Soul: Reflections on Prayer.* Worcester, MA: Twenty-Third, 2016.

Christ, Carol P., and Judith Plaskow, eds. *Womanspirit Rising: A Feminist Reader in Religion.* San Francisco: Harper, 1992.

Coakley, Sarah. *God, Sexuality, and the Self: an Essay 'On the Trinity'.* Cambridge: Cambridge University Press, 2013.

———. *Powers and Submissions: Spirituality, Philosophy and Gender.* Oxford: Blackwell, 2002.

———. "What Does Chalcedon Solve and What Does It Not? Some Reflections on the Status and Meaning of the Chalcedonian Definition." In *The Incarnation*, edited by Stephen T. Davis et al., 143–63. Oxford: Oxford University Press, 2002.

Colbert, Joanna Powell. *Journey through the Gaian Tarot.* Woodbury, MN: Llewellyn, 2011.

College of Saint Benedict. "Stella Maris Chapel." https://www.csbsju.edu/sju-archives/sjuhistory/sjubuildings/stellamarischapel/

Davidson, Jennifer W. "Beyond Trigger Warnings: Toward a Trauma-Informed Androgogy for the Graduate Theological Classroom." *Review and Expositor* 117 (2020) 243–56.

Deardorff, Daniel. *The Other Within: the Genius of Deformity in Myth, Culture, and Psyche.* Introduction by Robert Bly. Berkeley, CA: North Atlantic, 2009.

Dorje, Rig'dzin. *Dangerous Friend: The Teacher-Student Relationship in Vajrayana Buddhism.* Boston: Shambhala, 2001.

Eliot, T. S. "Little Gidding." In *Collected Poems 1909–1962.* New York: Faber, 1974. https://poetryarchive.org/poem/four-quartets-extract/.

Elsheimer, Janice. *The Creative Call: An Artist's Response to the Way of the Spirit.* Colorado Springs: Shaw, 2001.

Ensler, Eve. "Suddenly My Body." Filmed December 7–8, 2010 at the International Trade Center, Washington, DC. https://www.ted.com/talks/eve_ensler_suddenly_my_body?subtitle=en.

Estes, Clarissa Pinkola. *Untie the Strong Woman: Blessed Mother's Immaculate Love for the Wild Soul*. Boulder, CO: SoundsTrue, 2017.

Evans, Rachel Held. *Inspired: Slaying Giants, Walking on Water, and Loving the Bible Again*. Nashville: Nelson, 2018.

Fierro, Rita Sinorita. *Digging Up the Seeds of White Supremacy*. Philadelphia: Collective Power Media, 2022.

Fortune, Marie M., and Cindy G. Enger. "Violence Against Women and the Role of Religion." *Applied Research Forum: National Online Resource Center on Violence Against Women*, March 2005. https://vawnet.org/material/violence-against-women-and-role-religion.

Gilbert, Elizabeth. *Big Magic: Creative Living Beyond Fear*. New York: Riverhead, 2015.

Gillian, Carol. *The Birth of Pleasure: A New Map of Love*. New York: Vintage, 2003.

Ginwright, Shawn A. *The Four Pivots: Reimagining Justice, Reimagining Ourselves*. Berkeley, CA: North Atlantic, 2022.

Grahn, Judy. *Blood, Bread and Roses: How Menstruation Created the World*. Boston: Beacon, 1994.

Grahn, Judy, and Betty de Shong Meador. *Inanna, Lady of Largest Heart: Poems of the Sumerian High Priestess*. Austin: University of Texas, 2001.

Grieco, Mary Hayes. *Unconditional Forgiveness: a Simple and Proven Method to Forgive Everyone and Everything*. New York: Atria, 2011.

Griffin, Susan. *Woman and Nature: The Roaring Inside Her*. San Francisco: Harper&Row, 1978.

Haines, Staci. *The Politics of Trauma: Somatics, Healing, Social Justice*. Berkeley: North Atlantic, 2019.

Heclo, Hugh. *On Thinking Institutionally*. Boulder: Paradigm, 2008.

Hemphill, Prentis. *What It Takes to Heal: How Transforming Ourselves Can Change the World*. New York: Random House, 2024. https://www.theembodimentinstitute.org/.

Hess, Carol Lakey. *Caretakers of Our Common House: Women's Development in Communities of Faith*. Nashville: Abingdon, 1997.

Hess, Lisa M. *Artisanal Theology: Intentional Formation in Radically Covenantal Companionship*. Eugene, OR: Cascade, 2009.

———. *A Companionable Way: Path of Devotion in Conscious Love*. Eugene, OR: Cascade, 2016.

———. "Conscious Feminine Leadership: Plenary Address." United Seminary (OH). January 29, 2019.

———. "A Contemplative Empiricism: Mindfulness, Wisdom, and Expertise in Teaching Spirituality in Seminaries." Association of Practical Theology Biennial Meeting, St. John's University, Collegeville, MN, April 2008.

———. *Learning in a Musical Key: Insight for Theology in Performative Mode*. Princeton Theological Monograph series. Eugene, OR: Pickwick, 2011.

———. "Scarred, Scared and Sacred." Filmed February 29, 2020 at TedXDaytonSalon for Women, Dayton, OH. https://www.youtube.com/watch?v=TLLazM5dMbA.

———. "Shadowdancing: Fear as Pathway to Transformation." *Review and Expositor* 115 (2018) 76–86.

Hess, Lisa M., and Brad Hirschfield. "It's More Complicated Than We Know: Pilgrimage as Metaphor and Method." *Spiritus* 23 (2023) 116–34.

Hollis, James. *The Eden Project: In Search of the Magical Other*. Toronto: Inner City, 1998.

Irenaeus of Lyons. "Against Heresies." In *The Apostolic Fathers with Justin Martyr and Irenaeus. The Ante-Nicene Fathers*, 1:309–567. Peabody, MA: Hendrickson, 1999.

Isherwood, Lisa. *The Power of Erotic Celibacy: Queering Heteropatriarchy*. London: T. & T. Clark, 2006.

Izzard, Eddie. *Dress to Kill*. Vision Video, 1998.

Jennings, Willie James. *After Whiteness: an Education in Belonging*. Grand Rapids, MI: Eerdmans, 2020.

Johns, Cheryl Bridges. "Grieving, Brooding, and Transforming: the Spirit, the Bible, and Gender." In *Grieving, Brooding and Transforming: the Spirit, the Bible, and Gender*, edited by Cheryl Bridges Johns and Lisa Stephenson, 7–19. Boston: Brill, 2021.

———. "Job and the Deconstruction of Benevolent Patriarchy." In *Grieving, Brooding and Transforming: the Spirit, the Bible, and Gender*, edited by Cheryl Bridges Johns and Lisa Stephenson, 63–77. Boston: Brill, 2021.

Johnson, Elizabeth. *She Who Is: The Mystery of God in Feminist Theological Discourse*. New York: Crossroad, 1993.

Johnson, Will. *The Spiritual Practices of Rumi: Radical Techniques for Beholding the Divine*. Rochester, VT: Inner Traditions, 2007.

Kidd, Sue Monk. *The Book of Longings*. New York: Viking, 2020.

Kula, Irwin with Linda Loewenthal. *Yearnings: Embracing the Sacred Messiness of Life*. New York: Hatchett, 2007.

Laird, Martin. "The Fountain of His Lips: Desire and Divine Union in Gregory of Nyssa's *Homilies on the Song of Songs*," *Spiritus* 7 (2007) 40–57.

Leidenfrost, Isadora, and Alisa Starkweather. *The Red Tent Movement: A Historical Perspective*. Tampa: Soul Media, 2015. In conjunction with "The Things We Don't Talk About."

Lerner, Gerda. *The Creation of Patriarchy*. Oxford: Oxford University Press, 1987.

Levandoski, Alana, and James Finley. "Do Not Perpetuate Violence." *Sanctuary: Exploring the Healing Path Within*. https://alanalevandoski.com/store/sanctuary-exploring-the-healing-path.

———. "Palace to Nowhere." *Point Vierge: Thomas Merton's Journey in Song*. N.d., 2017. https://alanalevandoski.com/store/point-vierge-thomas-merton-s-journey-in-song.

Lloyd, Dana. "Politicizing Kierkegaardian Repetition: On Schmitt and Kierkegaard." In *Kierkegaard and Political Theology*, edited by Roberto Sirvent, Silas Morgan, 213–25. Eugene, OR: Wipf & Stock, 2018.

Loder, James E. *The Knight's Move: the Relational Logic of the Spirit in Science and Theology*. Colorado Springs: Helmers & Howard, 1992.

———. *The Transforming Moment*. 2nd ed. Colorado Springs: Helmers & Howard, 1989.

Lorde, Audre. *Sister Outsider: Essays and Speeches*. Berkeley: Crossing, 2007.

Luke, Helen. *The Way of Woman: Awakening the Perennial Feminine*. New York: Doubleday, 1995.

———. *Woman Earth and Spirit: the Feminine Symbol and Myth*. New York: Crossroad, 1989.

MacIntyre, Alisdair. *After Virtue*. 2nd ed. Notre Dame: University of Notre Dame Press, 1984.

Macy, Joanna with Jessica Serrante. *We Are the Great Turning*. https://resources.soundstrue.com/we-are-the-great-turning-podcast/.

Malancharuvil, Joseph M. "Projection, Introjection, and Projective Identification: a Reformulation." *The American Journal of Psychoanalysis* 64 (2004) 375–82.

Marion, Jean-Luc. *The Erotic Phenomenon*. Translated by Stephen Lewis. Chicago: University of Chicago Press, 2007.

———. *God Without Being: Hors-Texte*. Translated by Thomas A. Carlson. Chicago: University of Chicago Press, 1991.

Markell, Kara. "Rewilding Religious Leadership: Engaging the Big Book of Revelation for the Future." *Journal of Religious Leadership* (forthcoming 2024).

May, Gerald. "From Cruelty to Compassion: The Crucible of Personal Transformation." In *Essays on Deepening the American Dream*, 1–35. Kalamazoo, MI: Fetzer Institute, 2005.

McDonald, Lee Martin. "Wherein Lies Authority? A Discussion of Books, Texts, and Translations." *Exploring the Origins of the Bible: Canon Formation in Historical, Literary, and Theological Perspective*, edited by Craig A. Evans and Emanuel Tov, 203–40. Ada, MI: BakerAcademic, 2008.

McGowan, Kathleen. *The Book of Love*. The Magdalene Line 2. New York: Atria, 2007.

Menakem, Resmaa. *My Grandmother's Hands: Racialized Trauma and the Pathway to Mending Our Hearts and Bodies*. Las Vegas: Central Recovery, 2017.

Merritt, Carol Howard and James Fenimore. *Wounded Pastors: Navigating Burnout, Finding Healing, and Discerning the Future of Your Ministry*. Louisville, KY: Westminster John Knox, 2024.

Millin, Peggy Tabor. *Women, Writing, and Soul-Making: Creativity and the Sacred Feminine*. Asheville, NC: StoryWater, 2009.

Mizen, Richard "On the Capacity to Suffer One's Self." *The Journal of Analytical Psychology* 59 (2014) 314–32.

Moltmann-Wendel, Elizabeth. *I Am My Body: A Theology of Embodiment*. New York: Continuum, 1995.

Morrison, Toni. "Ohio Arts Council Speech." Cited in *The African Courier* (August 8, 2019). https://www.theafricancourier.de/culture/toni-morrisons-quintessential-message-to-black-people-everywhere/.

Myers, Alicia D. *Blessed Among Women? Mothers and Motherhood in the New Testament*. Oxford: Oxford University Press, 2019.

Myss, Carolyn. *Sacred Contracts: Awakening Your Divine Potential*. New York: Harmony, 2003.

Noble, Vicki. *The Double Goddess: Women Sharing Power*. Rochester, VT: Bear & Company, 2003.

———. *Motherpeace: A Way to the Goddess through Myth, Art, and Tarot*. San Francisco: HarperOne, 1994. https://motherpeace.com/.

Nsoroma, Jojopahmaria. *The Wisdom Walk to Self-Mastery: Ancient Wisdom for Transforming Pain*. Bloomington, IN: Balboa, 2019.

Oliver, Mary Anne McPherson. *Conjugal Spirituality: The Primacy of Mutual Love in Christian Tradition*. New York: Sheed & Ward, 1994.

Ong, Walter, SJ. *Orality and Literacy: Technologizing the Word*. 3rd ed. London: Routledge, 2012.

———. *The Presence of the Word.* Albany: Global Academic, 2000.
Ostriker, Alicia. *Feminist Revision and the Bible: The Unwritten Volume.* The Bucknell Lectures in Literary Theory. Oxford: Wiley-Blackwell, 1993.
———. *The Nakedness of the Fathers: Biblical Visions and Revisions.* New Brunswick, NJ: Rutgers University Press, 1997.
Palmer, Parker. "Thirteen Ways of Looking at Community (With a Fourteenth Thrown in for Free)." *Inner Edge.* Center for Courage and Renewal (August/September 1998). https://couragerenewal.org/library/thirteen-ways-of-looking-at-community/.
Parmenter, Dorina Miller. "The Bible as Icon: Myths of the Divine Origins of Scripture." In *Jewish and Christian Scripture as Artifact and Canon,* edited by Craig A. Evans and H. D. Zacharias, 298–309. New York: Bloomsbury.
Pass, David B. *Music and the Church.* Nashville: Broadman, 1989.
Prechtel, Martin. *Smell of Rain on Dust: Grief and Praise.* Berkeley: North Atlantic, 2015.
Potts, Matthew Ichihashi. *Forgiveness: an Alternative Account.* New Haven, CT: Yale University Press, 2022.
Reinhart, Peter. "What Is an Artisanal Loaf?" In *Brother Juniper's Bread Book: Slow Rise as Method and Metaphor,* 157–65. New York: Perseus, 1991.
Rich, Adrienne. "Notes on the Erotic: The Erotic as Power." *Sister Outsider: Essays and Speeches.* Berkeley: Crossing, 2007.
Richardson, Jan L. *In Wisdom's Path: Discovering the Sacred in Every Season.* Frederick, MD: Wanton Gospeller, 2012.
Riley, Cole Arthur. *This Here Flesh: Spirituality, Liberation, and the Stories That Make Us.* New York: Convergent, 2022.
Roberson, Quanita. "Individuals, Teams, Tribes and Communities." https://www.nzuzu.com/post/individuals-teams-tribes-communities.
Roberson, Quanita, and Amy Howton. *Innerground Railroad: A Forty-Day Journey to Remembering Soul and Spirit.* Cincinnati: Akan, 2023.
Rohr, Richard. *Falling Upward: A Spirituality for the Two Halves of Life.* Jossey-Bass, 2011.
———. *Daily Meditations.* https://cac.org/daily-meditations/transforming-pain-2018-10-17/.
Rolling Stones. "You Can't Always Get What You Want." Track 9 on *Let It Bleed.* Decca, 1969.
Ross, Maggie. *Pillars of Flame: Power, Priesthood, and Spiritual Maturity.* New York: Seabury, 1988, 2007.
———. *Silence: A User's Guide.* 2 vols. Eugene, OR: Wipf & Stock, 2018.
———. *Writing the Icon of the Heart: In Silence Beholding.* Eugene, OR: Cascade, 2013.
Russell, Letty M. *Church in the Round: Feminist Interpretation of the Church.* Louisville, KY: Westminster/John Knox, 1993.
Sancken, Joni S. *All Our Griefs to Bear: Responding with Resilience After Collective Trauma.* Huntington, IN: Herald, 2022.
Schnarch, David. *Passionate Marriage: Keeping Love and Intimacy in Emotionally Committed Relationships.* New York: W.W. Norton & Company, 1997.
Schneiders, Sandra. *The Revelatory Text: Interpreting the New Testament as Sacred Scripture.* 2nd ed. Collegeville, MN: Liturgical, 1999.

Schüssler Fiorenza, Elisabeth. *Bread Not Stone: The Challenge of Feminist Biblical Interpretation*. Boston: Beacon, 1995.
Shlain, Leonard. *The Alphabet Versus the Goddess: the Conflict Between Word and Image*. New York: Arkana, 1998.
———. *Sex, Time, and Power: How Women's Sexuality Shaped Human Evolution*. New York: Viking, 2003.
Shriver, Donald W. *An Ethic for Enemies: Forgiveness in Politics*. Oxford: Oxford University Press, 1998.
Silk, Mark. "Defining Religious Pluralism in America: a Regional Analysis." *Annals, AAPSS* 612 (2007) 64–81.
Slaughter, Michael. *Unlearning Church*. Nashville: Abingdon, 2008.
Smith, James K. A. *How to Inhabit Time: Understanding the Past, Facing the Future, Living Faithfully Now*. Ada, MI: Brazos, 2022.
———. *How (Not) to Be Secular: Reading Charles Taylor*. Grand Rapids, MI: Eerdmans, 2014.
Sosler, Alexander. "Prodigal Love and a Hermeneutic of Charity." *Pro Rege* 48 (2020) 23–28. https://digitalcollections.dordt.edu/pro_rege/vol48/iss3/4/.
Sovatsky, Stuart. *Eros, Consciousness, and Kundalini: Deepening Sensuality through Tantric Celibacy and Spiritual Intimacy*. Rochester, VY: Park Street, 1999.
Sprinkle, Steven. "A God at the Margins? Marcella Althaus-Reid and the Marginality of LGBT People." *Journal of Religious Leadership* 8 (2009) 57–83.
Stewart, David. "The Hermeneutics of Suspicion." *Journal of Literature and Theology* 3 (1989) 296–307.
Stone, Merlin. *When God Was a Woman*. Boston: Mariner, 1978.
Strand, Clark, and Perdita Finn. *The Way of the Rose: The Radical Path of the Divine Feminine Hidden in the Rosary*. New York: Random, 2019.
Sue, Derald Wing. *Race Talk and the Conspiracy of Silence: Understanding and Facilitating Difficult Dialogues on Race*. Oxford: Wiley, 2016.
———. *Microaggressions in Everyday Life: Race, Gender, and Sexual Orientation*. Wiley, 2010.
Taylor, Barbara Brown. *Learning to Walk in the Dark*. San Francisco: HarperOne, 2015.
Taylor, Charles. *The Secular Age*. Cambridge, MA: Harvard University Press, 2018.
Tutu, Desmond, and Mpho Tutu. *The Book of Forgiving: The Fourfold Path for Healing Ourselves and the World*. Glasgow: William Collins, 2014.
Ullman, Robert, and Judyth Reichenberg-Ullman, *Mystics, Masters, Saints and Sages: Stories of Enlightenment*. Newburyport, MA: Conari, 2001.
Umbreit, Mark S., et al. *The Energy of Forgiveness: Lessons from Those in Restorative Dialogue*. Eugene, OR: Cascade, 2015.
United Theological Seminary. "To Protect the Learning Environment For All." https://united.edu/faculty-statement/.
Walker, Alice. *In Search of Our Mothers' Gardens*. Reprint. Boston: Mariner, 2003.
Washburn, Michael. *The Ego and the Dynamic Ground: A Transpersonal Theory of Human Development*, 2nd ed. Albany: State University of New York Press, 1995.
———. *Embodied Spirituality in a Sacred World*. Albany, NY: State University of New York Press, 2003.
Webster, Bethany. *Discovering the Inner Mother: A Guide to Healing the Mother Wound and Claiming Your Personal Power*. New York: William Morrow, 2021.

Weil, Simone. "The Right Use of School Studies." In *Waiting for God*, 57–65. New York: G.P. Putnam's Sons, 1951.

Weller, Francis. *The Wild Edge of Sorrow: Rituals of Renewal and the Sacred Work of Grief*. Berkeley: North Atlantic, 2015.

Winter, Miriam Therese. *Paradoxology: Spirituality in a Quantum Universe*. Maryknoll, NY: Orbis, 2009.

Woodman, Marion. *Coming Home to Myself: Reflections for Nurturing a Woman's Body and Soul*. Newburyport, MA: Conari, 2001.

———. *Conscious Femininity: Interviews with Marion Woodman*. Toronto: Inner City, 1993.

———. *Sitting by the Well: Bringing the Feminine to Consciousness Through Language, Dreams and Metaphor*. Boulder, CO: SoundsTrue, 2015.

World Health Organization. "Violence Against Women: Key Facts." Edited March 25, 2024. https://www.who.int/news-room/fact-sheets/detail/violence-against-women.

Wittlinger, Carlton O. *Quest for Piety and Obedience: The Story of the Brethren in Christ* Nappanee, IN: Evangel, 1978.

Wright, Dana. "Biography of James E. Loder." https://www.biola.edu/talbot/ce20/database/james-edwin-loder-jr#biography.

Index

abandonment, xi, xiii, 3, 9, 12, 18, 20, 22, 24–30, 33–34, 37, 41, 46, 51–54, 63–64, 68, 70, 72, 78, 86–87, 94–95, 98, 100–2, 106, 114, 121, 123, 128–29, 131, 137, 156, 160, 167, 178, 187–88, 197, 199, 202
absence, 12, 24, 82–83, 196, 199
accountability, 3, 93, 168, 177
ancestral, xii, xiv, 5–7, 9, 12, 24–25, 29, 35, 37, 39, 41, 76, 87–89, 117–18, 125, 138–39, 140–41, 145, 167, 170n10, 175–76, 193, 196–97, 199
anger, 2, 39, 41–45, 72, 101, 104, 134, 136–38, 144, 157, 162, 198
anointing, 9, 40–41, 167
archetypal, xv, 13, 47–48, 50–51, 170
artisanal way, 8, 190, 192
authority
    decentered, 180
    derived, 180, 183
    of scripture, 137, 179–80, 182–83, 199
    institutional, 59, 121, 170
    sacred, 114, 145
awakening
    anti-matter of, 148
    desire, 9–10, 37–38, 78, 94–95, 142, 152, 196
    F/feminine, xiv–xv, xviii, 1, 10, 20, 29, 49–50, 59–60, 64, 73, 83, 87, 97, 103, 109, 117–18, 124–25

insight, 190
tears, 27
theological-spiritual, 9, 11, 35, 37, 51, 53, 59, 73–74, 79, 87, 104, 138, 145, 157, 162–63, 167
awareness
    lack, of xv, 37, 43, 130, 163
    desire, 158
    general, 60, 67, 71, 74, 91, 95, 109, 111, 122, 118, 128, 134, 136, 171, 189
    projections, 165
    visceral, 9, 18, 23, 27–29, 31, 40, 51, 75, 130, 138, 141, 156, 194, 196

Bacon, Kevin 52, 54
baptism, waters of, 44
belonging, xi, xvii–xviii, 4, 11, 15, 22, 36, 50, 80, 83–84, 87–89, 92, 99, 119, 132, 136–37, 141–43, 153, 165, 168–69, 181, 194, 196, 203
Berry, Thomas, 182
betrayal, 22, 46, 54, 86, 132, 143
bewilderment
    conscious, 10, 74
    embodied, 75, 137, 195
    human, xii, 2, 10, 12, 44, 126, 143, 185, 187
    sacred, xvii–xviii, 4, 15, 17, 24, 24n17, 79, 106, 122, 133, 168, 190, 203
Berezan, Jennifer, 25

Body of Humanity, xi–ii, xiv, xviii–xix, 2, 4, 9, 11–12, 19, 23, 34, 44, 71–72, 75, 80, 86, 92–93, 107, 115, 133, 137, 144, 147–48, 159, 165, 167–69, 177, 185, 187, 194–96, 203
Boehme, Jacob, 112
Bolen, Jean Shinoda, 50, 181n32
Bourgeault, Cynthia, 7, 10, 24, 108–9, 188
Brethren in Christ, 5
brooding, 70
Brosmer, Mary Pierce, 16n4, 48
brown, adrienne marie, 89n26

Cameron, Julia, 138, 189
cauldron, 42–43, 45, 135, 137, 173, 186
certainty, xii, 1–3, 12, 24, 24n17, 30, 71, 142, 152, 172, 192n47, 199
Chalcedonian, 10n22, 67, 114
chiasmic, xii, 8, 196
Christ, Carol P., 64
Christ, 15n2, 67, 90, 106, 114, 183, 199. *See also* Jesus
Christianity
    congregational, xi, xvi, 97, 111, 114, 148, 159–60, 199
    lunar, xiii
    root tradition, 71, 109, 114
    orthodox, 128n6, 183
    Protestant, 182
    solar, xii, 199
Church of the Holy Sepulchre, 31, 33
circle-way, xi, 16, 19, 136, 165, 168, 177, 195
climate crisis, xvii
Coakley, Sarah, 9–10, 108, 116, 167
Coates, Ta-Nehisi, 126
community
    Beloved, xviii
    Conscious Feminine, xix, 16, 71, 78, 81, 83–84, 86, 136, 144, 159, 180
    ecclesial, 19, 95, 113, 121, 146, 151, 154n6, 161, 171–72, 178, 195
    emergent, 168–69, 171, 200
    faith, xiii, 30, 45, 58, 72–73, 85, 98, 100, 126, 162
    historic Christian, xviii, 17, 30, 33, 67, 74–75, 81, 114, 137, 198–99
    human, xiv, xvii, 3, 11, 16, 34, 40, 47, 49, 53, 57, 70, 89–92, 115, 167, 170, 182
    intentional, 46, 94, 161
    interpretation, 81
    TedX, 74
    wisdom, 136
    witnessing, 10–11, 43, 51, 75, 78, 85–86, 93, 106, 142, 162, 165, 175, 179
    worshipping, 122
companionship, 23, 129, 168, 181, 190–91, 195, 202
conscious feminine, xvi, xviii, 1, 9–10, 13, 15, 17, 23–26, 31, 46–52, 58, 63–64, 68, 71, 79–80, 82–83, 87, 96, 107–9, 124, 130, 132–33, 139, 144, 148, 150, 154, 161, 166, 172, 178, 185, 191, 199
consciousness, xi, xv, 10, 24, 37, 50, 59–62, 84, 102, 114, 131, 179, 193
    visceral, 28, 107
container, xviii, 19, 23, 39, 45, 90–91, 106, 114–15, 117, 126, 165, 177, 190
contemplative, xviii, 7–8, 10, 17, 23, 30, 94, 111, 125–26, 190, 192, 192n47
courage, xii, 49–50, 55, 71, 74, 135, 180, 181n32, 197
    "catching courage," xvii, 79, 179
    ethical, 164
covenant, xix, 11, 13, 18, 23, 26, 29, 58, 67, 90–92, 95, 122, 130, 144, 149–50, 152–56, 159–61, 166, 176–77, 188, 190, 198
Covid, 89, 158, 173
crucible, xix, 9, 15, 18–19, 38, 116, 155, 159
cycle-breaker, 6

Dalai Lama, 2
Days in the Weeds, 9, 18–20, 24, 28–30, 34, 36, 38, 75–78, 85, 95–96, 98, 103, 108, 118, 125, 127, 131–32, 169, 199

Deardorff, Daniel, 2
Dickinson, Emily, 21
delight, ix, xi, 6, 15, 22, 86, 113, 120, 123–24, 152, 190
  expressive, 3, 12, 49, 108, 120, 175
desire, ix, xiii, xvii–xviii, 18, 35–36, 52, 74, 78, 87, 102, 108, 117, 125, 128, 148, 150, 152, 155–56, 170, 195
  concentration of, 107, 112, 115, 136
  eros, 119, 164
  God/de's desire, 9, 35, 79, 86, 89–90, 92–95, 108, 111, 115, 117–20, 123, 127, 131, 145, 167–68
  hermeneutics of, 67–68
  justified, 1
  man's, 77, 164
  mimicked, 158
  ontology of, 9–12, 90, 107, 118–20, 136, 138, 196
  physiological, 118
  polarizing, 92
  and prayer, 121
  refined, 115, 117
  right ordering of, 116, 130
  sensual, 9, 85, 106, 129, 142, 177, 198
  sexual, 117–19, 121
  shamed, 37, 86–87, 101 108, 115, 118, 142
  undesired, xv, 11, 19, 42, 118, 132, 149, 152, 154, 158–60, 165
devotion, ix, 9, 17, 19–22, 70–71, 89–90, 93, 102, 121, 123, 159–60, 198
  act of, 21
  Christian, 10, 111, 166
  as prayer, 20, 22–23, 120, 192
  as writing, 20, 22
discipline, 9, 21–23, 62
  academic, 8, 15n2, 55, 63–64, 67, 94
  punishment, 36
  spiritual, 103
dissociation, 29, 36–37, 43, 70, 87–88, 92–93
Dorje, Rig'dzin, 191
doubt, 7, 88, 96, 164
doxology, 71–72 (see also paradoxology)
dualism, xiv, 1

ecclesia, xin1
  ecclesial (systemic), xin1, xv, xvii, 1, 16–19, 26, 35, 41, 76–78, 81, 95–97, 103–4, 106, 108, 110, 116, 120–24, 130, 134, 137–38, 146, 149–50, 157, 160–61, 177–79, 184, 198–99
  non-sectarian, xi, xvii, 23, 86
  traditional, xiv, 30, 47, 49, 114
embodied-enspirited, 19
empathy, 11, 141, 149, 158–59, 177
Ensler, Eve, 203
eros, 80, 86, 92, 119, 163
erotic, 25, 36, 67, 79–80, 90–91, 93, 119, 121–22, 190
expertise, xvi, 1–2, 148, 161–62, 170, 179, 189

faith, viii–ix, xi, xvii, 1, 4, 6–7, 11, 20–21, 53, 59, 66, 72, 128, 133, 136, 146, 153, 160, 169, 184, 197
  community/people of, xiii–xiv, xviii–xix, 5, 30, 41, 43–44, 51, 70, 72–73, 85, 96, 98–100, 115, 133, 135, 144, 148, 158, 161–62, 182, 193, 195, 199
  defined, 187–90
  embodied, xiii–xiv, 149, 166, 168–69, 184
  faithfulness, xviii, 19, 37, 103, 124, 130, 152, 179, 199
  language of, xii, 12, 39
  luminous perception, 180–81, 185, 188, 203
  mysteries, xix
  practices, 35
  renewal, xvi, 2, 170
  righteousness in, 3, 108
  rupture/trauma, 17, 46, 100, 120
  seal of, 41, 161
  triumphalist/grounded in certainty, xii, 30
  unfaithful, 3
fear, xviii, 2, 26, 35, 39–40, 69, 74, 77, 79–80, 96, 103, 107, 118, 125, 127, 129, 141–42, 152–53, 156, 172, 180–81, 186, 193, 196, 202
  body, 25–26, 41–42, 84, 95, 117–18, 181, 185, 199

fear *(continued)*
   congregational, 16, 30, 83, 93
   inherited, 138
   path to resilience, 162–64, 193
   projecting, 176
   unconscious, 25, 39, 69, 183, 185
fearlessness, 180, 188, 192, 199, 203
fearmongering, 80, 114, 172, 184
F/feminine, xiv–xviii, 3n6, 4, 10, 13, 16, 20, 22, 25–26, 29, 31, 35, 37–38, 46–48, 50–51, 53, 59, 72–75, 78–84, 86–87, 91, 96–97, 102–3, 106–9, 124–25, 127, 130, 135, 159, 168, 175, 177, 182, 184, 187
feminist, xiv, xvi, 10, 13, 15, 37, 49, 52, 63–68, 73, 79, 96, 101, 107, 124, 130, 132–33, 135, 137, 144–45, 148, 150, 154, 166
Finley, James, 100, 142
Fiorenza, Elisabeth Schussler, 64, 67
flesh, xiii, xv, 15, 23, 26, 34, 38, 41, 46, 51, 63, 70, 74, 78, 85, 87, 90–91, 96, 106, 112, 114–15, 124–25, 144, 172, 190, 198
F/flow, 3, 11, 33–34, 38, 41–42, 46, 72, 85, 90, 94–95, 98, 106, 111–13, 120, 128, 138, 147, 165, 172, 188, 200, 202
Flower Duet, 197–99
forbearance, 15, 47, 146–47, 173, 177
forgiveness, xvii, xix, 5, 115–16, 126, 128–30, 133–35, 137, 142, 144–45, 196
   finding, 136–37, 144–46, 149, 157, 168, 177, 203
   forgiving the divine, 136, 142
   fourfold path, 143
   Jesus, 128–30
   not reconciliation, 135, 143
   problem, 15, 96, 124, 130, 133, 145, 148, 166
   rooted in grieving, 133–35
   salvific peripheral vision, 144–45, 166
   social, 145–46, 177
   traditional-Scriptural, 137, 178
   unconditional, 143
   unforgiveness, forces of, xii, xiv, 3, 146–47
   without will, viii, 11–12
Fortune, Marie, 53
freedom, viii, xvii, 2, 4–5, 7, 11, 41, 53, 80, 88, 116, 132–33, 137–38, 145, 148, 154, 158, 166, 174, 194, 196, 203
   capacity to forgive, 132–33
   sacred, 15
   unwilled, xiii

gaze, 54, 106, 118, 126–27, 201
   feminine, 54
   icon, 183
   masculine, 63, 77, 83, 108, 132
   portal, 106–7
   spiritual discipline, 103, 106, 127
gender, xiv, xvii, 10, 13, 47, 50–51, 53, 68, 72, 75, 79–80, 88–90, 119, 121, 136, 149
   and the Bible, 68
   cisgender, 6, 47
   roles, 149
Gilbert, Elizabeth, xvi, 167
Gilligan, Carol, 80, 86, 101, 119
Godde, xiv, 11, 19–20, 24, 34–36, 38, 41–42, 79, 85–86, 91–92, 103, 106, 108, 111, 113, 117, 119–20, 181–82, 198
Goddess, xiv, 56, 58, 61, 64, 100, 102
Grahn, Judy, 59, 63
Great Turning, xvii
Griffin, Susan, 75
Grosser Gott, 4, 198–99
grief, viii, xii, 2, 34–35, 39, 69, 86, 91, 97, 104, 130–31, 136, 138–40, 144, 200
   ancestral, 139–41
   and praise, 125, 135–36, 170n10, 188, 196
   body, 34, 125, 203
   gates of, 34, 138, 142
   root of forgiveness, 134
   sacred art, 125
   unresolved, 137–38, 145, 186, 192

Habakkuk, 39, 40, 41
healing, viii, xi–xii, xiv–xvii, 2–3, 15n2,
    26, 38, 50–51, 69, 72, 93, 96,
    133–34, 174, 178, 186, 200
  communal, 5, 85, 93, 144, 169, 193
  intergenerational, xii, 2, 5, 123, 159,
    164–65
  in the F/feminine, xviii, 3, 86
  Jesus's, 186
  journey/work, 9, 35, 145, 165, 167,
    170n10, 173, 181, 183, 195, 203
  spaces, 19, 39, 175, 191
  superficial, 134
Heclo, Hugh, 173
hermeneutics, 64–69
  of desire, 67–68
  of indeterminacy, 68
  of revelation, 67
herstory, 10, 55, 63
Hess, Elizabeth M. Musser, 139
Hess, Ruth Berger, 5n11
Hess, Benjamin Musser, 6
Hollis, James, 163
Holy God, We Praise Your Name, 198–99

icon, 33, 103–5, 198, 202
  audible, 198–99
  contemporary, 105–6
  scripture, 183
  Sinai Jesus, 103, 126–27
imaginal realm, xii, 39, 114, 197
incarnational, 19, 51, 91
Inanna, 59
institutional thinking, 169, 175–76
interconnected/ness, xii–xiii, xvi, 74, 93,
    102, 107, 170n10, 196, 203
intimacy, 34, 127, 132, 154, 164, 169,
    191, 199
  acoustics of, 179
  container, 45
  covenantal, 155
  with God/de, 11, 24
  raw, 149–50, 154–55
  Spirit-spirit, xv, 90, 199
Irenaeus of Lyon, vi, 2, 17
Isherwood, Lisa, 90–91, 93

Jensen, Jean, 104
Jesus, 7, 31, 33, 67, 75, 103, 127–30, 137,
    143, 147, 183–84, 191
  bodycentric healing, 186
  Sinai icon, 103, 126–28, 132–33
  truly human, 129
Johns, Cheryl Bridges, xviii, 186
Johnson, Elizabeth, 64
Johnson, Will, 103

Kidd, Sue Monk, 139
Kierkegaard, Søren, 20–21, 107
koinonia, 19, 195

leadership, 48–49, 53, 60, 80, 134, 156–
    57, 161, 166, 168–71, 173
  conscious feminine academy, 48, 80,
    83, 108, 139, 191, 199
  emergent, 177, 190, 193, 203
  religious, 166, 184, 187
Lerner, Gerda, 54
Lerner, Michael, 34, 141
Lewis, C. S., 41
Levandoski, Alana, 142
Levi-Strauss, Claude, 57
Lion of Judah, 40
Loder, James E., xv, 15, 15n2, 21, 95, 136
love without being, 90, 113
Luke, Helen, 50

matriarchy, 56
Marion, Jean-Luc, 19
Markell, Kara, 187
masculine, xiii, xix, 11, 13, 47, 50–51,
    54–55, 63, 75, 77, 81, 83, 96,
    108–9, 128, 132, 170, 177–78,
    187
menarche/menstruation, 59–62
Merton, Thomas, 98
microaggression, 156
Möbius, 10, 94–95
monotheism, 58
Morrison, Toni, xvi
Mother Emanuel AME Church, 126,
    134
MotherPeace, 78, 80–81

nonbinary, xiii, 47, 55, 132–33
New Moon, 16, 83–84
nothingness, 9, 18, 24, 28, 30, 41, 64, 78, 99, 148
Nsoroma, Jojopah, 27
Nugent, Sister Shirley, 35, 84

O'Connor, Sinead, 25
oikonomia, 114
Oliver, Mary Anne McPherson, 91
open space, 11, 192, 195
orthodoxy, 1, 108, 114, 116, 121
    dance of, 120, 122
    ecclesial, 121–23, 178
    Modern Orthodox
    Orthodoxy Christian, 95, 111, 120
    Spirit-project, 121–22, 167
Ostriker, Alicia, xviii, 66–67, 186

Palmer, Parker, 169
paradoxology, 71–72
participation, xvii, 10, 34, 94, 97, 107, 111, 115, 119–20
patriarchy/patriarchal, 13, 54, 55–58, 66, 132–33, 186, 202
Pennsylvania-Dutch, 5–6, 37–38, 43
Plaskow, Judith, 63
pleasure, ix, xvii, 10–12, 34, 36–37, 67, 75, 82, 86–87, 89–90, 92, 94, 123, 125, 177, 196
    activism, 89n26
    beyond pleasure, 75
    displeasure, 25
    as grief, 125
    of learning and teaching, 71
    in communion, synchrony, 89
    rebirth of, 87
    sacred calling, 92
    as sinful, 117
polarization, 1, 93, 162, 172, 196
Potts, Matthew Ichihashi, 126, 134
power-principle, xiv, 56–57, 59
practice, xv, 3, 11, 18–19, 37, 52, 103, 113, 119–20, 132, 161, 164, 166, 173, 175, 191–93, 195–96
    choir, 45
    community of, xix, 16, 46–47, 78, 81, 144, 169, 177, 180, 192

covenantal, 177, 190
faith practice, xii, 12, 35, 97, 108, 178–79, 185
forgiveness as, 134, 143, 146–47
prayer as, 19, 41, 93–94, 96, 98, 103, 126, 180, 192n47
self-reflective, 165, 172
socializing, 24, 34, 57, 126, 150
spiritual, xii–xiii, 86, 91–92, 106, 161, 163
theory-practice, 10, 48, 54, 94–95, 114, 190
praise, viii, xii, 2, 4, 17, 72, 125, 135–37, 139–40, 198–99, 203
    as grief, 125, 135–40, 149, 170n10, 186–88, 196
    prayer of, 140, 199
prayer, viii, 1, 9, 19, 23, 39, 41, 81, 94, 96, 109, 117, 180, 192
    active waiting, 17, 22, 160
    attention, 22
    devotion, viii, 19–20, 23, 26
    embodied, 10, 19, 34, 93–5, 98 103, 107
    with icons, 103, 126
    intensification, 74, 116
    Lord's, 128
    in the Spirit, 121
    practice, 11, 41, 192n47
    of praise, 140
    silent, 106, 111
    spoken, 97–98, 126
    problem of, 10, 94–95, 98–99
    without ceasing, 97
    writing, 17, 22
preacher's wife, xviii, 11, 13, 16, 83, 96, 124, 130, 147–66
Prechtel, Martin, 125, 138
presence, xi, xvii, xix, 21, 23, 53, 121, 135, 139–40, 176–77, 187, 190, 193–94
    dialectical, 67
    of God/de, 12, 24, 30, 70, 91, 120, 126, 178, 196
    with horses, 97
    Feminine, 52, 97, 106, 110, 125, 177, 201–3
    prayer, 97, 123

professionalism, 2
projection, 1, 13, 156, 162–65, 176, 193
  defined, 163
  withdrawing, 163–64
purgation, 93, 119–20

queer/ing, xiii, 47, 55, 65, 80, 133
quest for assurance, 12

rage, viii, xii, xvi–xvii, 55, 59, 63, 69–70, 72, 87, 97, 99, 123–24, 126, 132, 134, 139, 143–44, 156–58, 172, 185, 197, 202–3
  ancient, 78
  becoming holy, viii, 42–44, 51, 53, 143
  cauldron of, 135, 137, 186
  collective anger, 46, 138
  fired by, 45, 114, 142
  fruit of rage, 1
  at God/de, 36, 39
  righteousness of, 51, 72, 102, 106–7, 133, 166
  sacred purpose, 52, 135
  sadness, 34, 128, 147, 177
  un/resolved, xiv, 1–3, 9–12, 18, 24–26, 28, 32–34, 41, 122, 130, 145
rationality (reason), 7, 120, 152, 190
receptivity, 16, 170
Red Tent/Temple, 16, 47, 63, 78, 83–85, 200
resilience, 19, 149, 162, 165
resistance, xiv, 33, 117, 119, 126, 128, 132, 143, 147, 149–50, 159, 166, 171, 185
respect-in-depth, 169, 175
restoration, 69, 107, 111, 114
revelation, 8, 77, 120, 182, 185
  Big Book (nature), 187
  God/de's, 24, 67
  hermeneutics of, 67–68
  Little Book (Bible), 187
  self-revelation, 87
Richardson, Jan, 47
Ricouer, Paul, 21, 66
Roberson, Quanita, xii, xix, 13, 89, 131, 170n10, 171, 189
Rohr, Richard, 24, 27

Roof, Dylann, 126
Ross, Maggie, 154n6
Russell, Letty, 174

salvation, 17, 40, 113, 168, 203
salvific, 144–45, 166–67, 184
Schnarch, David, 154
Schneiders, Sandra, 64
S/scripture, 1, 11, 22, 24, 34, 40–41, 52, 63, 65, 67–70, 92, 116, 130, 132, 154n6, 169, 171, 177, 187, 193
  authority of, 137, 178–80, 183
  decentering, 184, 189
  egoic use of, 69–70, 181
  Hebrew and Christian, 95, 101, 132, 181–83
  interpretation of, xiii, 81, 184
  sanctifying role, 69
  yardstick of judgment, 178
seeing with the eye of the heart, xii, 7, 11
shadow, 10, 97, 125, 155, 160–62, 165, 172–73, 184, 186
  defined, 162
  and projection, 162–63, 165
shadowdancing, 161–63, 165, 193
Shalem Institute, 30, 126–27, 133, 197
shame, 35–36, 38, 135, 141, 162, 172, 202
  body-, 91, 108, 142, 198
  defined, 141
  in desire, 37, 118
  free of, 80, 115, 198
  imposed, xv, 2, 9, 21, 26, 36, 86–87, 117, 138–39, 181, 186, 193
  imprisoned in, 63, 142
  ingested/internalized, 1, 84–85, 101, 158, 179
  lineages of, 38, 86, 141
  as sacred path, 118
Shriver, Donald, 146, 177
silence, 26, 29, 78, 97–98, 136
  Great Silence, 132–33, 197
  practices, 126–27, 132, 179, 197
  shared, 103, 126–27
  to silence, (v.) 3, 76, 158, 177, 181
  spacious, 116
silenced, xv, 16, 29, 46, 74, 101, 177
Smith, James K.A., 3n5

226 INDEX

somatic, 1, 165
speaking in tongues, 40–41
S/spirit, xv, xviii, 15–18, 20, 37–38, 49,
    68–70, 72, 87, 91, 95–96, 107–8,
    111, 114, 118, 121, 123, 126,
    149, 184, 190, 203
  body-mind-spirit, 35, 37, 39, 48,
    52, 132, 137, 143, 159, 168–69,
    185, 191
  enspirited-embodied method, 19,
    22, 47, 51
  fruit of Spirit, 1, 182, 195
  life of the Spirit, 15n2, 69
  logic of the Spirit, 94, 113–14
  power of the Spirit, 9, 74, 79, 93,
    183, 199
  Spirit of Christ, 15n2
  Spirit-spirit intimacy, xv, 20, 44, 67,
    90, 94–95, 115, 181
  Spirit-led, xv, xviii, 11, 51, 121–23,
    185
  Spirit's interruption, 120
  Spirit's tether, 17, 148
  SpiriT's work, 39, 125, 159, 182
  spirit/ual, 24, 27, 39, 50, 64, 69,
    72, 82, 85, 91–92, 97, 103–4,
    121–23, 151, 154–55, 160–63,
    183–84, 190, 195, 198, 200
  spiritual pain, 16, 35, 145
spirit-friendship, xviii–xix, 19, 24,
    27–28, 31, 33–34, 76, 78, 81, 83,
    85–86, 89–90, 98 103, 106, 118,
    129, 159, 166, 168–69, 191–92,
    197
spiritual maturity, xii, 3, 154, 154n6,
    162–63, 165, 195
spirituality, 6, 116
  conjugal, 91–92
  of connection, 175
  discipline of, 8, 65
  women's, 64
Stone, Merlin, 60
suffering, viii–ix, xi, 24, 33, 39, 96, 141,
    154n6, 155, 162–63, 171–72
  leadership's, 171–72
  redeemed, 143
  of self and other, 3–4, 12, 49, 120,
    175
  women's, 33, 44, 53
surrender, viii–ix, xii–xiii, xviii, 11, 15,
    19, 74, 115, 119, 128, 131, 133,
    138, 145, 147, 148–61, 166,
    168–69, 171, 178, 183, 185, 188,
    190, 192n47

taboo, 57, 59, 62, 88, 92
Taylor, Barbara Brown, xii
Taylor, Charles, 3n5
TedX Dayton, 74, 79,
Temple Mount (*Haram al-Sharif*), 31,
    202
terror, 9, 18, 24, 27–28, 33–34, 41, 44,
    129, 131
theodicy, 96
theologie totale, 9, 120
tradition, xiii, xv–vi, 1, 4, 8–9, 18, 23,
    59–60, 63–64, 66–67, 71–72, 81,
    83, 89, 98, 122, 126, 143, 172,
    181–82, 187, 195
  cross-traditional, 146, 182
  faith, 1, 108
  historic Christian, 10–11, 15, 17,
    33–34, 52, 68, 75, 87–89, 91,
    93–94, 103–4, 106, 111, 113–14,
    116–17, 137, 141, 184
  institutions, xi, 2, 16, 53, 65, 168,
    199
  integrity, 111, 114
  liturgical, xviii
  masculinized, 76, 121
  non-traditional, 46, 48, 86, 96
  religious, 15, 19, 31, 53–54, 85, 90,
    97, 109, 175, 192
  root-, xi, xvi, 2–3, 10–11, 16, 19,
    22, 50, 52, 54, 59, 79, 83, 86, 96,
    103, 107–8, 113–14, 132, 166,
    168–69, 176, 189, 192
  to tradition (verb), 3, 37, 63, 70, 75,
    85, 103, 117–18, 171, 193
  traditionalist, xiv–v, 1, 9, 53, 91, 145,
    174, 177, 187

wisdom-, xii, xv–xvii, 3, 9–11, 15, 19, 24, 46–47, 58, 96, 116, 132, 147, 167, 173, 186, 190, 192, 202
transcendental psychology, 28
transfiguration, 3, 3n6, 122, 162, 199
transformation, 2, 3n6, 8, 61, 78, 94, 114, 118, 120, 122, 167, 172, 175, 198
trauma-informed, xii, 181, 193
Trinity, 10, 50, 95, 106–8, 111–14, 117, 121–22
  driveshaft of creation, 111
  economic, 11, 15, 17, 151, 165
  immanent, 17
  incorporative, 108, 117, 123
  participation, 10, 111, 115
  Pentecostal, 111, 114, 123
  praying the, 10, 116, 120–21, 123
trinitarian, xviii, 47, 92, 113, 116–19, 122
  flow, 111, 113
  language, 95
  life, 119, 121, 123
  logic, 117, 143
  Möbius, 94
  nature, 118
  renewed-renewing, xvi–ii, 3, 8–10, 12, 17, 86, 107–8, 116–17, 121, 123–24, 136, 138, 168, 196
trust, xiii, xvii, 3, 11, 19, 22–23, 25, 38, 69–70, 80–81, 83, 85–86, 89, 93, 124, 131, 133, 135, 160, 162, 165, 172, 174–75, 185, 188, 196, 203
  distrust, xv, 66, 134, 144, 173–76, 188
  entrusted, 51
  God/divine order of things, 39, 168, 189–90
  regrounded, ix
  trustworthiness, 8, 111–12, 170–71
T/truth, 1, 4, 17, 21–22, 67–69, 120, 143–44, 148, 161–62, 165, 167, 178, 184
  Emily Dickinson, 21–23, 135
  public, 30
  radical, 111
  untruthful, 5, 167

(un)conscious, xv–xvi, 9–10, 13, 16, 25, 33, 43, 57, 64, 69, 73, 75, 77, 86–87, 95, 97, 121, 130, 149, 154, 157, 160, 168, 177
United Nations, 53

Void, 9, 18, 24, 28, 30, 64, 78, 131, 148
vulnerability, 82, 85, 132, 141, 150, 162

Walker, Alice, 49
Weil, Simone, 22
Weller, Francis, 34, 89, 138, 140
Wild Church, 187
Winter, Miriam Therese, 71
W/wisdom, xii, 1–3, 23, 26, 35, 43, 51, 73–74, 80, 92, 102, 112, 146, 159, 166, 172, 182
  body, 38, 42, 76, 81, 83, 115, 133, 168
  communal, xi, 136, 168
  cross-traditional, 146, 182, 191
  feminine, xix, 4, 37–38, 49, 72, 82, 87, 98–99, 106, 114–15, 170
  historic, xvi–ii, 46, 58, 88, 132, 167, 186
  Holy Wisdom (Monastery), xviii, 46, 67, 75, 122, 182, 192, 199
  literature, 186
  non-sectarian communities, 71, 136–38, 169
  restorative, 192
  of serpents, 3, 168
  Throne of, 108–10
  tradition, xi–ii, xv–vii, 9–11, 15–16, 19, 24, 46, 58, 66, 96, 116–17, 119, 132, 147–48, 150, 167, 173–74, 184–90, 192, 202
witness, xvii–xiii, 2–3, 10–11, 19, 25, 44, 51, 67, 72, 85, 91, 93, 102, 113, 123, 133, 199
  authoritative, 178, 182–83
  ill-witness, 128–29
  without judgment, 23, 34, 165, 168, 193
  community, 43, 75–76, 78, 85–86, 106, 122, 142, 162, 165, 175, 179, 193, 203
womanist, xiv, xvi, 10, 49, 65

woman-centric, 54–55, 58–59, 63, 78–79, 81, 186
womanheart, 23, 47, 52, 59, 75, 79–80, 82–83, 85–86, 104, 125–26, 132
Women Writing for (a) Change (WWfaC), 16n4, 47–48, 159
women's mysteries, 83, 104, 125–26
Woodman, Marion, xiii, 46, 48
wordless/ness, 40, 75, 97
Word of God as event, 178–80, 184
woundedness, xiii, 2, 3n6, 6, 9, 34, 69, 96, 117, 136, 156, 165, 167, 172, 176, 181, 184, 192, 197, 199

yearning, ix, 4n8, 20, 55, 59, 95, 97, 127, 132, 145, 163, 202

www.ingramcontent.com/pod-product-compliance
Lightning Source LLC
Chambersburg PA
CBHW031808220426
43662CB00007B/569